Scala in Depth

Scala in Depth

JOSHUA D. SUERETH

MANNING
SHELTER ISLAND

Manning Publications Co.   Development editor: Katharine Osborne
20 Baldwin Road   Technical proofreader: Justin Wick
PO Box 261   Copyeditors: Linda Kern, Benjamin Berg
Shelter Island, NY 11964   Proofreader: Elizabeth Martin
Typesetter: Dottie Marsico
Cover designer: Marija Tudor

ISBN 9781935182702
Printed in the United States of America
1 2 3 4 5 6 7 8 9 10 – MAL – 17 16 15 14 13 12

contents

foreword

Joshua Suereth is one of the most complete programmers I know. Familiar with a whole gamut of programming languages and techniques, he is an expert in high-performance systems, build tools, type theory, and many other areas. He is also a gifted teacher, and all that combined is what makes *Scala in Depth* special.

This book provides in-depth coverage of several of the more intricate areas of Scala, including advanced aspects of its type system, implicits, composition techniques with traits, collections, actors, functional categories. But this is not a dry recollection of language and library concepts. The book is full of practical advice on how to apply these lesser known parts of Scala in useful ways, and what the best practices are. The explanations and examples demonstrate Joshua's great experience constructing large-scale systems in Scala.

Scala in Depth is not a beginner's introduction; it should primarily appeal to competent Scala programmers who want to become experts. The techniques that are taught are handy for constructing flexible and type-safe library abstractions. Many of these techniques were folklore until now; they have been, for the first time, written-up here.

I am particularly happy about one other thing: The book fills a gap in that it explains key parts of the formal Scala specification to programmers who are not language lawyers. Scala is one of few languages that actually has a specification. That specification consists mainly of definitions written in highly stylized prose and mathematical formulas; so it's not everybody's piece of cake. Joshua's book manages to be both authorative and understandable as it explains these concepts.

MARTIN ODERSKY
CREATOR OF SCALA
HEAD OF PROGRAMMING
RESEARCH GROUP, EPFL

preface

In fall 2010 Michael Stephens from Manning contacted me about writing a Scala Book. I was working for a small virtualization/security startup where I had been learning Scala and applying it to our codebase. During that first conversation Michael and I discussed the Scala ecosystem and what kind of a book would best serve the community.

I believed Scala needed a "practical Scala" book to help guide those new to the language. Scala is a beautiful language, but it brings many new concepts to the table. I had watched as the community slowly discovered best practices and a code style that was wholly "Scala." But I wasn't sure whether I was the right person to write such a book. When it came down to it, I was passionate about the topic, had enough free time to do the research, and had the support of the magnates of the community to help achieve what you are reading today—so I decided to go ahead.

I've learned a lot during the writing process. One reason it took so long was the evolving nature of Scala and the emergence of new best practices. Another reason was that I realized my own knowledge was woefully inadequate in some areas of Scala. To all aspiring authors out there, I will tell you that writing a book makes you an expert. You may think you are one before you start, but true expertise grows from the blood, sweat, and tears of teaching, of trying to convey complex concepts to your readers with clarity.

Working on this book was a journey that I never could have completed without a very supportive and loving wife, a great publisher, and an amazing community of Scala developers and readers willing to read my manuscript in various stages, point out my typos and misspellings, and offer advice on how to make *Scala in Depth* a much better book than I could have achieved alone.

acknowledgments

Many people helped get this book off the ground and into print. While I'm going to try to list them all, I'm sure I'll miss a few as there were just too many for my tiny brain to remember. This book showed me that I have a lot of high quality friends, coworkers, and family.

The biggest thank you is for my wife and children, who had to deal with a husband/father who was constantly hiding in a corner, writing, when he should have been helping out. There's no way an author can write a book without the support of immediate family, and mine was no exception.

Next, I'd like to thank Manning Publications and all the work the staff did to ensure I became a real author. Not only did they review and lay out the book, they also helped improve my technical writing skills for clear communication. I can't give enough thanks to the whole team, but I'd especially like to thank Katherine Osborne for putting up with my missed deadlines, Pennsylvania-Dutch sentence structures, and overall poor spelling. Katherine was instrumental to the voice of this book, and those who've been reading the MEAPs will notice the improvement.

The next group that deserves thanks are the Scala experts and nonexperts who helped me improve my technical material and descriptions. Tim Perret was authoring *Lift in Action* for Manning around the same time I was writing *Scala in Depth*. Discussions with Tim were both encouraging and motivating. Unfortunately for me, he finished first. Justin Wick was a reviewer and collaborator on a lot of the content, and definitely helped me reach a wider audience than I had initially attempted to attract. He also reviewed the final manuscript and code one last time, just before the book went into production. Adriaan Moors, as usual, pointed out all my mistakes when discussing the type system and implicit resolution and helped make the discussions both practical and correct. Eric Weinberg was an old coworker of mine who helped provide guidance for reaching non-Scala developers in the book. Viktor Klang reviewed the "Actors" chapter (and the whole book) and offered improvements. Thank you also to Martin Odersky for his endorsement and kind words on the final product that you will read in the foreword, Josh Cough for being a guy I can bounce ideas off when needed, and Peter Simanyi for an email with a very detailed, thorough, complete, and awesome review of the entire book.

Manning also contacted the following reviewers, who read the manuscript at various stages of its development, and I would like to thank them for their invaluable insights and comments: John C. Tyler, Orhan Alkan, Michael Nash, John Griffin, Jeroen Benckhuijsen, David Biesack, Lutz Hankewitz, Oleksandr Alesinskyy, Cheryl Jerozal, Edmon Begoli, Ramnivas Laddad, Marco Ughetti, Marcus Kazmierczak, Ted Neward, Eric Weinberg, Dave Pawson, Patrick Steger, Paul Stusiak, Mark Thomas, David Dossot, Tariq Ahmed, Ken McDonald, Mark Needham, and James Hatheway.

Finally, I'd like to thank all of the MEAP reviewers. I received great feedback from them and appreciate the support and good reviews this book received before it was even in print. You guys had to bear with lots of typos and errors and deserve credit for persevering through my rough initial cuts and making it to this final version.

about this book

Scala in Depth is a practical guide to using Scala with deep dives into necessary topics. This book, picking up where introductory books drop off, enables readers to write idiomatic Scala code and understand trade-offs when making use of advanced language features. In particular, this book covers Scala's implicit and type systems in detail before discussing how these can be used to drastically simplify development. The book promotes the "blended style" of Scala, where paradigms are mixed to achieve something greater.

Who should read this book?

Scala in Depth is for new or intermediate Scala developers who wish to improve their skills with the language. While this book covers very advanced concepts in Scala, it attempts to pull along those new to Scala.

This book was written for readers who know Java or another object-oriented language. Prior experience with Scala is helpful but not required. It covers Scala 2.7.x through Scala 2.9.x.

Roadmap

Scala in Depth begins with a philosophical discussion of the "xen" of Scala—that Scala is a blending of concepts that achieve a greater whole when combined. In particular, three dichotomies are discussed: static typing versus expressiveness, functional programming versus object-oriented programming, and powerful language features versus dead simple Java integration.

Chapter 2 is a discussion of the core rules of Scala. These are the things that every Scala developer should be aware of and make use of in daily development. This chapter is for every Scala developer and covers the basics that make Scala a great language.

Chapter 3 is a digression in code style and associated issues. Scala brings a few new players to the table, and any Scala style guide should reflect that. Some common conventions from popular languages like Ruby and Java can actually be deterrents to good Scala code.

Chapter 4 covers new issues arising in object-oriented design due to Scala's mixin inheritance. One topic of interest to any Scala developer is the early initializer coverage, which gets little coverage in other books.

After object orientation, the book moves into the implicit system. In chapter 5, rather than simply discussing best practices, a deep dive is taken into the mechanics of implicits in Scala. This chapter is a must for all Scala developers who wish to write expressive libraries and code.

Chapter 6 is devoted to Scala's type system. The discussion covers all the ways types appear in Scala and how to utilize the type system to enforce constraints. The chapter moves into a discussion of higher-kinded types and finishes with a dive into existential types.

Chapter 7 discusses the most advanced usage patterns in the language, the intersection of types and implicits. This intersection is where a lot of interesting and powerful abstractions occur, the epitome of which is the type class pattern.

Having covered the most advanced aspects of Scala, in chapter 8 we move into a discussion of Scala's collection library. This includes the design and performance of Scala's collections as well as how to deal with the powerful type mechanisms.

Chapter 9 kicks off the discussion on actors in Scala. Actors are a concurrency mechanism that can provide great throughput and parallelism when used appropriately. The chapter dives into issues of designing actor-based systems and finishes with a demonstration of how the Akka actors library provides best practices by default.

Chapter 10 covers Java integration with Scala. While Scala is more compatible with Java than most other JVM languages, there's still a mismatch in features between the two. It's at these corners that issues arise in Scala-Java integration and this chapter provides a few simple rules that help avoid these issues.

Chapter 11 takes concepts from category theory and makes them practical. In pure functional programming, a lot of concepts from category theory have been applied to code. These are akin to object-oriented design patterns, but far more abstract. While they have terrible names, as is common in mathematics, these concepts are immensely useful in practice. No coverage of functional programming would be complete without a discussion of some of these abstractions, and Scala in Depth does its best to make these concepts real.

Code downloads and conventions

All source code in the book is in a `fixed-width font like this`, which sets it off from the surrounding text. In many listings, the code is annotated to point out the key concepts. I have tried to format the code so that it fits within the available page space in the book by adding line breaks and using indentation carefully. Sometimes, however, very long lines include line-continuation markers.

Source code for all the working examples is available from www.manning.com/ ScalainDepth and at https://github.com/jsuereth/scala-in-depth-source. To run the examples, readers should have Scala installed and, optionally, SBT (http://scala-sbt.org).

Code examples appear throughout this book. Longer listings appear under clear listing headers; shorter listings appear between lines of text.

Author online

Purchase of *Scala in Depth* includes free access to a private web forum run by Manning Publications where you can make comments about the book, ask technical questions, and receive help from the authors and from other users. To access the forum and subscribe to it, point your web browser to www.manning.com/ScalainDepth. This page provides information on how to get on the forum once you're registered, what kind of help is available, and the rules of conduct on the forum.

Manning's commitment to our readers is to provide a venue where a meaningful dialog between individual readers and between readers and the authors can take place. It's not a commitment to any specific amount of participation on the part of the authors, whose contribution to the AO forum remains voluntary (and unpaid). We suggest you try asking the author some challenging questions lest his interest stray.

The Author Online forum and the archives of previous discussions will be accessible from the publisher's website as long as the book is in print.

About the author

Josh Suereth is a Senior Software Engineer at Typesafe Inc., the company behind Scala. He has been a Scala enthusiast since he came to know this beautiful language in 2007. He started his professional career as a software developer in 2004, cutting his teeth with C++, STL, and Boost. Around the same time, Java fever was spreading and his interest was migrating to web-hosted distributed Java-delivered solutions to aid health departments in the discovery of disease outbreaks.

He introduced Scala into his company code base in 2007, and soon after he was infected by Scala fever, contributing to the Scala IDE, maven-scala-plugin and Scala itself. Today, Josh is the author of several open source Scala projects, including the Scala automated resource management library and the PGP sbt plugin, as well as contributing to key components in the Scala ecosystem, like the maven-scala-plugin. His current work at Typesafe Inc., has him doing everything from building MSIs to profiling performance issues.

Josh regularly shares his expertise in articles and talks. He likes short walks on the beach and dark beer.

about the cover illustration

On the cover of *Scala in Depth* is a figure dressed in "An old Croatian folk costume." The illustration is taken from a reproduction of an album of Croatian traditional costumes from the mid-nineteenth century by Nikola Arsenovic, published by the Ethnographic Museum in Split, Croatia, in 2003. The illustrations were obtained from a helpful librarian at the Ethnographic Museum in Split, itself situated in the Roman core of the medieval center of the town: the ruins of Emperor Diocletian's retirement palace from around AD 304. The book includes finely colored illustrations of figures from different regions of Croatia, accompanied by descriptions of the costumes and of everyday life.

While the caption for the illustration on the cover does not tell us the town or region of origin, the blue woolen trousers and richly embroidered vest and jacket that the figure is wearing are typical for the mountainous regions of central Croatia. Dress codes and lifestyles have changed over the last 200 years, and the diversity by region, so rich at the time, has faded away. It's now hard to tell apart the inhabitants of different continents, let alone of different hamlets or towns separated by only a few miles. Perhaps we have traded cultural diversity for a more varied personal life—certainly for a more varied and fast-paced technological life.

Manning celebrates the inventiveness and initiative of the computer business with book covers based on the rich diversity of regional life of two centuries ago, brought back to life by illustrations from old books and collections like this one.

Scala— a blended language

In this chapter

- Short introduction to Scala
- Insights into Scala's design

Scala was born from the mind of Martin Odersky, a man who had helped introduce generics into the Java programming language. Scala was an offshoot from the Funnel language, an attempt to combine functional programming and Petri nets. Scala was developed with the premise that you could mix together object orientation, functional programming, and a powerful type system and still keep elegant, succinct code. It was hoped that this blending of concepts would create something that real developers could use and that could be studied for new programming idioms. It was such a large success that industry has started adopting Scala as a viable and competitive language.

Understanding Scala requires understanding this mixture of concepts. Scala attempts to blend three dichotomies of thought into one language. These are:

- Functional programming and object-oriented programming
- Expressive syntax and static typing
- Advanced language features and rich Java integration

1

Functional programming is programming through the definition and composition of functions. Object-oriented programming is programming through the definition and composition of objects. In Scala, functions *are* objects. Programs can be constructed through both the definition and composition of objects or functions. This gives Scala the ability to focus on "nouns" or "verbs" in a program, depending on what is the most prominent.

Scala also blends expressive syntax with static typing. Mainstream statically typed languages tend to suffer from verbose type annotations and boilerplate syntax. Scala takes a few lessons from the ML programming language and offers static typing with a nice expressive syntax. Code written in Scala can look as expressive as dynamically typed languages, like Ruby, while retaining type safety.

Finally, Scala offers a lot of advanced language features that are not available in Java. But Scala runs on the Java virtual machine (JVM) and has tight integration with the Java language. This means that developers can make direct use of existing Java libraries and integrate Scala into their Java applications while also gaining the additional power of Scala. This integration makes Scala a practical choice for any JVM-based project.

Let's take a deeper look at the blending of paradigms in Scala.

1.1 *Functional programming meets object orientation*

Functional programming and object-oriented programming are two different ways of looking at a problem. Functional programming puts special emphasis on the "verbs" of a program and ways to combine and manipulate them. Object-oriented programming puts special emphasis on "nouns" and attaches verbs to them. The two approaches are almost inverses of each other, with one being "top down" and the other "bottom up."

Object-oriented programming is a top-down approach to code design. It approaches software by dividing code into nouns or objects. Each object has some form of identity (self/this), behavior (methods), and state (members). After identifying nouns and defining their behaviors, interactions between nouns are defined. The problem with implementing interactions is that the interactions need to live inside an object. Modern object-oriented designs tend to have *service classes*, which are a collection of methods that operate across several domain objects. Service classes, although objects, usually don't have a notion of state or behavior independent of the objects on which they operate.

A good example is a program that implements the following story: "A cat catches a bird and eats it." An object-oriented programmer would look at this sentence and see two nouns: cat and bird. The cat has two verbs associated with it: catch and eat. The following program is a more object-oriented approach:

```
class Bird
class Cat {
    def catch(b: Bird): Unit = ...
    def eat(): Unit = ...
```

```
}
val cat = new Cat
val bird = new Bird

cat.catch(bird)
cat.eat()
```

In the example, when a `Cat` catches a `Bird`, it converts the bird to a type of `Food`, which it can then `eat`. The code focuses on the nouns and their actions: `Cat.eat()`, `Cat.catch(...)`. In functional programming, the focus is on the verbs.

Functional programming approaches software as the combination and application of functions. It tends to decompose software into behaviors, or actions that need to be performed, usually in a bottom-up fashion. Functions are viewed in a mathematical sense, purely operations on their input. All variables are considered immutable. This immutability aids concurrent programming. Functional programming attempts to defer all side effects in a program as long as possible. Removing side effects makes reasoning through a program simpler, in a formal sense. It also provides much more power in how things can be abstracted and combined.

In the story "A cat catches a bird and eats it," a functional program would see the two verbs *catch* and *eat*. A program would create these two functions and compose them to create the program. The following program is a more functional approach:

```
trait Cat
trait Bird
trait Catch
trait FullTummy

def catch(hunter: Cat, prey: Bird): Cat with Catch
def eat(consumer: Cat with Catch): Cat with FullTummy

val story = (catch _) andThen (eat _)
story(new Cat, new Bird)
```

In the example, the `catch` method takes a `Cat` and a `Bird` and returns a new value of type `Cat with Catch`. The eat method is defined as taking a `CatWithPrey` (a cat needs something to eat) and returns a `FullCat` (because it's no longer hungry). Functional programming makes more use of the type system to describe what a function is doing. The `catch` and `eat` methods use the type signatures to define the expected input and output states of the function. The `with` keyword is used to combine a type with another. In this example, the traits Catch and FullTummy are used to denote the current state of a Cat. The methods eat and catch return new instances of Cat attached to different state types. The `story` value is created by composing the functions catch and eat. This means that the `catch` method is called and the result is fed into the eat method. Finally, the `story` function is called with a `Cat` and a `Bird` and the result is the output of the story: a full cat.

Functional programming and object orientation offer unique views of software. It's these differences that make them useful to each other. Object orientation can deal with composing the nouns and functional programming can deal with composing

Table 1.1   Attributes commonly ascribed to object-oriented and functional programming

Object-oriented programming	Functional programming
Composition of objects (nouns)	Composition of functions (verbs)
Encapsulated stateful interaction	Deferred side effects
Iterative algorithms	Recursive algorithms and continuations
Imperative flow	Lazy evaluation
N/A	Pattern matching

verbs. In the example, the functional version was built by composing a set of functions that encompassed a story and then feeding the initial data into these functions. For the object-oriented version, a set of objects was created and their internal state was manipulated. Both approaches are useful in designing software. Object orientation can focus on the nouns of the system and functional programming can compose the verbs.

In fact, in recent years, many Java developers have started moving toward splitting nouns and verbs. The Enterprise JavaBeans (EJB) specification splits software into *Session beans*, which tend to contain behaviors, and *Entity beans*, which tend to model the nouns in the system. Stateless Session beans start looking more like collections of functional code (although missing most of the useful features of functional code).

This push of functional style has come along much further than the EJB specifications. The Spring Application Framework promotes a functional style with its Template classes, and the Google Collections library is very functional in design. Let's look at these common Java libraries and see how Scala's blend of functional programming with object orientation can enhance these Application Program Interfaces (APIs).

1.1.1   Discovering existing functional concepts

Many modern API designs have been incorporating functional ideas without ascribing them to functional programming. For Java, things such as Google Collections or the Spring Application Framework make popular functional concepts accessible to the Java developer. Scala takes this further and embeds them into the language. To illustrate, you'll do a simple translation of the methods on the popular Spring Jdbc-Template class and see what it starts to look like in Scala.

```
public interface JdbcTemplate {
  List query(PreparedStatementCreator psc,          ⟵   Query for list of objects
          RowMapper rowMapper)
  ...
}
```

Now for a simple translation into Scala, you'll convert the interface into a trait having the same method(s):

```
trait JdbcTemplate {
  def query(psc: PreparedStatementCreator,
          rowMapper: RowMapper): List[_]
}
```

The simple translation makes a lot of sense but it's still designed with a distinct Java flair. Let's start digging deeper into this design. Specifically, let's look at the Prepared-StatementCreator and the RowMapper interfaces.

```
public interface PreparedStatementCreator {
  PreparedStatement createPreparedStatement(Connection con)
      throws SQLException;
}
```

The PreparedStatementCreator interface contains only one method: create-PreparedStatement. This method takes a JDBC connection and returns a Prepared-Statement. The RowMapper interface looks similar:

```
public interface RowMapper {
  Object mapRow(ResultSet rs, int rowNum)
        throws SQLException;
}
```

Scala provides first-class functions. This feature lets us change the JdbcTemplate query method so that it takes functions instead of interfaces. These functions should have the same signature as the sole method defined on the interface. In this case, the PreparedStatementCreator argument can be replaced by a function that takes a connection and returns a PreparedStatement. The RowMapper argument can be replaced by a function that takes a ResultSet and an integer and returns some type of object. The updated Scala version of the JdbcTemplate interface would look as follows:

```
trait JdbcTemplate {
  def query(psc: Connection => PreparedStatement,        Use first-class
      rowMapper: (ResultSet, Int) => AnyRef          <----  functions
      ): List[AnyRef]
}
```

The query method is now more functional. It's using a technique known as the *loaner pattern*. This technique involves some controlling entity (the JdbcTemplate) creating a resource and delegating the use of it to another function. In this case, there are two functions and three resources. Also, as the name implies, JdbcTemplate is part of a template method in which pieces of the behavior were deferred for the user to implement. In pure object-orientation, this is usually done via inheritance. In a more functional approach, these behavioral pieces become arguments to the controlling function. This provides more flexibility by allowing mixing/matching arguments without having to continually use subclasses.

You may be wondering why you're using AnyRef for the second argument's return value. AnyRef is equivalent in Scala to java.lang.Object. Because Scala has supported generics, even when compiling for 1.4 JVMs, we should modify this interface further to remove the AnyRef and allow users to return specific types.

```
trait JdbcTemplate {
  def query[ResultItem](psc: Connection => PreparedStatement,
      rowMapper: (ResultSet, Int) => ResultItem          Typed
      ): List[ResultItem]                            <----  return list
}
```

With a few simple transformations, you've created an interface that works directly against functions. This is a more functional approach because Scala's function traits allow composition. By the time you're finished reading this book, you'll be able to approach the design of this interface completely differently.

Functional programming also shines when used in a collections library. The Ruby and Python programming languages support some functional aspects directly in their standard library collections. For Java users, the Google Collections library bring practices from functional programming.

1.1.2 Examining functional concepts in Google Collections

The Google Collections API adds a lot of power to the standard Java collections. Primarily it brings a nice set of efficient immutable data structures, and some functional ways of interacting with your collections, primarily the `Function` interface and the `Predicate` interface. These interfaces are used primarily from the `Iterables` and `Iterators` classes. Let's look at the `Predicate` interface and its uses.

```
interface Predicate<T> {
    public boolean apply(T input);
    public boolean equals(Object other);
}
```

The `Predicate` interface is simple. Besides equality, it contains an `apply` method that returns true or false against its argument. This is used in an `Iterators/Iterables-filter` method. The `filter` method takes a collection and a predicate. It returns a new collection containing only elements that pass the predicate `apply` method. Predicates are also used in the `find` method. The `find` method looks in a collection for the first element passing a Predicate and returns it. The filter and find method signatures are shown in the following code.

```
class Iterables {
    public static <T> Iterable<T> filter(Iterable<T> unfiltered,     ⟵ Filters
        Predicate<? super T> predicate) {...}                          using
    public static <T> T find(Iterable<T> iterable,                     predicate
        Predicate<? super T> predicate) {...}                        ⟵ Find using
    ...                                                                 predicate
}
```

There also exists a `Predicates` class that contains static methods for combining predicates (ANDs/ORs) and standard predicates for use, such as "not null." This simple interface creates some powerful functionality through the potential combinations that can be achieved with terse code. Also, because the predicate itself is passed into the filter function, the function can determine the best way or time to execute the filter. The data structure may be amenable to lazily evaluating the predicate, making the iterable returned a "view" of the original collection. It might also determine that it could best optimize the creation of the new iterable through some form of parallelism. This has been abstracted away, so the library could improve over time with no code changes on our part.

The Predicate interface is rather interesting, because it looks like a simple function. This function takes some type T and returns a Boolean. In Scala this would be represented `T => Boolean`. Let's rewrite the filter/find methods in Scala and see what their signatures would look like:

```
object Iterables {
    def filter[T](unfiltered: Iterable[T],
        predicate: T => Boolean): Iterable[T] = {...}
    def find[T](iterable: Iterable[T],
            predicate: T => Boolean): T = {...}
    ...
}
```

No need for ? ◁

You'll immediately notice that in Scala we aren't using any explicit ? super T type annotations. This is because Scala defines type variance at declaration time. For this example, that means that the variance annotation is defined on the `Function1` class rather than requiring it on every method that used the class.

What about combining predicates in Scala? We can accomplish a few of these quickly using some functional composition. Let's make a new `Predicates` module in Scala that takes in function predicates and provides commonly used function predicates. The input type of these combination functions should be `T => Boolean` and the output should also be `T => Boolean`. The predefined predicates should also have a type `T => Boolean`.

```
object Predicates {
  def or[T](f1: T => Boolean, f2: T => Boolean) =
        (t: T) => f1(t) || f2(t)
  def and[T](f1: T => Boolean, f2: T => Boolean) =
        (t: T) => f1(t) && f2(t)
  val notNull[T]: T => Boolean = _ != null
}
```

Explicit anonymous function ◁

Placeholder function syntax ◁

We've now started to delve into the realm of functional programming. We're defining first-class functions and combining them to perform new behaviors. You'll notice the or method take two predicates, f1 and f2. It then creates a new anonymous function that takes an argument t and ORs the results of f1 and f2. Playing with functions also makes more extensive use of generics and the type system. Scala has put forth a lot of effort to reduce the overhead for generics in daily usage.

Functional programming is more than combining functions with other functions. The essence of functional programming is delaying side effects as long as possible. This predicate object defines a simple mechanism to combine predicates. The predicate isn't used to cause side effects until passed to the `Iterables` object. This distinction is important. Complex predicates can be built from simple predicates using the helper methods defined on the object predicates.

Functional programming grants the means to defer state manipulation in a program until a later time. It provides a mechanism to construct verbs that delay side effects. These verbs can be combined in a fashion that makes reasoning through a program simpler. Eventually the verbs are applied against the nouns of the system. In traditional FP, side effects are delayed as long as possible. In blended OO-FP, the idioms merge.

1.2 Static typing and expressiveness

The Scala type system allows expressive code. A common misconception among developers is that static typing leads to verbose code. This myth exists because many of the languages derived from C, where types must be explicitly specified in many different places. As software has improved, along with compiler theory, this is no longer true. Scala uses some of these advances to reduce boilerplate in code and keep things concise.

Scala made a few simple design decisions that help make it expressive:

- Changing sides of type annotation
- Type inference
- Scalable syntax
- User-defined implicits

Let's look at how Scala changes the sides of type annotations.

1.2.1 Changing sides

Scala places type annotations on the right-hand side of variables. In some statically typed languages, like Java or C++, it's common to have to express the types of variables, return values, and arguments. When specifying variables or parameters, the convention, drawn from C, is to place type indicators on the left-hand side of the variable name. For method arguments and return values, this is acceptable, but causes some confusion when creating different styles of variables. C++ is the best example of this, as it has a rich set of variable styles, such as volatile, const, pointers, and references. Table 1.2 shows a comparison of C++ variables   and Scala variables.

The more complicated a variable type, the more annotations are required directly on the type of the variable. In C++, this is maximized in the usage of a pointer, because a pointer can be constant. Scala defines three variable types on the left-hand side, like var, val, and lazy val. These leave the type of the variable clean. In all instances, the type of the name x is Int.

Table 1.2   Variable definition in C++ versus Scala

Variable type	C++	Java	Scala
Mutable integer variable	`int x`	`int x`	`var x: Int`
Immutable integer value	const int x	`final int x`	`val x: Int`
Constant pointer to a volatile integer	`volatile int * const x`	N/A	N/A
Lazily evaluated integer value	N/A	N/A	`lazy val x: Int`

In addition to separating the concerns of how a variable behaves from the variable type, the placement of types on the right allows type inference to determine the type of the variables.

1.2.2 Type inference

Scala performs type inference wherever possible. Type inference is when the compiler determines what the type annotation should be, rather than forcing the user to specify one. The user can always provide a type annotation, but has the option to let the compiler do the work.

```
val x: Int = 5
val y = 5
```

This feature can drastically reduce the clutter found in some other typed languages. Scala takes this even further to do some level of inference on arguments passed into methods, specifically with first-class functions.

```
def myMethod(functionLiteral: A => B): Unit
myMethod({ arg: A => new B })
myMethod({ arg => new B })
```

If a method is known to take a function argument, the compiler can infer the types used in a function are literal.

1.2.3 Dropping verbose syntax

Scala syntax takes the general approach that when the meaning of a line of code is straightforward, the verbose syntax can be dropped. This feature can confuse users first using Scala but can be rather powerful when used wisely. Let's show a simple refactoring from the full glory of Scala syntax into the simplistic code that's seen in idiomatic usage. Here is a function for Quicksort in Scala.

```
def qsort[T <% Ordered[T]](list:List[T]):List[T] = {        ◁——  <% means "view"
  list.match({
    case Nil => Nil;
    case x::xs =>
      val (before,after) = xs.partition({ i => i.<(x) });
      qsort(before).++(qsort(after).::(x)));                  ◁┐ ++ and ::
  });                                                         │ mean aggregate
}
```

This code accepts a list whose type, T, is able to be implicitly converted into a variable of type Ordered[T] (T <% Ordered[T]). We'll discuss type parameters and constraints in great detail in chapter 6, so don't focus too much on these. We're requiring that the list contain elements that we have some notion of ordering for, specifically a less than function (<). We then examine the list. If it's empty, or Nil, then we return a Nil list. If it encounters a list, we extract the head (x) and tail (xs) of the list. We use the head element of the list to partition the tail into two lists. We then recursively call the Quicksort method on each partition. In the same line, we combine the sorted partitions and the head element into a complete list.

You may be thinking, "Wow, Scala looks ugly." In this case you would be right. The code is cluttered and difficult to read. There's a lot of syntactic noise preventing the meaning of the code from being clear. There's also a lot of type information after qsort. Let's pull out our surgical knife and start cutting out cruft. First we'll start with Scala's semicolon inference. The compiler will assume that the end of a line is the end of an expression, unless you leave some piece of syntax hanging, like the . before a method call.

But removing semicolons isn't quite enough to reduce the clutter. We should also use an *operator notation*. This is the name Scala gives to its ability to treat methods as operators. A method of no arguments can be treated as a postfix operator. A method of one argument can be treated as an infix operator. There's also the special rule for certain characters (for example, :) at the end of a method name that reverses the order of a method call. These rules are demonstrated as follows:

```
x.foo();   /*is the same as*/ x foo
x.foo(y);  /*is the same as*/ x foo y
x.::(y);   /*is the same as*/ y :: x
```

Scala also provides placeholder notation when defining anonymous functions (aka, lambdas). This syntax uses the _ keyword as a placeholder for a function argument. If more than one placeholder is used, each consecutive placeholder refers to consecutive arguments to the function literal. This notation is usually reserved for simple functions, such as the less-than (<) comparison in our Quicksort.

We can apply this notation paired with operator notation to achieve the following on our quick sort algorithm:

```
def qsort[T <% Ordered[T]](list:List[T]):List[T] = list match {
    case Nil => Nil
    case x :: xs =>
        val (before, after) = xs partition ( _ < x )
        qsort(before) ++ (x :: qsort(after));
}
```

Placeholder notation used instead of =>

Scala offers syntactic shortcuts for simple cases, and it provides a mechanism to bend the type system via implicits conversions and implicits arguments.

1.2.4   *Implicits are an old concept*

Scala implicits are a new take on an old concept. The first time I was ever introduced to the concept of implicit conversions was with primitive types in C++. C++ allows primitive types to be automatically converted as long as there is no loss of precision. For example, we can use an int literal when declaring a long value. The types *double, float, int,* and *long* are different to the compiler. It does try to be intelligent and "do the right thing" when mixing these values. Scala provides this same mechanism, but using a language feature that's available for anyone.

The scala.Predef object is automatically imported into scope by Scala. This places its members available to all programs. It's a handy mechanism for providing convenience functions to users, like directly writing println instead of Console

.println or System.out.println. Predef also provides what it calls *primitive widenings*. These are a set of implicit conversions that automatically migrate from lower-precision types to higher precision types. The following listing shows the set of methods defined for the Byte type.

```
implicit def byte2short(x: Byte): Short = x.toShort
  implicit def byte2int(x: Byte): Int = x.toInt
  implicit def byte2long(x: Byte): Long = x.toLong
  implicit def byte2float(x: Byte): Float = x.toFloat
  implicit def byte2double(x: Byte): Double = x.toDouble
```

These methods are calls to the runtime-conversion methods. The implicit before the method means the compiler may attempt to apply this method to a type Byte, if it's required for correct compilation. This means if we attempt to pass a Byte to a method requiring a Short, it will use the implicit conversion defined as byte2short. Scala also takes this one step further and looks for methods via implicit conversions if the current type doesn't have the called method. This comes in handy for more than just primitive conversions.

Scala also uses the implicit conversion mechanism as a means of extending Java's base classes (Integer, String, Double, and so on). This allows Scala to make direct use of Java classes, for ease of integration, and provide richer methods that make use of Scala's more advanced features. Implicits are a powerful feature and are mistrusted by some. The key to implicits in Scala are knowing how and when to use them.

1.2.5 Using Scala's implicit keyword

Utilizing implicits is key to manipulating Scala's type system. They're primarily used to automatically convert from one type to another as needed, but can also be used to limited forms of compiler time metaprogramming. To use, implicits must be associated with a lexical scope. This can be done via companion objects or by explicitly importing them.

The implicit keyword is used in two different ways in Scala. First it's used to identify and create arguments that are automatically passed when found in the scope. This can be used to lexically scope certain features of an API. As implicits also have a lookup policy, the inheritance linearization, they can be used to change the return type of methods. This allows some advanced APIs and type-system tricks such as that used in the Scala collections API. These techniques are covered in detail in chapter 7.

The implicit keyword can also be used to convert from one type to another. This occurs in two places, the first when passing a parameter to a function. If Scala detects that a different type is needed, it will check the type hierarchy and then look for an implicit conversion to apply to the parameter. An implicit conversion is a method, marked implicit, that takes one argument and returns something. The second place where Scala will perform an implicit conversion is when a method is called against a particular type. If the compiler can't find the desired method, it will apply implicit conversations against the variable until it either finds one that contains the method or it runs out of conversions. This is used in Scala's "pimp my library" pattern, described in chapter 7.

These features combine an expressive syntax with Scala, despite its advanced type system. Creating expressive libraries requires a deep understanding of the type system, as well as thorough knowledge of implicit conversions. The type system will be covered more fully in chapter 6. The type system also interoperates well with Java, which is a critical design for Scala.

1.3   Transparently working with the JVM

One of Scala's draws is its seamless integration with Java and the JVM. Scala provides a rich compatibility with Java, such that Java classes can be mapped directly to Scala classes. The tightness of this interaction makes migrating from Java to Scala rather simple, but caution should be used with some of Scala's advanced feature sets. Scala has some advanced features not available in Java, and care was taken in the design so that seamless Java interaction can be achieved. For the most part, libraries written in Java can be imported into Scala as is.

1.3.1   Java in Scala

Using Java libraries from Scala is seamless because Java idioms map directly into Scala idioms. Java classes become Scala classes; Java interfaces become abstract Scala traits. Java static members get added to a pseudo-Scala object. This combined with Scala's package import mechanism and method access make Java libraries feel like natural Scala libraries, albeit with more simplistic designs. In general, this kind of interaction just works. For example, the following listing shows a Java class that has a constructor, a method, and a static helper method.

Listing 1.2   Simple Java object

```
class SimpleJavaClass {
  private String name;
  public SimpleJavaClass(String name) {          ◁──── Constructor
    this.name = name;
  }
  public String getName() {                      ◁──── Class method
    return name;
  }
  public static SimpleJavaClass create(String name) {   ◁──── Static class helper
    return new SimpleJavaClass(name);
  }
}
```

Now, let's use this in Scala.

```
val x = SimpleJavaClass.create("Test")          ◁──── Calling Java static methods

x.getName()                                      ◁──── Calling Java methods

val y = new SimpleJavaClass("Test")              ◁──── Using Java constructor
```

This mapping is rather natural and makes using Java libraries a seamless part of using Scala. Even with the tight integration, Java libraries usually have a form of thin Scala wrapper that provides some of the more advanced features a Java API could not provide. These features are apparent when trying to use Scala libraries inside Java.

1.3.2 *Scala in Java*

Scala attempts to map its features to Java in the simplest possible fashion. For the most part, simple Scala features map almost one-to-one with Java features (for example, classes, abstract classes, methods). Scala has some rather advanced features that don't map easily into Java. These include things like objects, first-class functions, and implicits.

SCALA OBJECTS IN JAVA

Although Java statics map to Scala objects, Scala objects are instances of a singleton class. This class name is compiled as the name of the object with a $ appended to the end. A MODULE$ static field on this class is designed to be the sole instance. All methods and fields can be accessed via this MODULE$ instance. Scala also provides *forwarding* static methods when it can; these exist on the companion class (that is, a class with the same name as the object). Although the static methods are unused in Scala, they provide a convenient syntax when called from Java.

```
object ScalaUtils {
  def log(msg : String) : Unit = Console.println(msg)    ⟵— Simple Scala method

  val MAX_LOG_SIZE = 1056                                ⟵— Simple Scala field
}

ScalaUtils.log("Hello!");                                ⟵— Acts like static call

  ScalaUtils$.MODULE$.log("Hello!");                     ⟵— Use the singleton instance

  System.out.println(ScalaUtils$.MODULE$.MAX_LOG_SIZE());  ⟵— Variables become

  System.out.println(ScalaUtils.MAX_LOG_SIZE());         ⟵— Static forwarder
```

SCALA FUNCTIONS IN JAVA

Scala promotes the use of function as object, or first-class functions. As of Java 1.6, there is no such concept in the Java language (or the JVM). Therefore, Scala creates the notion of *function traits.* These are a set of 23 traits that represent functions of arity 0 through 22. When the compiler encounters the need for passing a method as a function object, it creates an anonymous subclass of an appropriate function trait. As traits don't map into Java, the passing of first-class functions from Java into Scala is also inhibited but not impossible.

```
object FunctionUtil {
  def testFunction(f : Int => Int) : Int = f(5)
}
                                                        Special abstract
abstract class AbstractFunctionIntIntForJava extends    class to use
    (Int => Int) {                                  ⟵— from Java
}
```

We've created an abstract class in Scala that Java can implement more easily than a function trait. Although this eases the implementation in Java, it doesn't make things 100% simple. There's still a mismatch between Java's type system and Scala's encoding of types that requires us to coerce the type of the function when making the Scala call, as you can see in the following listing.

> **Listing 1.3   Implementing a first-class function in Java**

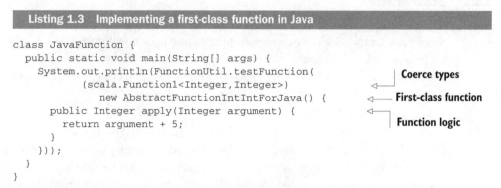

```
class JavaFunction {
  public static void main(String[] args) {
    System.out.println(FunctionUtil.testFunction(
          (scala.Function1<Integer,Integer>)                    Coerce types
              new AbstractFunctionIntIntForJava() {             First-class function
      public Integer apply(Integer argument) {
        return argument + 5;                                    Function logic
      }
    }));
  }
}
```

It's possible to use first-class functions and with them a more functional approach when combining Scala and Java. But other alternatives exist to make this work. A more detailed discussion of this tweak, along with other Java–Scala related issues can be found in chapter 10. As you can see, Scala can integrate well with existing Java programs and be used side by side with existing Java code. Java–Scala interaction isn't the only benefit of having Scala run inside the JVM; the JVM itself provides a huge benefit.

1.3.3   *The benefits of a JVM*

As alluded to earlier, the JVM provides many of the benefits associated with Java. Through bytecode, libraries become distributable to many differing platforms on an as is basis. The JVM has also been well tested in many environments and is used for large-scale enterprise deployments. It has also been a big focus on performance of the Java platform. The HotSpot compiler can perform various optimizations on code at runtime. This also enables users to upgrade their JVM and immediately see performance improvements, without patches or recompiling.

HOTSPOT-ING

The primary benefit of Scala running on the JVM is the HotSpot runtime optimizer. This allows runtime profiling of programs, with automatic optimizations applied against the JVM bytecode. Scala acquires these optimization "for free" by nature of running against the JVM. Every release of the JVM improves the HotSpot compiler, and this improves the performance of Scala. The HotSpot compiler does this through various techniques. Including the following:

- Method inlining
- On Stack Replacement (OSR)
- Escape Analysis
- Dynamic deoptimization

Method inlining is HotSpot's ability to determine when it can inline a small method directly at a call-spot. This was a favorite technique of mine in C++, and HotSpot will dynamically determine when this is optimal. *On Stack Replacement* refers to HotSpot's ability to determine that a variable could be allocated on the stack versus the heap. I remember in C++ the big question when declaring a variable was whether to place it on the stack or the heap. Now HotSpot can answer that for me. HotSpot performs *escape analysis* to determine if various things "escape" a certain scope. This is primarily used to reduce locking overhead when synchronized method calls are limited to some scope, but it can be applied to other situations. *Dynamic deoptimization* is the key feature of HotSpot. It's the ability to determine whether an optimization did *not* improve performance and undo that optimization, allowing others to be applied. These features combine into a pretty compelling picture of why new and old languages (for example, Ruby) desire to run on the JVM.

1.4 Summary

In this chapter, you've learned a bit about the philosophy of Scala. Scala was designed with the idea of blending various concepts from other languages. Scala blends functional and object-oriented programming, although this has been done in Java as well. Scala made choices about syntax that drastically reduced the verbosity of the language and enabled some powerful features to be elegantly expressed, such as type inference. Finally, Scala has tight integration with Java and runs on top of the Java virtual machine, which is perhaps the single most important aspect to make Scala relevant to us. It can be utilized in our day-to-day jobs with little cost.

As Scala blends various concepts, users of Scala will find themselves striking a balance among functional programming techniques, object orientation, integration with existing Java applications, expressive library APIs, and enforcing requirements through the type system. Often the best course of action is determined by the requirements at hand. It's the intersection of competing ideas where Scala thrives and also where the greatest care must be taken. This book will help guide when to use each of these techniques.

Let's start looking at a few key concepts every Scala developer needs to know when coding Scala.

The core rules

In this chapter
- Using the Scala Read Eval Print Loop
- Expression-oriented programming
- Immutability
- The Option class

This chapter covers a few topics that every newcomer to Scala needs to know. Not every topic is covered in depth, but we cover enough to allow you to explore the subject. You'll learn about the Read Eval Print Loop and how you can use this to rapidly prototype software. Next we'll learn about expression-oriented programming, and how to look at control flow in a different light. From this, we'll spring into immutability and why it can help to greatly simplify your programs, and help them run better concurrently.

2.1 Learn to use the Read Eval Print Loop (REPL)

Scala provides many materials to learn the core language. You can investigate many tutorials, examples, and projects online. But the single most important thing Scala provides is a *Read Eval Print Loop (REPL)*. The REPL is an interactive shell that compiles Scala code and returns results/type immediately. The Scala REPL is instantiated by running scala on the command line, assuming you have Scala installed on your machine and your path is set correctly. The Scala REPL should output something like the following:

```
$ scala
Welcome to Scala version 2.8.0.r21454-b20100411185142
  (Java HotSpot(TM) 64-Bit Server VM, Java 1.6.0_15).
Type in expressions to have them evaluated.
Type :help for more information.

scala>
```

From now on, in code examples I'll use the scala> prompt to imply that these were entered into the REPL. The following line will be the output. Let's do a few quick samples in the REPL and see what it shows us.

```
scala> "Hello"
res0: java.lang.String = Hello

scala> "Hello".filter(_ != 'l')
res1: String = Heo

scala> "Hello".map(_.toInt + 4)
res2: scala.collection.immutable.IndexedSeq[Int] =
  Vector(76, 105, 112, 112, 115)

scala> "Hello".r
res3: scala.util.matching.Regex = Hello
```

You'll notice that after every statement we enter into the interpreter, it prints a line like res0: java.lang.String = Hello (see figure 2.1). The first part of this expression is a variable name for the expression. In the case of these examples, the REPL is defining a new variable for the result of each expression (res0 through res3). The next part of the result expression (after the :) is the static type of the expression. The first example has a type of java.lang.String, whereas the last has a type of scala.util.matching.Regex. The last part of the result expression is the stringified value of the result. This normally comes from calling the toString method defined on all classes within the JVM.

As you can see, the REPL is a powerful way to test the Scala language and its type system. Most build tools also include a mechanism to start the REPL with the same classpath as your current working project. This means libraries and compiled classes from your project are available within the REPL. You can make API calls and remote server hits inside the REPL. This can be a great way to test out a web service or REST API in a quick manner. This leads to what I refer to as *experiment-driven development*.

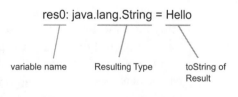

Figure 2.1   REPL return values

2.1.1   *Experiment-driven development*

Experiment-driven development is where you, the developer, first spend some time experimenting with a live interpreter or REPL before writing tests or production code. This gives you time to fully understand the external pieces of software you're interacting with and get a feel for the comings and goings of data within that API. It's a great way to learn about a new web service or RESTful API that has just been published, that latest Apache library, or even learn about something one of your coworkers have written. After determining the workings of the API, you can then better write your own code. If you also ascribe to test-driven development, this means that you would then write your tests.

Rule 1

Experiment in the REPL

Scala provides the REPL tool so every developer can toy around in the language before committing any final code. It's by far the most useful tool in the Scala ecosystem. Development should start inside the REPL in Scala.

There has been a big push for developers to embrace test-driven development (TDD). This is an approach to development where one writes the unit tests first, and then any implementation of those classes. You don't always know what your API should be before you write the tests. Part of TDD is defining the API through the tests. It allows you to see your code in context and get a feel for whether it's something you would want to use. Strongly typed languages can present more issues than dynamic languages with TDD because of expressiveness. Using the REPL, experiment-driven development brings this API definition phase before test generation, allowing a developer to ensure an API is possible in the type system.

Scala is a strongly typed language with flexible syntax, and as such sometimes requires some finagling with the type system to attain the API you desire. Because a lot of developers don't have strong type theory backgrounds, this often requires more experimentation. Experiment-driven development is about experimenting in the REPL with the type system to utilize types as effectively as possible in your API. Experiment-driven design is more about adding larger features or domains into your code, rather than new methods or bug fixes.

Experiment-driven design can also help drastically when defining domain-specific languages (DSLs). A DSL is a pseudo programming language that deals with a particular domain. This language is specific to the domain at hand—for example, querying for data from a database. A DSL may be either internal, as seen in many Scala libraries, or external like SQL. In Scala, it is popular among library developers to create DSLs covering the same domain as the library. For example, the Scala actors library defines a DSL for sending and receiving messages in a thread-safe manner.

One of the challenges when defining a DSL in Scala is to make effective use of the type system. A good type-safe DSL can be expressive and easy to read and can catch many programming errors at compiler time rather then runtime. Also having static knowledge of types can drastically improve performance. The REPL will let you experiment with how to express a particular domain and make sure that expression will compile. When developing Scala, one finds himself adopting the following creative flow:

- Experiment in the REPL with API design
- Copy working API into project files
- Develop unit tests against API
- Adapt code until unit tests pass

When used effectively, experiment-driven development can drastically improve the quality of your API. It will also help you become more comfortable with Scala syntax as you progress. The biggest issue remaining is that not every possible API in Scala is expressible in the REPL. This is because the REPL is interpreted on the fly, and it eagerly parses input.

2.1.2 *Working around eager parsing*

The Scala REPL attempts to parse input as soon as it possibly can. This, and a few other limitations, means that there are some things that are hard to impossible to express with the REPL. One important function to express are *companion objects and classes*.

A companion object and class are a set of object and class definitions that use the same name. This is easy to accomplish when compiling files; declare the object and class like so:

```
class Foo
```

These statements will also evaluate in the REPL, but they won't function as companions of each other. To prove this, in the following listing let's do something that a companion object can do, that a regular object can't: access private variables on the class.

Listing 2.1   Companion objects in REPL

```
scala>class Foo {
     | private var x = 5
     | }
defined class Foo

scala> object Foo {                              This would
     | def im_in_yr_foo(f: Foo) = f.x            compile normally
     | }
<console>:7: error: variable x cannot be accessed in Foo
       def im_in_yr_foo(f: Foo) = f.x
```

To fix this issue, we need to embed these objects in some other accessible scope within the interpreter. In the following listing, let's place them inside some scope so we can interpret/compile the class and companion object at the same time:

Listing 2.2   Correct companion object in REPL

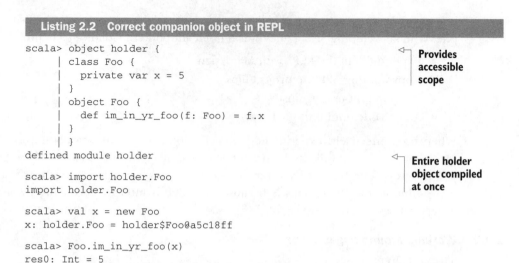

```
scala> object holder {
     |   class Foo {                                    Provides
     |     private var x = 5                            accessible
     |   }                                              scope
     |   object Foo {
     |     def im_in_yr_foo(f: Foo) = f.x
     |   }
     | }
defined module holder                                  Entire holder
                                                       object compiled
scala> import holder.Foo                                at once
import holder.Foo

scala> val x = new Foo
x: holder.Foo = holder$Foo@a5c18ff

scala> Foo.im_in_yr_foo(x)
res0: Int = 5
```

What we've done is create a *holder object*. This gives us our accessible scope, and defers the REPL's compilation until the close of the holder object. We then have to import Foo from the holder object. This allows us to test/define companion objects within the REPL.

> **PASTE AND SCALA 2.9.X**   Starting in Scala 2.9.x, the REPL supports a `:paste` command, where all code copied into the prompt is compiled in the same run. This provides an alternative to using a container object.

2.1.3   *Inexpressible language features*

Even working around eager parsing, there are still some language features that the REPL can't reproduce. Most of these issues revolve around packages, package objects, and package visibility restrictions. In particular, you're unable to effectively create a package or package object in the REPL the same way you can within a source file. This also means that other language features dealing with packages, particularly visibility restrictions using the `private` keyword, are also inexpressible. Usually packages are used to namespace your code and separate it from other libraries you might use. This isn't normally needed inside the REPL, but there may be times when you're toying with some advanced feature of Scala—say, package objects and implicit resolution— and you would like to do some experiment-driven development. In this case, you can't express what you want solely in the REPL; see the following listing.

Listing 2.3   Inexpressible language features in the REPL

```
package foo                                          Package definitions

package object bar {                                 Package objects
  private[foo] def baz(...) = ...                    Package private
}
```

Hope isn't lost. As stated before, most build utilities allow you to create a Scala REPL session against your current project. As a last resort you can toy with some concept in a Scala file, recompile, and restart your REPL session.

A tool known as JRebel (http://mng.bz/8b4t) can dynamically reload class files within a running JVM. The JRebel team has graciously provided free licenses when used with Scala. This tool, combined with some form of continuous compilation, available in most Scala build tools, will allow you to modify your project files and have the changed behavior be immediately available within you REPL session. For the maven-scala-plugin, the details for continuous compilation are located at http://mng.bz/qG78. The Simple Build Tool (http://mng.bz/2f7Q) provides the cc target for continuous compilation. Whatever build tool you use to start a REPL session must be integrated with a JRebel classloader so that dynamic class reloading can happen. This technique is a bit detailed and prone to change, so please check your build tool's documentation or the JRebel website for help.

The REPL will allow you to try out Scala code and get a real feel for what you're doing before attempting to create some large complicated system. It's often important in software development to get a slightly more than cursory knowledge of a system before tackling a new feature. The Scala REPL should allow you to do so with a minimal amount of time, allowing you to improve your development skills.

This entire book is enriched with examples of code from the REPL, as it's the best tool to teach and learn Scala. I often find myself running sample programs completely via the REPL before I even create some kind of "main" method, or a unit test, as is standard within Java development. To help encourage this, the book favors demonstrating concepts in the REPL using a few simple scripts. Please feel free to follow along with a REPL of your own.

> **USE THE REPL EVERYWHERE!**   No matter what build environment you use, the REPL can dramatically improve your development process. All the major IDEs have support for running the Scala REPL and most of the major build tools. Consult the documentation of the Scala integration for your IDE or build system for details on how to ensure a good REPL experience. For bonus points, use the REPL in combination with a graphical debugger.

The REPL is also a great way to begin learning how to use expressions rather than statements.

Rule 2 | **Use expressions not statements**

In Scala, a lot of code can be written as small methods of one expression. This style is not only elegant, but helps in code maintenance.

2.2   *Think in expressions*

Expression-oriented programming is a term I use to refer to the use of expressions rather than statements in code. What's the difference between an expression and a statement? A statement is something that executes, but an expression is something that evaluates.

What does this mean in practice? Expressions return values. Statements execute code, but there's no value returned. In this section, we'll learn all about expression-oriented programming and how it can help simplify your programs. We'll also look at mutability of objects, and how it interacts with expression-oriented programming.

> **STATEMENT VERSUS EXPRESSION**   A statement is something that executes; an expression is something that evaluates to a value.

Expressions are blocks of code that evaluate to a value. In Scala, some control blocks are also expressions. This means that if the control were to branch, each of these branches must evaluate to a value as well. The if clause is a great example; this checks a conditional expression and returns one expression or another, depending on the value of the conditional expression. Let's look at a simple REPL session:

```
scala> if(true) "true string" else "false string"
res4: String = true string

scala> if(false) 5 else "hello"
res5: Any = hello
```

As you can see, in Scala an if block is an expression. Our first if block returns "true string", the true expression. The second if block returns *hello*, the result of the false expression. To accomplish something similar in Java, you would use the ?: syntax as shown in the following:

```
String x = true ? "true string" : "false string"
```

An if block in Java is therefore distinct from a ?: expression in that it doesn't evaluate to a value. You can't assign the result of an if block in Java, but Scala has unified the concept of ?: with its if blocks. Scala has no ?: syntax; you merely use if blocks. This is the beginning of expression-oriented programming. In fact, Scala has few statements that do *not* return values from their last expression.

2.2.1   *Don't use return*

One of the keys to using expressions is realizing that there's no need for a return statement. An expression evaluates to a value, so there's no need to return.

While programming in Java, there was a common practice of having a single point of return for any method. This meant that if there was some kind of conditional logic, the developer would create a variable that contained the eventual return value. As the method flowed, this variable would be updated with what the method should return. The last line in every method would be a return statement. The following listing shows an example.

Listing 2.4   Java idiom: one return statement

```
def createErrorMessage(errorCode: Int) : String = {
  var result : String = _                          ⊲——— Initialized to default
  errorCode match {
    case 1 =>
```

```
      result = "Network Failure"                    ◁──── Directly assign result
    case 2 =>
      result = "I/O Failure"
    case _ =>
     result = "Unknown Error"
  }
  return result;
}
```

As you can see, the `result` variable is used to store the final result. The code falls through a pattern match, assigning error strings as appropriate, then returns the result variable. We can improve this code slightly by using the expression-oriented syntax that pattern matching allows. A pattern match returns a value. The type of the value is determined as a common super type from all case statement returns. Pattern matching also throws an exception if no pattern is matched, so we're guaranteed a return or error here. The following listing shows the code translated for an expression-oriented pattern match.

Listing 2.5   Updated `createErrorMessage` with expression-oriented pattern match

```
def createErrorMessage(errorCode : Int) : String = {
  val result = errorCode match {                    ◁── Assigning pattern match

    case 1 => "Network Failure"
    case 2 => "I/O Failure"                          Returns
    case 3 => "Unknown Error"                        expression
  }
  return result
}
```

You'll notice two things. First, we changed the result variable to a `val` and let the type inferencer determine the type. This is because we no longer have to change the `val` after assignment; the pattern match should determine the unique value. Therefore, we reduced the size and complexity of the code, and we increased immutability in the program. *Immutability* refers to the unchanging state of an object or variable; it's the opposite of mutability. *Mutability* is the ability of an object or variable to change or mutate during its lifetime. We'll cover mutability and expression-oriented programming in the next section. You'll frequently find that expression-oriented programming and immutable objects work well together.

The second thing we've done is remove any kind of assignment from the case statements. The last expression in a case statement is the "result" of that case statement. We could have embedded further logic in each case statement if necessary, as long as we eventually had some kind of expression at the bottom. The compiler will also warn us if we accidentally forget to return, or somehow return the wrong type.

The code is looking a lot more concise, but we can still improve it somewhat. In Scala, most developers avoid return statements in their code; they prefer to have the last expression be the return value (similar to all the other expression-oriented styles). In fact, for the `createErrorMessage` method, we can remove the intermediate `result` variable altogether. The following listing shows the final transformation.

Listing 2.6   Final expression-oriented `createErrorMessage` method

```
def createErrorMessage(errorCode: Int) : String = errorCode match {
  case 1 => "Network Failure"
  case 2 => "I/O Failure"
  case _ => "Unknown Error"
}
```

Note how we haven't even opened up a code block for the method? The pattern match is the only statement in the method, and it returns an expression of type `String`. We've completely transformed the method into an expression-oriented syntax. Note how much more concise and expressive the code is. Also note that the compiler will warn us of any type infractions or unreachable case statements.

2.2.2   *Mutability*

Expression-oriented programming becomes slightly more interesting when mixed with mutability, or the ability to change an object's state during its lifetime. This is because code utilizing mutable objects tends to be written in an imperative style.

Imperative coding is a style that you're probably used to. Many early languages such as C, Fortran, and Pascal are imperative. Imperative code tends to be made of statements, not expressions. Objects are created which have state. Then statements are executed that "mutate" or change the state of an object. In the case of languages that don't have objects, the same mechanisms apply, except with variables and structures. The following listing shows an example of imperative code.

Listing 2.7   Example of imperative style code

```
val x = Vector2D(0.0,0.0)
x.magnify(2.0)
```

Note how a vector is constructed and then mutated via the magnify method. Expression-oriented code prefers having all statements return some expression or value, which would include the move method. In the case of object mutation, what value should be returned? One option is to return the object that was just mutated, as in the following listing.

Listing 2.8   Example mutable expression-oriented method

```
class Vector2D(var x: Double, var y: Double) {
  def magnify(amt: Double) : Vector2D = {
    x *= amt
    y *= amt
    this
  }
}
```

This may seem a great option but has some serious drawbacks. In particular, it can get confusing determining when an object is being mutated, especially when combined with immutable objects. See if you can determine what values should print at the end of this block of code. Assume that the - method defined on `Vector2D` follows the mathematical definition. Now for the listing.

Listing 2.9   Mixing immutable and mutable objects with expression

```scala
scala> val x = new Vector2D(1.0, 1.0)
x : Vector2D = Vector2D(1.0,1.0)

scala> val y = new Vector2D(-1.0, 1.0)
y : Vector2D = Vector2D(1.0, 1.0)

scala> x.magnify(3.0) - (x - y).magnify(3.0)
res0 : mutable.Vector2D = ???
```

What is the result of the preceding expression, then? On first look, we would expect it to be the vector (3.0,3.0) minus the vector (6.0,0.0), which is (-3.0,3.0). But each of these variables is mutable. This means that the operations are modifying the variables in the order they're used. Let's evaluate this as it's compiled. First the x vector, (1.0,1.0) is magnified by 3 to become (3.0,3.0). Next, we subtract y from x to give x the value (2.0,4.0). Why? Because the right-hand side of the - method must be evaluated next, and (x-y) is the first part of this expression. We then magnify x by 3.0 again, bringing the value to (6.0,12.0). Finally we subtract x from itself, bringing the resulting value to (0.0,0.0). That's right—x is subtracted from itself. Why? Because the expression on the left-hand side of the - and the right-hand side of the minus both start with the x variable. Because we're using mutability, this means that each expression returns x itself. So no matter what we do, we wind up calling x - x which results in the vector (0.0, 0.0).

Because of this confusion, it's best to prefer immutability when using objects and expression-oriented programming. This is particularly the case with operator overloading, as with the previous example. Some examples can demonstrate where mutability works well with expression-oriented programming, particularly with pattern matching or if statements.

Code has a common task where you need to look up values on an object based on some value. These objects may be immutable or mutable. But expression-oriented programming comes in to simplify the lookup. Let's consider a simple example of looking up the action to perform based on a Menu button click. When we click the Menu button, we receive an event from our event system. This event is marked with the identifier of the button pressed. We want to perform some action and return a status. Let's check out the code in the following listing.

Listing 2.10   Mutable objects and expressions—the right way

```scala
def performActionForButton(buttonEvent: ButtonEvent,
                     form: Form) : Boolean =
  buttonEvent.getIdentifier match {
    case "SUBMIT" if form.isValid() =>
        try {
          form.submit()
```

```
          true
        } catch {
        case t: FormSubmitError =>
          false
        }
    case "CLEAR" =>
        form.clear()
        true
    case _ =>
        false
    }
```

Return
values

Note how we're mutating the objects in place and then returning our result. Instead of an explicit return statement, we state the expression we wish to return. You can see the code here is more succinct than creating a variable to hold the result variable. You'll also notice that mixing mutation statements with our expressions has reduced some of the clarity of the code. This is one of the reasons why it's better to prefer immutable code—the topic of our next section.

Expression-oriented programming can reduce boilerplate and provide elegant code. It's accomplished through having all statements return meaningful values. You can now reduce clutter and increase expressiveness within your code.

Expression-oriented programming tends to pair favorably with immutable programming, but less so with mutable objects. Immutability is a term to denote that something doesn't change, in this case the state of an object, once constructed.

2.3   *Prefer immutability*

Immutability, in programming, refers to the unchanging state of objects after construction. This is one of the capstones of functional programming and a recommended practice for object-oriented design on the JVM. Scala is no exception here and prefers immutability in design, making it the default in many cases. This can be tricky. In this section, you'll learn how immutability can help when dealing with equality issues or concurrent programs.

Rule
3

Prefer Immutability

Creating immutable classes drastically reduces the number of potential runtime issues. When in doubt, it's safest to stay immutable.

The most important thing to realize in Scala is that there's a difference between an immutable object and an immutable reference. In Scala, all variables are references to objects. Defining a variable as a `val` means that it's an immutable *reference*. All method parameters are immutable references, and class arguments default to being immutable references. The only way to create a mutable variable is through the `var` syntax. The immutability of the reference doesn't affect whether the object referred to is immutable. You can have a mutable reference to an immutable object and vice versa. This means it's important to know whether the object itself is immutable or mutable.

Determining immutability constraints on objects isn't obvious. In general, it's safe to assume that if the documentation states an object is immutable, then it is;

otherwise, be careful. The Scala standard library helps make the delineation obvious in its collections classes by having parallel package hierarchies, one for immutable classes and one for mutable classes.

In Scala immutability is important because it can help programmers reason through their code. If an object's state doesn't change, then you can determine where objects are created to see where state changes. It can also simplify methods that are based on the state of an object. This benefit is particularly evident when defining equality or writing concurrent programs.

2.3.1 *Object equality*

One critical reason to prefer immutability is the simplification of object equality. If an object won't change state during its lifetime, one can create an equals implementation that is both deep and correct for any object of that type. This is also critical when creating a hash function for objects. A hash function is one that returns a simplified representation of an object, usually an integer, that can be used to quickly identify the object. A good hash function and equals method are usually paired, if not through code, then in logical definition. If state changes during the lifetime of an object, it can ruin any hash code that was generated for the object. This in turn can affect the equality tests of the object. The following listing shows a simple example of a two-dimensional geometric point class.

Listing 2.11 Mutable `Point2` class

```
class Point2(var x: Int, var y: Int) {
  def move(mx: Int, my: Int) : Unit = {
    x = x + mx
    y = y + my
  }
}
```

The Point2D class is simple. It consists of *x* and *y* values, corresponding to locations on the x and y axes. It also has a move method, which is used to move the point around the two-dimensional plane. Imagine we want to tie labels to particular points on this 2-D plane, where each label is only a string. To do so, we'd like to use a map of Point2D to string values. For efficient lookup, we're going to use a hashing function and a HashMap. Let's try the simplest possible thing, hashing with the *x* and *y* variables directly, in the following listing.

Listing 2.12 Mutable `Point2` class with hashing function

```
class Point2(var x: Int, var y: Int) {
  def move(mx: Int, my: Int) : Unit = {
    x = x + mx
    y = y + my
  }
  override def hashCode(): Int = y + (31*x)
}
```

```
scala> val x = new Point2(1,1)
x: Point2 = Point2@20

scala> x.##
res1: Int = 32

scala> val y = new Point2(1,2)
y: Point2 = Point2@21

scala> import collection.immutable.HashMap
import collection.immutable.HashMap

scala> val map = HashMap(x -> "HAI", y -> "ZOMG")
map: scala.collection.immutable.HashMap[
  Point2,java.lang.String] =
  Map((Point2@21,ZOMG), (Point2@20,HAI))

scala> map(x)
res4: java.lang.String = HAI

scala> val z = new Point2(1,1)
z: Point2 = Point2@20

scala> map(z)
java.util.NoSuchElementException: key not found: Point2@20
...
```

Things appear to be working exactly as we want—until we attempt to construct a new point object with the same values as point *x*. This point should hash into the same section of the map, but the equality check will fail because we haven't created our own equality method. By default, Scala uses object location equality and hashing, but we've only overridden the hash code. Object location equality is using the address in memory for an object as the only factor to determine if two objects are equal. In our Point2 case, object location equality can be a quick check for equality, but we can also make use of the *x* and *y* locations to check for equality.

You may have noticed that the Point2 class overrides the hashCode method, but I'm calling the ## method on the instance x. This is a convention in Scala. For compatibility with Java, Scala utilizes the same equals and hashCode methods defined on java.lang.Object. But Scala also abstracts primitives such that they appear as full objects. The compiler will box and unbox the primitives as needed for you. These primitive-like objects are all subtypes of scala.AnyVal whereas "standard" objects, those that would have extended java.lang.Object, are subtypes of scala.AnyRef. scala.AnyRef can be considered an alias for java.lang.Object. As the hashCode and equals methods are defined on AnyRef, Scala provides the methods ## and == that you can use for both AnyRef and AnyVal.

> **HASHCODE AND EQUALS SHOULD ALWAYS BE PAIRED**   The equals and hashCode methods should always be implemented such that if x == y then x.## == y.##.

Let's implement our own equality method in the following listing and see what the results are.

Listing 2.13 Mutable `Point2` class with hashing and equality

```
class Point2(var x: Int, var y: Int) extends Equals {
  def move(mx: Int, my: Int) : Unit = {
    x = x + mx
    y = y + my
  }
  override def hashCode(): Int = y + (31*x)
  def canEqual(that: Any): Boolean = that match {
      case p: Point2 => true
      case _ => false
  }
  override def equals(that: Any): Boolean = {
    def strictEquals(other: Point2) =
        this.x == other.x && this.y == other.y
    that match {
      case a: AnyRef if this eq a => true
      case p: Point2 => (p canEqual this) && strictEquals(p)
      case _ => false
    }
  }
}

scala> val x = new Point2(1,1)
x: Point2 = Point2@20

scala> val y = new Point2(1,2)
y: Point2 = Point2@21

scala> val z = new Point2(1,1)
z: Point2 = Point2@20

scala> x == z
res6: Boolean = true

scala> x == y
res7: Boolean = false
```

The implementation of `equals` may look strange, but will be covered in more detail in section 2.5.2. For now, note that the `strictEquals` helper method compares the *x* and *y* values directly. This means that two points are considered equal if they are in the same location. We've now tied our `equals` and `hashCode` methods to the same criteria, the x and y values. Let's throw our *x* and *y* values into a `HashMap` again, only this time we're going to move the *x* value, and see what happens to the label attached to it.

Listing 2.14 Mutating `Point2` with `HashMap`

```
scala> val map = HashMap(x -> "HAI", y -> "WORLD")
map: scala.collection.immutable.HashMap[Point2,java.lang.String] =
  Map((Point2@21,WORLD), (Point2@20,HAI))

scala> x.move(1,1)

scala> map(y)
res9: java.lang.String = WORLD
```

```
scala> map(x)
java.util.NoSuchElementException: key not found: Point2@40
...

scala> map(z)
java.util.NoSuchElementException: key not found: Point2@20
...
```

What happened to the label attached to *x*? We placed it into the HashMap when *x* has a value of (1,1). This means it had a hash code of 32. We then move *x* to (2,2), changing its hash code to 64. Now when we try to look up the label in the map using *x*, it can't be found because *x* was encoding with the hash bucket of 32, and it's looking in the hash bucket for 64. Well, what if we try to look up the value using a new point, *z*, that still has a hash code of 32? It also fails, because *x* and *z* aren't equal according to our rules. You see, a HashMap uses the hash at the time of insertion to store values but doesn't update when an object's state mutates. This means we've lost our label for *x* when using hash-based lookup, but we can still retrieve the value when traversing the map or using traversal algorithms:

```
scala> map.find( _._1 == x)
res13: Option[(Point2, java.lang.String)] = Some((Point2@40,HAI))
```

As you can see, this behavior is rather confusing, and can cause no end of strife when debugging. As such, it's generally recommended to ensure the following constraints when implementing equality:

- If two objects are equal, they should have the same hashCode.
- A hashCode computed for an object won't change for the life of the object.
- When sending an object to another JVM, equality should be determined using attributes available in both JVMs.

As you can see, the second constraint implies that all criteria used in creating a hash-Code should *not* change with the life of an object. The last statement, when applicable, means that an object's hash and equals method should be computed using its own internal state. Combine this with the first statement, and you find that the only way to satisfy these requirements is through the use of immutable objects. If the state of an object never changes, it's acceptable to use it in computing a hash code or when testing equality. You can also serialize the object to another JVM and continue to have a consistent hash code and equality.

You may be wondering, why do I care about sending objects to other JVMs? My software will never run on more than one JVM. In fact, my software runs on a mobile device, where resources are critical. The problem with that thinking is that serializing an object to another JVM need not be done in real time. I could save some program state to disk and read it back later. This is effectively the same as sending something to another JVM. Although you may not be directly sending it over the network, you're sending it through time, where the JVM of today is the writer of data, and the JVM started tomorrow is the user of the data. In these instances, having a hash code and equals implementation is critical.

The last constraint makes immutability a necessity. Remove this constraint, and there are only two simple ways to satisfy the first two constraints:

- Utilize only immutable object internal state in hashCode computation
- Use default concepts for equals and hashCode

As you can see, this means that *something* in the object must be immutable. Making the entire object immutable simplifies this whole process greatly.

2.3.2 Concurrency

Immutability doesn't merely simplify object equality; it can also simplify concurrent access of data. Programs are becoming increasingly parallelized, and processors are splitting into multiple cores. The need to run concurrent threads of control in programs is growing across all forms of computing. Traditionally, this meant using creative means to protect access to shared data across these various threads of control. Protected mutable data usually means some form of locking. Immutability can help share state while reducing the need for locking.

Locking entails a performance overhead. Threads that wish to read data can't do so unless the lock is available to obtain. Even using read-write locks can cause issues, because a writer may be slow in preventing readers from accessing the data they desire. On the JVM, there are optimizations in the JIT to attempt to avoid locks when they aren't necessary. In general, you want to have as few locks in your software as possible, but you want enough to encourage a high degree of parallelism. The more you can design your code to avoid locking the better. For instance, let's try to measure the effect of locking on an algorithm and see if we can design a new algorithm that reduces the amount of locking.

We'll create an index service that we can query to find particular items by their key. The service will also allow users to add new items into the index. We expect to have many users looking up values and a smaller amount of users adding additional content to the index. Here's the initial interface:

```
trait Service[Key,Value] {
  def lookUp(k: Key): Option[Value]
  def insert(k: Key, v: Value): Unit
}
```

The service is made up of two methods: lookUp, which will look up values in the index by the key, and insert, which will insert new values into the service. This service is like a map of key-to-value pairs. Let's implement this using a locking and a mutable HashMap.

```
import collection.mutable.{HashMap=>MutableHashMap}

class MutableService[Key, Value] extends Service[Key, Value] {
  val currentIndex = new MutableHashMap[Key, Value]
  def lookUp(k: Key): Option[Value] = synchronized(currentIndex.get(k))
  def insert(k: Key, v: Value): Unit = synchronized {
    currentIndex.put(k,v)
  }
}
```

This class contains three members. The first is the currentIndex, which is a reference to the mutable HashMap that we use to store values. The lookUp and insert methods are both surrounded by a synchronized block, which synchronizes against the MutableService. You'll notice that all operations on a MutableService require locking. But given what was stated about the usage of this service, the lookUp method will be called far more often than the insert method. A read-write lock could help in this situation, but let's look at using immutability instead.

We'll change the currentIndex to be an ImmutableHashMap that get overwritten when the insert method is called. The lookUp method can then be free of any locking, as shown in the following code:

```
class ImmutableService[Key, Value] extends Service[Key, Value] {
  var currentIndex = new ImmutableHashMap[Key,Value]
  def lookUp(k: Key): Option[Value] = currentIndex.get(k)
  def insert(k: Key, v: Value): Unit = synchronized {
    currentIndex = currentIndex + ((k, v))
  }
}
```

The first thing to notice is that the currentIndex is a mutable reference to an immutable variable. We update this reference every time there's an insert operation. The second thing to notice is that this service isn't completely immutable. All that's happened is the reduction of locking by utilizing an immutable HashMap. This simple change can cause a drastic improvement in running time.

I've set up a simple micro-performance benchmark suite for these two classes. The basics of the suite are simple. We construct a set of tasks that will write items into the service and a set of tasks that will attempt to read items from the index. We then interleave the two sets of tasks and submit them to a queue of two threads for execution. We time the speed that this entire process takes and record the results. Figure 2.2 shows some worst-case results.

The y-axis is the execution time of running a test. The x-axis corresponds to the number of insert/lookUp tasks submitted to the thread pools. You'll notice that the mutable service's execution time grows faster than the immutable service's execution time. This graph certainly shows that extra locking can severely impact performance. But note that the execution times of this test can greatly vary. Due to the uncertainty of parallelism, this graph could look anywhere from the one shown above to a graph where the immutable service and mutable service execution times track relatively the same. In general, the MutableService implementation was slower than the ImmutableService, but don't judge performance from one graph or on execution alone.

Figure 2.3 shows another graph where you can see, for one particular test, the MutableService had all of its stars align and ran with a drastically reduced locking overhead. You can see in the preceding run where a single test case had all its timing align so that the MutableService could outperform the ImmutableService. Though possible for this specific case, the general case involved the ImmutableService outperforming the MutableService. If the assumptions stated here hold true for a real-life program,

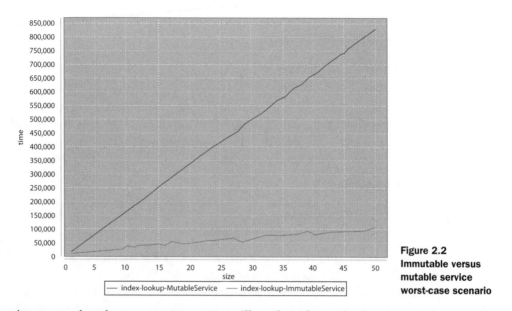

**Figure 2.2
Immutable versus
mutable service
worst-case scenario**

it appears that the `ImmutableService` will perform better in the general case and not suffer from random contention slowdowns.

The most important thing to realize is that immutable objects can be passed among many threads without fear of contention. The ability to remove locks, and all the potential bugs associated with them, can drastically improve the stability of a codebase. Combined with the improved reasoning one can get, as seen with the equals method, immutability is something to strive to maintain within a codebase.

Immutability can ease concurrent development by reducing the amount of protection a developer must use when interacting with immutable objects. Scala also

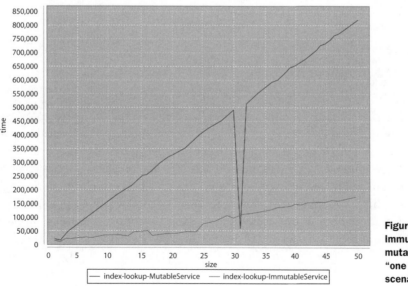

**Figure 2.3
Immutable versus
mutable service
"one golden run"
scenario**

provides a class called `Option` that allows developers to relax the amount of protection they need when dealing with `null`.

2.4   *Use None instead of null*

Scala does its best to discourage the use of null in general programming. It does this through the `scala.Option` class found in the standard library. An `Option` can be considered a container of something or nothing. This is done through the two subclasses of `Option`: `Some` and `None`. `Some` denotes a container of exactly one item. `None` denotes an empty container, a role similar to what `Nil` plays for `List`.

Rule 4

Use None instead of null

While it was habit in Java to initialize values to null, Scala provides an `Option` type for the same purpose. `Option` is self-documenting for developers and, used correctly, can prevent unintended null pointer exceptions when using Scala.

In Java, and other languages that allow `null`, `null` is often used as a placeholder to denote a nonfatal error as a return value or to denote that a variable isn't yet initialized. In Scala, one can denote this through the `None` subclass of `Option`. Conversely, one can denote an initialized, or nonfatal variable state through the `Some` subclass of `Option`. Let's look at the usage of these two classes in the following listing.

Listing 2.15   Simple usage of Some and None

```
scala> var x : Option[String] = None
x: Option[String] = None

scala> x.get
java.util.NoSuchElementException: None.get in

scala> x.getOrElse("default")
res0: String = default

scala> x = Some("Now Initialized")
x: Option[String] = Some(Now Initialized)

scala> x.get
res0: java.lang.String = Now Initialized

scala> x.getOrElse("default")
res1: java.lang.String = Now Initialized
```

An `Option` containing no value can be constructed via the `None` object. An `Option` that contains a value is created via the `Some` factory method. `Option` provides many differing ways of retrieving values from its inside. Of particular use are the `get` and `getOrElse` methods. The `get` method will attempt to access the value stored in an `Option` and will throw an exception if it's empty. This is similar to accessing nullable values within other languages. The `getOrElse` method will attempt to access the value stored in an `Option`, if one exists; otherwise it will return the value supplied to the method. You should always prefer `getOrElse` over using `get`.

Scala provides a factory method on the `Option` companion object that will convert from a Java style reference, where `null` implies an empty variable, into an `Option` where this is more explicit. Let's take a quick look in the following listing.

Listing 2.16   Usage of the `Option` factory

```
scala> var x : Option[String] = Option(null)
x: Option[String] = None

scala> x = Option("Initialized")                          ◁──── Option.apply("Initialized")
x: Option[String] = Some(Initialized)
```

The `Option` factory method will take a variable and create a `None` object if the input was `null`, or it will create a `Some` if the input was initialized. This makes it rather easy to take inputs from an untrusted source—that is, another JVM language—and wrap them into `Option`s. You might be asking yourself why you would want to do this. Isn't checking for `null` just as simple in code? `Option` provides advanced features that make it far more ideal than using `null` and `if` checks.

2.4.1   *Advanced Option techniques*

The greatest feature of `Option` is that you can treat it as a collection. This means you can perform the standard `map`, `flatMap`, and `foreach` methods, as well as utilize it inside a `for` expression. This helps ensure a nice concise syntax, and it opens a variety of different methods to handling uninitialized values. Let's look at some common issues solved using `null` and their solutions using `Option`, starting with creating an object or returning a default.

CREATE AN OBJECT OR RETURN A DEFAULT

You'll have many times in code when you'll need to construct something if some other variable exists, or supply some sort of default. Let's pretend that we have an application that requires some kind of temporary file storage for its execution. The application is designed so that a user may optionally specify a directory to store temporary files on the command line. If the user doesn't specify a new file, if the argument provided by the user is not a real directory, or if they didn't provide a directory, then we want to return a sensible default temporary directory. The following listing shows a method that will return this temporary directory:

Listing 2.17   Creating an object or returning a default

```
def getTemporaryDirectory(tmpArg: Option[String]): java.io.File = {
    tmpArg.map(name => new java.io.File(name)).              ◁──── Create if defined
        filter(_.isDirectory).                              ◁──── Only directories
        getOrElse(new java.io.File(                         ◁──── Specify default
          System.getProperty("java.io.tmpdir")))
}
```

The `getTemporaryDirectory` method takes the command-line parameter as an `Option` containing a `String` and returns a `File` object referencing the temporary directory we should use. The first thing we do is use the `map` method on `Option` to create a `java.io.File` if there was a parameter. Next, we make sure that this newly constructed file object is a directory. To do that, we use the `filter` method. This will check whether the value in an `Option` abides by some predicate, and if not, convert to a `None`. Finally, we check to see if we have a value in the `Option`; otherwise we return the default temporary directory.

This enables a powerful set of checks without resorting to nested `if` statements or blocks. Sometimes we would like a block, such as when we want to execute a block of code based on the availability of a particular parameter.

EXECUTE BLOCK OF CODE IF VARIABLE IS INITIALIZED

`Option` can be used to execute a block of code if the `Option` contains a value. This is done through the `foreach` method, which, as expected, iterates over all the elements in the `Option`. As an `Option` can only contain zero or one value, this means the block either executes or is ignored. This syntax works particularly well with `for` expressions. Let's take a look at the following listing.

> **Listing 2.18   Executing code if option is defined**

```
val username: Option[String] = ...

for(uname <- username) {
    println("User: " + uname)
}
```

As you can see, this looks like a normal "iterate over a collection" control block. The syntax remains similar when we need to iterate over several variables. Let's look at the case where we have some kind of Java servlet framework, and we want to be able to authenticate users. If authentication is possible, we want to inject our security token into the `HttpSession` so that later filters and servlets can check access privileges for this user, as in the following listing.

> **Listing 2.19   Executing code if several options are defined**

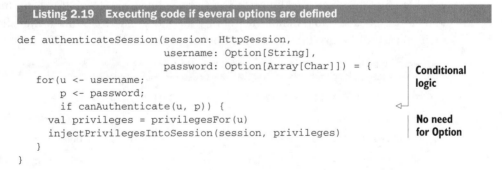

```
def authenticateSession(session: HttpSession,
                        username: Option[String],
                        password: Option[Array[Char]]) = {
    for(u <- username;                                          Conditional
        p <- password;                                          logic
        if canAuthenticate(u, p)) {
      val privileges = privilegesFor(u)                         No need
      injectPrivilegesIntoSession(session, privileges)          for Option
    }
}
```

Note that you can embed conditional logic in a `for` expression. This helps keep less nested logical blocks within your program. Another important consideration is that all the helper methods do *not* need to use the `Option` class. `Option` works as a great front-line defense for potentially uninitialized variables, but it doesn't need to pollute the rest of your code. In Scala, `Option` as an argument implies that something may not be initialized. The opposite should be true as well. If a method takes a value that is not labeled as an `Option`, you should not pass it null or uninitialized parameters.

Scala's `for` expression syntax is rather robust, even allowing you to produce values, rather then execute code blocks. This is handy when you have a set of potentially uninitialized parameters that you want to transform into something else.

USING POTENTIAL UNINITIALIZED VARIABLES TO CONSTRUCT ANOTHER VARIABLE

Sometimes we want to transform a set of potentially uninitialized values so that we have to deal with only one. To do this, we need to use a `for` expression again, but this time using a `yield`. The following listing shows a case where a user has input some database credentials, or we attempted to read them from an encrypted location, and we want to create a database connection using these parameters. We don't want to deal with failure in our function, as this is a utility function that won't have access to the user. In this case, we'd like to transform our database connection configuration parameters into a single option containing our database.

Listing 2.20   Merging options

```
def createConnection(conn_url: Option[String],
                     conn_user: Option[String],
                     conn_pw: Option[String]) : Option[Connection] =
  for {
    url <- conn_url
    user <- conn_user
    pw <- conn_pw
  } yield DriverManager.getConnection(url, user, pw)
```

This function does exactly what we need it to. It does seem, though, that we're merely deferring all logic to `DriverManager.getConnection`. What if we wanted to abstract this such that we can take *any* function and create one that's option-friendly in the same manner? The following listing shows what we'll call the "lift" function.

Listing 2.21   Generically converting functions

```
scala>  def lift3[A,B,C,D](
     |    f: Function3[A,B,C,D]): Function3[Option[A], Option[B],
     |                                      Option[C], Option[D]] = {
     |      (oa : Option[A], ob : Option[B], oc : Option[C]) =>
     |        for(a <- oa; b <- ob; c <- oc) yield f(a,b,c)
     |    }
lift3: [A,B,C,D](f: (A, B, C) => D)(Option[A],
                                    Option[B],
                                    Option[C]) => Option[D]            Using lift3
                                                                      directly
scala> lift3(DriverManager.getConnection)
res4: (Option[java.lang.String],
       Option[java.lang.String],
       Option[java.lang.String]) => Option[java.sql.Connection] =
  <function3>
```

The `lift3` method looks somewhat like our earlier `createConnection` method, except that it takes a function as its sole parameter. The `Function3` trait represents a function that takes three arguments and returns a result. The `lift3` function takes a function of three arguments as input and outputs a new function of three arguments. As you can see from the REPL output, we can use this against existing functions to create option-friendly functions. We've directly taken the `DriverManager.get-Connection` method and lifted it into something that's semantically equivalent to our earlier `createConnection` method. This technique works well when used with the "encapsulation" of uninitialized variables. You can write most of your code, even utility methods, assuming that everything is initialized, and then lift these functions into `Option`-friendly variants when needed.

One important thing to mention is that `Option` derives its equality and `hashCode` from what it contains. In Scala, understanding equality and `hashCode`, especially in a polymorphic setting, is very important.

2.5   *Polymorphic equality*

Let's discuss how to properly implement an `equals` and `hashCode` function in Scala. This can be tricky in a polymorphic language, but can be done by following some basic rules. In general, it's best to avoid having multiple concrete levels with classes that also need equality stronger then referential equality. In some cases, classes only need referential equality, the ability to differentiate two objects to determine if they're the same instance. But if the equality comparison needs to determine if two differing instances are equivalent *and* there are multiple concrete hierarchies, then things get a bit more tricky.

To understand this issue, we'll look at how to write a good equality method.

2.5.1   *Example: A timeline library*

We'd like to construct a time line, or calendar, widget. This widget needs to display dates, times, and time ranges as well as associated events with each day. The fundamental concept in this library is going to be an `InstantaneousTime`.

`InstantaneousTime` is a class that represents a particular discrete time within the time series. We could use the `java.util.Date` class, but we'd prefer something that's immutable, as we've just learned how this can help simplify writing good `equals` and `hashCode` methods. In an effort to keep things simple, let's have our underlying time storage be an integer of seconds since midnight, January 1, 1970, Greenwich Mean Time on a Gregorian calendar. We'll assume that all other times can be formatted into this representation and that time zones are an orthogonal concern to representation. We're also going to make the following common assumptions about our equality usage in the application:

- When `equals` is called and it will return `true`, it's because both objects are the same reference.
- Most calls to `equals` result in a return of `false`.

- Our implementation of `hashCode` is sufficiently sparse that for most equality comparisons, the `hashCode`s will be different.
- Computing a `hashCode` is more efficient than a deep equality comparison.
- Testing referential equality is more efficient than a deep equality comparison.

These assumptions are standard for most equality implementations. They might not always hold for your application. Let's take a first crack at the class and a simple equals and `hashCode` method pair in the following listing, and see what this looks like.

Listing 2.22   Simple `InstantaneousTime` class

```scala
trait InstantaneousTime {
  val repr: Int

  override def equals(other: Any) : Boolean = other match {
    case that: InstantaneousTime =>              Referential
      if(this eq that) {                          equality
        true
      } else {                                   Hash code
        (that.## == this.##) &&                    check
        (repr == that.repr)             Deep equality
      }
    case _ => false
  }                                       Linked to equals
  override def hashCode() : Int = repr.##    implementation
}
```

The class contains only one member, `repr`, which is a number representing the seconds since midnight, January 1, 1970 Greenwich Mean Time. As this is the only data value in the class, and it's immutable, `equals` and `hashCode` will be based on this value. When implementing an `equals` method within the JVM, it's usually more performant to test referential equality before doing any sort of deep equality check. In the case of this class, it's not necessary. For a sufficiently complex class, it can drastically help performance, but this class doesn't need it. The next piece to a good `equals` method is usually using the `hashCode` for an early false check. Given a sufficiently sparse and easy to compute `hashCode`, this would be a good idea. Once again, in this class it's not necessary, but in a sufficiently complex class, this can be performant.

> **`##` AND `==` VS. EQUALS AND HASHCODE**   In Scala, the `##` method is equivalent to the `hashCode` method in Java as the `==` method is equivalent to the `equals` method in Java. In Scala, when *calling* the `equals` or `hashCode` method it's better to use `##` and `==`. These methods provide additional support for value types. But the `equals` and `hashCode` method are used when *overriding* the behavior. This split provides better runtime consistency and still retains Java interoperability.

This class helps us illustrate two principles: the importance of a good equality method and always challenge the assumptions of your code. In this case, the "best practice" equality method, while great for a sufficiently complex class, provides little benefit for this simple class.

NOTE   When implementing equality for your own classes, test the assumptions in the standard equality implementation to make sure they hold true.

Our implementation of equals suffers from yet another flaw, that of polymorphism.

2.5.2   *Polymorphic equals implementation*

In general, it's best to avoid polymorphism with types requiring deep equality. Scala no longer supports subclassing case classes for this very reason. But there are still times in code where this is useful or even necessary. To do so, we need to ensure that we've implemented our equality comparisons correctly, keeping polymorphism in mind and utilizing it in our solution.

Let's create a subclass of `InstantaneousTime` that also stores labels. This is the class we'll use to save events in our timeline, so we'll call it `Event`. We'll make the assumption that events on the same day will hash into the same bucket, and hence have the same `hashCode`, but equality will also include the name of the event. Let's take a crack at an implementation in the following listing.

> **Listing 2.23   Event subclass of `InstantaneousTime`**

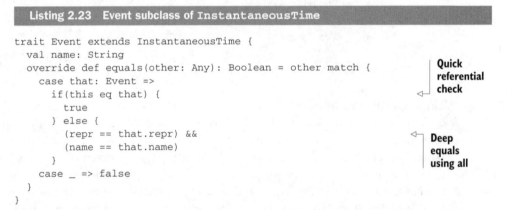

```scala
trait Event extends InstantaneousTime {
  val name: String
  override def equals(other: Any): Boolean = other match {     Quick
    case that: Event =>                                         referential
      if(this eq that) {                                        check
        true
      } else {
        (repr == that.repr) &&                                  Deep
        (name == that.name)                                     equals
      }                                                         using all
    case _ => false
  }
}
```

We've dropped the `hashCode` early exit in our code, as checking the `repr` member is just as performant in our particular class. The other thing you'll notice is that we've changed the pattern match so that only two `Event` objects can be equal to each other. Let's try to use this in the REPL in the following listing.

> **Listing 2.24   Using `Event` and `InstantaneousTime`**

```scala
scala> val x = new InstantaneousTime {
     | val repr = 2
     | }
x: java.lang.Object with InstantaneousTime = $anon$1@2

scala> val y = new Event {
     | val name = "TestEvent"
     | val repr = 2
     | }
y: java.lang.Object with Event = $anon$1@2

scala> y == x                                    Subclass to original
```

```
res8: Boolean = false

scala> x == y                                    ◁——— Original to subclass
res9: Boolean = true
```

Rule 5 | **Use scala.Equals for polymorphic equality**

Polymorphic equality is easy to mess up. scala.Equals provides a template to make it easier to avoid mistakes.

What's happened? The old class is using the old implementation of the equality method, and therefore doesn't check for the new name field. We need to modify our original equality method in the base class to account for the fact that subclasses may wish to modify the meaning of equality. In Scala, there's a scala.Equals trait that can help us fix this issue. The Equals trait defines a canEqual method that's used in tandem with the standard equals method. The canEqual method allows subclasses to opt out of their parent classes' equality implementation. This is done by allowing the other parameter in the equals method an opportunity to cause an equality failure. To do so, we override canEqual in our subclass with whatever rejection criteria our overridden equals method has. Let's modify our classes to account for polymorphism using these two methods in the following listing.

Listing 2.25   Using scala.Equals

```
trait InstantaneousTime extends Equals {
  val repr: Int
  override def canEqual(other: Any) =
    other.isInstanceOf[InstantaneousTime]          ◁——— Allows any subclass
  override def equals(other: Any) : Boolean =
    other match {
      case that: InstantaneousTime =>
        if(this eq that) true else {
            (that.## == this.##) &&                 ⎫ Call other
            (that canEqual this) &&                 ⎬ object's
            (repr == that.repr)                     ◁ canEqual
        }
    case _ => false
  }
  override def hashCode(): Int = repr.hashCode
}

trait Event extends InstantaneousTime {
  val name: String
  override def canEqual(other: Any) =               ⎫ Subclass opt
    other.isInstanceOf[Event]                       ⎬ out of equality
  override def equals(other: Any): Boolean = other match {  ◁ canEqual
    case that: Event =>
      if(this eq that) {
        true
      } else {
        (that canEqual this) &&
        (repr == that.repr) &&
        (name == that.name)
```

```
        }
      case _ => false
    }
  }
```

The first thing to do is implement `canEqual` on `InstantaneousTime` to return `true` if the other object is also an `InstantaneousTime`. Next let's account for the other object's `canEqual` result in the equality implementation. Finally, an overridden `canEqual` in the `Event` class will only allow equality with other `Event`s.

> **WHEN OVERRIDING EQUALITY OF A PARENT CLASS, ALSO OVERRIDES CANEQUAL**
> The `canEqual` method is a lever, allowing subclasses to opt out of their parent class's equality implementation. This allows a subclass to do so without the usual dangers associated with a parent class `equals` method returning `true` while a subclass would return `false` for the same two objects.

Let's look at our earlier REPL session and see if the new `equals` methods behave better, as in the following listing.

Listing 2.26   Using new `equals` and `canEquals` methods

```
scala> val x = new InstantaneousTime {
     |   val repr = 2
     | }
x: java.lang.Object with InstantaneousTime = $anon$1@2

scala> val y = new Event {
     |   val name = "TestEvent"
     |   val repr = 2
     | }
y: java.lang.Object with Event = $anon$1@2

scala> y == x
res10: Boolean = false

scala> x == y                                    ⟵—— No longer returns true
res11: Boolean = false
```

We've succeeded in defining an appropriate equality method. We can now write a general `equals` method that performs well with general assumptions about our programs, and we can handle the case where our classes are also polymorphic.

2.6   *Summary*

In this chapter, we looked at the first crucial items for using Scala. Leveraging the REPL to do rapid prototyping is crucial to any successful Scala developer. Favoring expression-oriented programming and immutability helps simplify a program and improve the ability to reason through code. `Option` can also help improve reasonability of the code by clearly delineating where uninitialized values are accepted. Also, writing a good equality method in the presence of polymorphism can be difficult. All of these practices can help make the first steps in Scala successful. For continued success, let's look at code style and how to avoid running into issues with Scala's parser.

Modicum of style— coding conventions

In this chapter

- The dangers of dragging old coding conventions into Scala
- Working with end-of-line inference
- Avoiding dangerous names for variables
- Ensuring correct behavior with annotations

This chapter presents style suggestions that will help you avoid compiler or runtime errors. Style issues are usually a "holy war" among developers, who each has her own opinions. But there are certain things that Scala allows from a style perspective that can cause logic or runtime issues in your programs. This chapter doesn't try to proselytize you into whether you should place spaces between parenthesis or what the best number of spaces for indentation is. This chapter merely presents a few styles that will cause real issues in Scala, and why you should modify your preferred style accordingly, if needed.

We discuss why placing opening braces for block expressions can convey different meanings to the compiler. Operator notation can cause issues if the compiler can't tell where a line ends. Also, when naming variables in Scala, there are some names that are syntactically valid but will cause compiler or runtime errors. Finally, we discuss the benefits of compile-time warnings and how you can use annotations to increase the helpfulness of the Scala compiler. Let's start by looking at some common coding conventions.

3.1   *Avoid coding conventions from other languages*

I've found that my style when writing in a new language tends to borrow heavily from styles I use in other languages until I've learned the language well. Scala is no exception. A lot of users come from Java or Ruby languages and you can see this influence in the syntax. Over time, this style will change and adjust to accommodate the new language as certain guidelines are found to cause issues in the new language. As such, it's important to understand exactly where your style is coming from and whether that style makes sense in the new language. In fact, it's not just the language itself that dictates style. You must consider many human social interactions, especially if you work in a company with a large developer base.

One thing that always frustrated me when using C++ was coding conventions that were developed before the ready availability of cheap mature C++ IDEs. An IDE can negate the need for a lot of coding conventions by visually altering code based on a good semantic parse. IDEs can also allow developers to click-through method calls into method definitions or declarations to quickly get a feel for what's going on in code. A good modern IDE makes a lot of "standard practice" coding conventions unnecessary. But this doesn't erase the need for *any* coding conventions. Coding conventions do serve a few purposes, which can be boiled down into three categories: code discovery, uniformity, and error prevention.

Error prevention conventions are style rules that help avoid bugs in production code. This could be anything from marking method arguments as final in Java to marking all single argument constructors as explicit in C++. The goal of these style rules will be obvious to any experienced developer of that language.

Uniformity rules are about keeping the look of code the same across a project. These are a necessary evil in development workshops and the cause of style wars. Without them, version control history can become misaligned as developers fight to push their own personal style, or lack thereof. With them, moving between source files requires little "readability" mental adjustments. These rules are things like how many spaces to put between parentheses.

Code discovery rules are about enabling engineers to easily reason through code and figure out what another developer intended. These rules usually take the form of variable naming rules, such as placing m_ in front of member variables or prefixing interfaces with a capital I. See table 3.1

Code discovery should align with the development environments that are expected in a team. If a team is using vanilla VI for editing, it will be more useful to add more code discovery guidelines than another project. If the team has a set of IDE

Table 3.1   Coding style examples

Error prevention rules	Uniformity rules	Code discovery rules
■ (C++) Don't use implicit conversions ■ (Java) Mark all arguments `final`	■ Indentations are three spaces ■ Place one space after opening parenthesis and one space before closing parenthesis	■ (C++) Member variables prefixed with `m_` ■ (Eclipse) Interface names prefixed with `I`

power users, it would need less code discovery rules, as the IDE will provide many alternative means of improving discovery.

The way you should develop coding conventions for a team is to:

1   Start with error prevention rules. These will usually be copied from other projects in the same language, but you may need to create new rules.

2   Develop discovery related rules, such as how to name packages and where to place source files. These should match the development environments used by team members.

3   Follow up the rules defined above with any uniformity related rules required for the team. These rules vary from team to team and can be fun to agree upon. When creating uniformity guidelines, you should keep in mind automated tool support.

AUTOMATED STYLE TOOLING   Many tools can automatically check style rules or refactor existing code into a given style. This can help new engineers on the project save time until they become accustomed to the style. For Scala, you should check out the Scalariform project http://mng.bz/78G9, which is a tool to automatically refactor Scala code given a set of style rules.

The issue nowadays is that most developers have a set of coding guidelines they prefer and pull them from project to project regardless of the language or the team. When starting a new project and developing new coding standards, make sure you don't just pull conventions from previous languages. Scala syntax isn't a direct C-clone; there are some pitfalls that certain coding styles will create in the language. We show an example with defining code blocks in Scala.

3.1.1   *The block debacle*

A common theme to C-style languages is code blocks, typically denoted with `{}`. Code blocks are sections of code that execute within loops, `if` statements, closures, or new variable namespaces. Coding standards tend to take two approaches with blocks: same line opening brace or next line opening brace.

```
if(test) {
  ...
}
```

This code shows a same line opening brace, which I prefer (go SLOBs!). In many languages, the choice between same line and next line opening brace doesn't matter. This is not the case in Scala, where semicolon inference can cause issues in a few key places. This makes the next line opening brace style error-prone. The easiest way to show the issue is with the definition of methods. Let's look at a common Scala method:

```
def triple(x: Int) =
{
  x * 3
}
```

The more idiomatic Scala convention for a function as simple as `triple` is to define it on one line with no code block. This is a toy example though, so we'll assume you have a good enough reason to use a code block, or your coding convention specifies you always having code blocks. In any case, the above function works perfectly fine. Now let's try to make a function that returns `Unit` using the convenience syntax:

```
def foo()
{
  println("foo was called")
}
```

This method will compile fine when used from the interpretive session, however it fails utterly when used inside a class, object, or trait definition in Scala 2.7.x and below. To reproduce the behavior in Scala 2.8, we add another line between the method name and the opening brace. In many C-style languages, including Java, this change is acceptable. In Scala, we see the issue, as shown in the following listing:

Listing 3.1   Next line opening brackets causing issues

```
class FooHolder
{
  def foo()

  {                              This block executed
                                 during construction
    println("foo was called")
  }
}
```

Inside of the `FooHolder` class definition block, Scala sees the `def foo()` line of code as an abstract method. This is because it doesn't catch the opening brace on the next line, so it assumes `def foo()` is a complete line. When it encounters the block expression, it assumes it found a new anonymous code block that should be executed in the construction of the class.

A simple solution to this problem exists: Add a new style guideline that requires the = syntax for all method definitions. This should solve any issues you might experience with opening brackets on the next line. Let's try it out in the following listing:

Listing 3.2 Next line opening brackets compiling correctly

```
trait FooHolder2
{
  def foo(): Unit =

  {
    println("foo2 was called")
  }
}
```

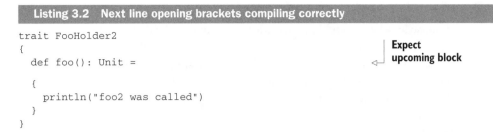

Expect
upcoming block

The = added after the `def foo(): Unit` tells the compiler that you're expecting an expression that contains the body of the foo function. The compile will then continue looking in the file for the code block. This solves the issue for method definitions. Other types of block expressions can still cause issues. In Scala, `if` statements don't require code blocks at all. This means the same kind of behavior could occur on an `if` statement if not properly structured. Luckily in that case, the compiler will catch and flag an error. The issue comes with `else` statements. Let's try the following:

```
if(true)
{
  println("true!")
}
else
{
  println("false!")
}
```

In an interpretive session, you can't enter this code because it will compile at the end of the first code block (the `if` statement) because it assumes the statement is complete. In a class, this *should* function as desired.

> **SHOULD MY CODING STYLE ALLOW ME TO PASTE CODE INTO AN INTERPRETIVE SESSION TO TEST IT?** The choice depends on your development environment. Most good tools allow you to automatically start an interpretive session against a compiled instance of your project. This means you wouldn't have to cut and paste code from your project into the session; however, in practice I find that sometimes my project isn't compiling and I want to test out a feature. In this case, I have to edit the files before pasting into the interpretive session.

Make sure when you're setting up a project, especially in a language you haven't used extensively before, that you rethink your style guidelines and choose ones that fit the new language and the environment you will be developing in. Don't merely pull what worked before in Language Foo and assume it will work well in Scala. Challenge your decisions!

A collaborative effort is in place to create a "good enough" style guide for Scala. This style guide should act as a good starting point and is currently located at http://mng.bz/48C2.

3.2   *Dangling operators and parenthetical expressions*

One style adjustment that can drastically help in Scala is to dangle operators at the end of lines. A dangling operator is an operator, such as + or - that's the last non-whitespace character in a line of code. Dangling operators will help the compiler determine the true end of a statement. Earlier, we described how this is important for block expressions. The concept works just as well with other types of expressions in Scala.

"Large string aggregation" is a great instance when dangling operators can help out the compiler or when you're trying to create a large string such that the whole definition doesn't fit on one line. Let's look at an example in Java:

```
class Test {
    private int x = 5;
    public String foo() {
      return "HAI"
        + x
        + "ZOMG"
        + "\n";
    }
}
```

The Test class has a foo method that's attempting to create a large string. Rather than having dangling aggregation operators, the + operator is found on the next line. A simple translation of this to Scala will fail to compile. Let's take a look:

```
object Test {
    val x = 5
    def foo = "HAI"
      + x
      + "ZOMG"
      + "\n"
}
```

This will fail to compile with the error message "error: value unary_+ is not a member of java.lang.String". Again, this is because the compiler is inferring the end of line before it should. To solve this issue, we have two options: dangling operators or parentheses. A dangling operator is an operator that ends a line, letting the compiler know there's more to come, as shown in the following listing:

> **Listing 3.3   Using dangling operators**

```
object Test {
    val x = 5
    def foo = "HAI" +
      x +
      "ZOMG" +
      "\n"
}
```

Dangling operators have the advantage of maintaining a minimal amount of syntax. This is the preferred style for the compiler itself.

An alternative to dangling operators is wrapping expressions in parentheses. You wrap any expression that spans multiple lines in parentheses. This has the advantage of allowing potentially arbitrary amount of whitespace between members of the expression. Let's take a look at the following listing:

Listing 3.4   Using parentheses

```
object Test {
   val x = 5
   def foo = ("HAI"
     + x
     + "ZOMG"
     + "\n")
}
```

Whichever one of these style guidelines you choose is up to you and your development shop. I prefer dangling operators, but both options are valid Scala syntax and will help you avoid parsing issues.

Now that we've discussed working around inference in the compiler, let's discuss another way to avoid issues in the compiler: the naming of variables.

3.3   *Use meaningful variable names*

One of the most common adages in any programming language is to use meaningful argument or variable names. Code clarity is a commonly ascribed benefit of meaningful argument names. Meaningful names can help take an arcane piece of code and turn it into something a new developer can learn in moments.

Some variables exist for which it is hard to determine appropriate names. In my experience this usually comes when implementing some kind of mathematical algorithm, like fast Fourier transforms, where the domain has well-known variable names. In this case, it's far better to use the standard symbols rather than invent your own names. In the case of Fourier transforms, the equation is shown in figure 3.1.

When implementing a Fourier transform, using a variable named N to represent the size of the input data, n to represent the index of a summing operation and k to represent the index to an output array is acceptable, as it's the notation used in the function. In many of languages, you end up "spelling" symbols because the language doesn't support mathematical symbols directly. In Scala, we can directly write ? rather than PI if we desire.

In this section well look at "reserved" characters that you shouldn't use for variable names, as well as using named and default parameters effectively. Reserved characters are characters the compiler reserves for internal use, but it doesn't warn you if you use them. This can cause issues at compile time or, even worse, runtime. These issues could be anything from a warning message on code that's perfectly valid, or exceptions thrown at runtime.

Scala provides a flexible naming scheme for variables and methods.

$$X_k = \sum_{n=0}^{N-1} x_n e^{-\mathrm{i}2\pi k \frac{n}{N}} \qquad k = 0,...,N-1.$$

Figure 3.1   Fourier transform equation

You use extended characters, if you desire to code mathematical equations directly. This allows you to write functions that look like mathematical symbols if you're writing some form of advanced mathematics library. My recommendation here is to ensure that whatever characters you use in your variable and method names, make sure that most developers in your shop know how to input them on their keyboards or ensure there's a direct key for it. Nothing is worse than having to copy and paste special characters into a program because you desire to use them.

An example of Scala's flexible naming is the duality of => and ? for defining closures and pattern matching. To even use the ? character in this book, I had to look it up and paste it into my editor. The best example of unicode and non-unicode operators comes from the Scalaz library. Let's look at one of the examples from the Scalaz source code:

```
val a, b, c, d = List(1)
...
a ? b ? c ? d apply {_ + _ + _ + _}
a |@| b |@| c |@| d apply {_ + _ + _ + _}
```

As you can see, Scalaz has provided both the |@| and the ? methods on its "Applicative Builder." We discuss applicative style application in detail in section 11.3. For now let's focus on the method names.

One name used for the applicative builder is a funny-looking unicode character (⊛), and the other is something someone could type without copy-paste or knowing what the correct keycode is ahead of time (|@|). By providing both, Scalaz has appealed to average developers and to those situations when using unicode characters proves you're the better nerd at the office. I would recommend following in Scalaz's footsteps if you wish to provide unicode operator support.

Although random unicode characters can be frustrating for developers, there's one character that's easy to type that can cause real issues in code: the dollar sign ($).

3.3.1   *Avoid $ in names*

Scala allows naming to be so flexible, you can even interfere with its own name mangling scheme for higher level concepts on the JVM. *Name mangling* refers to the compiler altering, or mangling, the name of a class or method to translate it onto the underlying platform. This means that if I looked at the classfile binaries Scala generates, I may not find a class with the same name as what I use in my code. This was a common technique in C++ so that it could share a similar binary interface with C but allow for method overloading. For Scala, name mangling is used for nested classes and helper methods.

As an example, let's create a simple trait and object pairing and look at how Scala names the underlying JVM classes and interfaces. When Scala has to generate anonymous function or classes, it uses a name containing the class it was defined in—the string anonfun and a number. These strings are all joined using the $ character to create an entity. Let's compile a sample and see what the directory looks like afterwards.

This sample will be a simple main method that computes the average of a list of numbers, as shown in the following listing:

Listing 3.5 Simple method to calculate an average

```
object Average {
   def avg(values: List[Double]) = {
     val sum = values.foldLeft(0.0) { _ + _ }
     sum / values.size.toDouble
   }
}
```

The class is rather simple. We define an `Average` object that contains a method: `avg`. In the `avg` method, we define a closure `{ _ + _ }` that will compile to an anonymous function class. Let's see the compiled files for this class:

```
$ ls *.class
Average$$anonfun$1.class  Average.class  Average$.class
```

Some interesting JVM classes are compiled here. The `Average` object gets compiled into the `Average$` class with the `Average` class having the static method forwarded to the `Average$` object. This is the mechanism Scala uses for "singleton objects" to ensure that they're true objects but look similar to static method invocations to Java. The anonymous closure we sent to `foldLeft` (`{ _ + _ }`) got compiled into the `Average$$anonfun$1` class. This is because it happens to be the first anonymous function defined in the `Average$` class As you can see, the `$` character is used heavily when creating real JVM classes for advanced Scala features.

Let's play a game called "break Scala's closures." This game will help outline the issues with using `$` in parameter names, something useful for those who are interested in adding plugin functionality to Scala, but not for general developers. Feel free to skip to section 3.3.2 if you're not interested in this.

What happens if we define our own class that has the same mangled name as the anonymous function? Either our class or the anonymous function class will be used at runtime. Let's create a new Average.scala file in the following listing and use the ` syntax to create a new mischievous class and see what happens:

Listing 3.6 Average.scala file with mischievous class

```
object Average {
   def avg(values: List[Double]) = {
     val sum = values.foldLeft(0.0) { _ + _ }       ⟵┐
      sum / values.size.toDouble
   }                                                   │ Same
}                                                      │ name
class `Average$$anonfun$1` {                          ⟵┘
    println("O MY!")
}
```

The `Average` object is the same as defined in listing 3.6, but we've created our mischievous class called `Average$$anonfun$1`. This compiles fine, so we know the compiler won't catch our mischievousness. Let's see what happens when we try to use it in an interactive interpreted session:

```
scala> Average.avg(List(0.0,1.0,0.5))
O MY!
java.lang.IncompatibleClassChangeError: vtable stub
  at ...LinearSeqLike$class.foldLeft(LinearSeqLike.scala:159)
  at scala.collection.immutable.List.foldLeft(List.scala:46)
  at Average$.avg(Average.scala:3)
```

The mischievous class is instantiated, as seen by the "O MY!" output. The mischievous class is even passed into the `foldLeft` method as seen in the stack trace. It isn't until the `foldLeft` function attempts to use the class instance that it realizes that this class isn't a closure. Well, what are the odds that someone would name a class the same kind of arcane string that occurs from name mangling? Probably low, but the $ character still gives Scala some issues. When defining nested classes, Scala also uses the $ character to mangle names, similar to Java inner classes. We can cause similar errors by defining mischievous inner classes, as shown in the following listing:

Listing 3.7   Average.scala with mischievous inner classes

```
object Average {
   def avg(values: List[Double]) = {
     val sum = values.foldLeft(0.0) { _ + _ }
     sum / values.size.toDouble
   }

   class `$anonfun` {            Conflicts
     class `1` {                 with closure
        println("O MY!")
     }
   }
}
```

In general then, it's best to avoid the $ character altogether in your naming schemes. It's also best to avoid making an inner class with the name `anonfun` or `$anonfun` that has its own numbered inner classes, although I have no idea why you would desire to do so. For completeness, it's best to totally avoid the mangling schemes of the compiler.

The compiler also uses name mangling for default parameters. In Scala default parameters are also encoded as a method with the name default and an ordinal representing the order the argument appears in the function. This is in the method namespace, not the classname namespace. To cause problems, we need to name a method something simple like `avg$default$1`.

```
object Average {
   def avg(values: List[Double] = List(0.0,1.0,0.5)) = {
     val sum = values.foldLeft(0.0) { _ + _ }
```

```
    sum / values.size.toDouble
  }

  def `avg$default$1` = List(0.0,0.0,0.0)
}
```

Luckily in this case the compiler will warn that the method avg$default$1 is a duplicate. This isn't the most obvious error message, but then again, the method name isn't
exactly common. So, although it's possible to use $ in method names and class names,
it can get you into trouble. The examples I've posted are somewhat extreme, but illustrate that name mangling issues can be rather tricky to track down. Therefore you
should avoid the $ character entirely.

3.3.2 Working with named and default parameters

Scala 2.8.x brings with it the ability to use named parameters. This means that the
names you give parameters of methods become part of the public API. Your parameter
names become part of the API, and changing them can and will break clients. Also,
Scala allows users to define different parameter names in subclasses. Let's look at the
named and default parameter feature.

> **Rule 6**
>
> **Use meaningful parameter names**
>
> In Scala, parameter names are part of the API and should follow all the coding conventions
> used for method and variable names.

Defining named parameters in Scala is easy, it's required syntax. Whatever name you
declare for a parameter is the name you can use when calling it. Let's define a simple
Foo class with a single method foo, but with several parameters. These parameters will
be set with default values. The following listing shows the various types of usage:

Listing 3.8 Simple named parameter usage

```
class Foo {
  def foo(one: Int = 1,                           Define
          two: String = "two",                    default
          three: Double = 2.5): String =          parameters
    two + one + three
}

scala> val x = new Foo
x: Foo = Foo@565902ca
                                                  Using all
scala> x.foo()                                    defaults
 res0: String = two12.5
                                                  Using named
scala> x.foo(two = "not two")                     parameter
 res1: String = not two12.5
                                                  Argument
scala> x.foo(0,"zero",0.1)                        placement
 res2: String = zero00.1
                                                  Mixed placement
scala> x.foo(4, three = 0.4)                      and named
 res3: String = two40.4
```

First, notice that the `foo` method declares defaults for all of its parameters. This allows us to call the method without passing any arguments. Things are more interesting when we pass arguments using their names, like when we write `x.foo(two = "not two")`.

Scala still allows argument placement syntax, where the order of the parameters is the same in the definition site and the call site. This can be seen in the line `x.foo(0,"zero",0.1)`. On this call, `0` is the first parameter and is referred to in the function as the argument one. This is a mixed mode usage.

Mixed mode is where you can use argument placement syntax for some arguments, and named parameters for the rest. This mode is obviously limited in that you can only use placement syntax for beginning arguments but is shown in the last line: `x.foo(4, three = 0.4)`. In this line, the first parameter, `4`, is passed as argument one and the argument `three` is passed as `0.4`.

So, why all the fuss over argument naming? Argument names become confusing with inheritance in the mix.

Scala uses the static type of a variable to bind parameter names, however the defaults are determined by the runtime type. Say it to yourself: *Names are static; values are runtime*. Let's look at a "simple" example of chaos ... er ... inheritance in the following listing:

Listing 3.9   Named parameters and inheritance

```
class Parent {                                          Initial method
  def foo(bar: Int = 1, baz: Int = 2): Int =            definition
    bar + baz
}
class Child extends Parent {                            Overridden with
  override def foo(baz: Int = 3, bar: Int = 4): Int =   poor names
    super.foo(baz,bar)
}
scala> val p = new Parent
p: Parent = Parent@271a2576

scala> p.foo()                                          Default
res0: Int = 3                                           arguments
                                                        on parent
scala> val x = new Child
x: Child = Child@3191394e

scala> x.foo()
res1: Int = 7

scala> val y: Parent = new Child
y: Parent = Child@6c5bdfae

scala> y.foo()
res2: Int = 7
                                                        Default
scala> x.foo(bar = 1)                                   arguments
                                                        on child
 res3: Int = 4
                                                        Static type
scala> y.foo(bar = 1)                                   determines name
 res4: Int = 5
```

Parent is a parent class that defined method foo. Child extends the foo method, but notice the naming difference. We've purposely reused the same names in differing orders to be confusing, but we've left the implementation of the method the same. If we instantiate a Parent class and execute foo, we see the value 3. When we instantiate a Child class, and execute foo we see 7 (*default values are runtime!*). The interesting part comes when we instantiate the Child class with the static type of Parent. When we call foo(bar = 1) on a Child instance with a static type of Child, we see the value 4. If we call foo(bar=1) on a Child instance with static type of Parent we see the value of 5.

What happened? In the Child class, we defined the argument names in the reverse order of the Parent class. The unfortunate circumstance of named parameters in Scala is that they use the static type to determine ordering. Remember our earlier mantra: *values are runtime; names are static.*

Renaming arguments in a child class isn't a warning in the compiler. As of Scala 2.8.0, there's no way to make this warning without writing your own compiler plugin. This naming issue may not be a huge deal when you're the author of an entire type hierarchy, but it might be when working on a larger team where others are consuming classes from others and are unhappy with parameter naming schemes from other developers.

> **DEPRECATING PARAMETER NAMES** In Scala 2.8.1, there will most likely be a mechanism for deprecating parameter names. This is to be done with an annotation on the parameter itself, declaring the old name. Clients of your library can then use both names, albeit the one will issue a warning. As the specifics may change, please follow the Scala mailing list and check the release notes of 2.8.1 for the mechanics of this.

For some shops, particularly ones I've worked in, developers were allowed to disagree on method naming conventions because they never mattered before. As of Scala 2.8.0, they do. Ensure that your developers are aware of naming in general, and of this particular surprising change (at least surprising when coming from a language without named parameters).

Remember that naming variables, classes, *and* parameters are all important in Scala. Misnaming can wind up in anything from a compile-time error to a subtle and hard-to-fix bug. This is one area where the compiler can't offer much assistance besides helpful error messages.

3.4   *Always mark overridden methods*

Scala did the world a great service when it introduced the override keyword. This keyword is used to demarcate when a method is intended to override vs. overload a method. If you neglect the keyword and the compiler finds you're overriding a superclass method, it will emit an error. If you add the override keyword and no superclass has the defined method, the compiler will warn you. Thankfully, this is mostly enforced by the compiler. One scenario remains where override isn't required but can cause issues: purely abstract methods. Scala has no abstract modifier: A purely abstract method is one that has no implementation.

<table>
<tr><td>Rule
7</td><td>**Always mark overridden methods**</td></tr>
</table>

In Scala, while the `override` keyword is optional in some situations, it's safe to always mark methods with `override`.

Let's take a look at example `override` usage. We want to define a business service for an application. This service will be for users. We'll allow them to log in, change their password and log out as well as validate that someone is still logged in. We're going to make an abstract interface for users of our service. It should look like the following:

```
trait UserService {
  def login(credentials: Credentials): UserSession
  def logout(session: UserSession): Unit
  def isLoggedIn(session: UserSession): Boolean
  def changePassword(session: UserSession,
                     credentials: Credentials): Boolean
}
```

The service is rather simple. We define a `login` method that takes the user's credentials and returns a new session for that user. We also define a `logout` method that takes a `UserSession` object and invalidates it and performs any cleanup that may be needed. Finally, we define two methods against the session. The `isLoggedIn` method will check to see if a `UserSession` is valid, meaning the user is logged in. The `changePassword` method will change the user's password but only if the new password is legal and the `UserSession` is valid. Now let's make a simple implementation that assumes any credentials are okay for any user and that all users are valid.

```
class UserServiceImpl extends UserService {
  def login(credentials: Credentials): UserSession =
    new UserSession {}
  def logout(session: UserSession): Unit
  def isLoggedIn(session: UserSession): Boolean = true
  def changePassword(session: UserSession,
      credentials: Credentials): Boolean = true
}
```

But wait, we forgot to add the override keyword. The method still compiles, so that means the override keyword wasn't needed. Why? Scala doesn't require the override keyword if your class is the first to define an abstract method. It also comes into play when using multiple inheritances, but we'll look into this in a moment. For now, let's see what happens in the following listing if we change the method signature in the parent class:

Listing 3.10   Changing the underlying method

```
trait UserService {
  def login(credentials: Credentials): UserSession
  def logout(session: UserSession): Unit
  def isLoggedIn(session: UserSession) : Boolean
  def changePassword(new_credentials: Credentials,      ◁─ Modified
                     old_credentials: Credentials): Boolean      definition
}
```

```
  }
class UserServiceImpl extends UserService {
  def login(credentials: Credentials): UserSession =
    new UserSession {}
  def logout(session: UserSession): Unit
  def isLoggedIn(session: UserSession): Boolean = true
  def changePassword(session: UserSession,
                  credentials: Credentials): Boolean = true
  }
```

Compile error

Notice we've changed the changePassword method in the UserService trait. The new method compiles fine, but the UserServiceImpl class won't compile. Because it's concrete, the compiler will catch the fact that changePassword defined in the User-Service isn't implemented. What happens if instead of an implementation, we're providing a library with partial functionality? Let's change UserServiceImpl to a trait, as shown in the following listing:

Listing 3.11 Traits won't cause compile errors

```
trait UserService {
  def login(credentials: Credentials): UserSession
  def logout(session: UserSession): Unit
  def isLoggedIn(session: UserSession) : Boolean
  def changePassword(new_credentials: Credentials,
    old_credentials: Credentials): Boolean
  }

trait UserServiceImpl extends UserService {
  def login(credentials: Credentials): UserSession =
    new UserSession {}
  def logout(session: UserSession): Unit
  def isLoggedIn(session: UserSession): Boolean = true
  def changePassword(session: UserSession,
    credentials: Credentials): Boolean = true
  }
```

Modified definition

Compiles

When we migrate UserServiceImpl to a trait, compilation now succeeds. This is an issue primarily when providing a library with no concrete implementations, or some form of DSL that's expected to be extended. Therefore, only users of the library will notice this easy-to-prevent issue. All that's required is to use the override modifier before any overridden method, as shown in the following listing:

Listing 3.12 Traits will cause compile errors

```
trait UserServiceImpl extends UserService {
  override def login(credentials: Credentials): UserSession =
    new UserSession {}
  override def logout(session: UserSession): Unit
  override def isLoggedIn(session: UserSession): Boolean = true
  override def changePassword(session: UserSession,
    credentials: Credentials): Boolean = true
  }
```

Compile error

Because this is such an easy error for the compiler to catch, there's no reason to run into the issue. What about the multiple inheritance we mentioned earlier? It's time to look into how `override` interacts with multiple inheritance.

Scala doesn't require the `override` keyword when implementing abstract methods. This was done to help multiple inheritance. Let's look at the classic "deadly diamond" inheritance problem. A deadly diamond occurs by creating a class that has two parent classes. Both of the parent classes must also be subclasses of the same parent-parent class. If you were to draw a picture of the inheritance relationship, you would see a diamond.

Let's start our own diamond by creating two traits, `Cat` and `Dog`, that extend a common base trait `Animal`. The `Animal` trait defines a method `talk` that's also defined in `Cat` and `Dog`. Now imagine some mad scientist is attempting to combine cats and dogs to create some new species, the `KittyDoggy`. How well could they do this using the `override` keyword? Let's define our three classes in the following listing and find out:

Listing 3.13   Animal hierarchy with `override`

```
trait Animal {
  def talk: String
}

trait Cat extends Animal {
  override def talk: String = "Meow"
}

trait Dog extends Animal {
  override def talk: String = "Woof"
}
```

We define the `talk` method on the Animal trait to return a `String`. We then create the `Cat` and `Dog` traits with their own implementation of the `talk` method. Let's pop open the REPL and try to construct our `KittyDoggy` experiment. Remember to cackle when typing, as shown in the following listing:

Listing 3.14   Multiple inheritance and `override`

```
scala> val kittydoggy = new Cat with Dog
kittydoggy: java.lang.Object with Cat with Dog = $anon$1@631d75b9

scala> kittydoggy.talk
res1: String = Woof

scala> val kittydoggy2 = new Dog with Cat
kittydoggy2: java.lang.Object with Dog with Cat = $anon$1@18e3f02a

scala> kittydoggy2.talk
res2: String = Meow
```

First we attempt to combine `Cat` with `Dog`. This results in the `talk` operation picking up the `Dog` behavior and ignoring the `Cat` behavior. That's not quite what our mad-scientist experiment wants to accomplish, so instead we try to combine a `Dog` with a `Cat`.

This ends up pulling in the Cat behavior and ignoring the Dog behavior! In Scala, the last trait "wins" when it comes to class linearization and method delegation, so this isn't unexpected.

Class linearization refers to the order in which parent calls occur for a particular class. In the preceding example, for the type Cat with Dog, the parent calls would first try the Dog trait, then Cat and then Animal. Class linearization will be covered in more detail in the section 4.2.

What happens now if we remove the override keyword from the Cat and Dog traits? Let's find out in the following listing:

Listing 3.15 Animal hierarchy without `override`

```
trait Animal {
  def talk: String
}

trait Cat extends Animal {
  def talk: String = "Meow"
}

trait Dog extends Animal {
  def talk: String = "Woof"
}
```

The definitions of Animal, Cat, and Dog are the same as before except that no override keyword is used. Let's put on our evil lab coat again and see if we can combine our cats and dogs in the following listing:

Listing 3.16 Multiple inheritance without `override`

```
scala> val kittydoggy = new Cat with Dog
<console>:8: error: overriding method talk in
  trait Cat of type => String;
 method talk in trait Dog of type => String
  needs `override' modifier
       val kittydoggy = new Cat with Dog
                            ^

scala> val kittydoggy2 = new Dog with Cat
<console>:8: error: overriding method talk in
  trait Dog of type => String;
 method talk in trait Cat of type => String
  needs `override' modifier
       val kittydoggy2 = new Dog with Cat
```

When we attempt to construct our Cat with Dog, the compiler issues an error that we're trying to override a method without the override keyword. The compiler is preventing us from combining two different concrete methods that aren't explicitly annotated with override. This means if I want to prevent mixing overrides of behavior, from mad scientist programmers, then I must not use the override modifier. This feature makes more sense when the traits don't share a common ancestor, as it requires the mad scientist to manually override the conflicting behaviors of two classes and unify them. But in the presence of the base class, things can get strange. Let's see what happens in the following listing if `Cat` defines its `talk` method with `override`, but `Dog` does not.

Listing 3.17   Multiple inheritance with mixed `override`

```
scala> val kittydoggy = new Cat with Dog
<console>:8: error: overriding method talk in
  trait Cat of type =>
    java.lang.String;
 method talk in trait Dog of type => String needs `override' modifier
       val kittydoggy = new Cat with Dog
                 ^

scala> val kittydoggy2 = new Dog with Cat
kittydoggy2: java.lang.Object with Dog with Cat = $anon$1@5a347448
```

Mixing a `Cat` with a `Dog` is still bad, because `Dog` doesn't mark `talk` method as being able to override. But extending a `Dog` with a `Cat` is acceptable because the `Cat`'s `talk` can override. We can't use the compiler to force users to pick a `talk` implementation every time they inherit from `Dog` and another `Animal`. In the case where any of the `Animals` defines a `talk` method with an `override`, we lose our error message. This reduces the utility of the feature, specifically for the inheritance case.

Multiple inheritance

Scala traits are linearized. For the purposes of overriding methods, a parent can be mixed in where we instantiate an object, rather than requiring the definition of a new class.

```
trait Animal { def talk: String }
trait Mammal extends Animal
trait Cat { def talk = "Meow" }
scala> val x = new Mammal with Cat
x: java.lang.Object with Mammal with Cat = $anon$1@488d12e4
scala> x.talk
res3: java.lang.String = Meow
```

In practice, the utility of not using the `override` keyword for subclass method overrides is far outweighed by the benefits of doing so. As such, you should annotate your objects with the `override` keyword. When it comes to multiple inheritance and overridden methods, you must understand the inheritance linearization and it consequences. We discuss traits and linearization in detail in section 4.2.

Another area where the compiler can drastically help us out is with error messages for missed optimizations.

3.5   *Annotate for expected optimizations*

The Scala compiler provides several optimizations of functional style code into performant runtime bytecodes. The compiler will optimize tail recursion to execute as a looping construct at runtime, rather than a recursive function call. Tail recursion is when a method calls itself as the last statement, or its tail. Tail recursion can cause the stack to grow substantially if not optimized. Tail call optimization isn't as much about improving speed as preventing stack overflow errors.

The compiler can also optimize a pattern match that looks like a Java `switch` statement to act like a `switch` statement at runtime. The compiler can figure out if it's more efficient and still correct to use a branch lookup table. The compiler will then emit a `tableswitch` bytecode for this pattern match. The `tableswitch` bytecode is a branching statement that can be more efficient than multiple comparison branch statements.

The switch and tail recursion optimizations come with optional annotations. The annotations will ensure the optimization is applied where expected or an error is issued.

3.5.1 *Using the tableswitch optimization*

The first optimization we'll look at is treating pattern matching as a `switch` statement. What this optimization does is try to compile a pattern match into a branch table rather than a decision tree. This means that instead of performing many different comparisons against the value in the pattern match, the value is used to look up a label in the branch table. The JVM can then jump directly to the appropriate code. This whole process is done in a single bytecode, the `tableswitch` operation. In Java, the `switch` statement can be compiled into a `tableswitch` operation. In Scala, the compiler can optimize a pattern match into a single `tableswitch` operation if all the stars align, or at least the right conditions apply.

For Scala to apply the `tableswitch` optimization, the following has to hold true:

- The matched value must be a known integer.
- Every match expression must be "simple." It can't contain any type checks, `if` statements or extractors. The expression must also have its value available at compile time: The value of the expression must not be computed at runtime but instead always be the same value.
- There should be more than two case statements, otherwise the optimization is unneeded.

Let's take a quick look at some successfully optimized code and what operations will break it. First let's start off with a simple switch on an integer. We're going to `switch` on an integer to handle three cases: the integer is one, the integer is two, and all other possible integer values.

```
def unannotated(x: Int) = x match {
    case 1 => "One"
    case 2 => "Two!"
    case z => z + "?"
}
```

This is a `match` statement with three cases. As previously stated, we're explicitly looking at the case when an integer is either one or two. The compiler is able to optimize this to a `tableswitch`, as you can see in the bytecode. Here's the Java output:

```
public java.lang.String unannotated(int);
  Code:
    0:  iload_1
    1:  tableswitch{ //1 to 2
            1: 51;
            2: 46;
            default: 24 }
...
```

What you're seeing here are the bytecode instructions for the unannotated method. The first instruction at label `0:` shows us loading the first argument as an integer (`iload_1`). The next instruction is our `tableswitch`. The `tableswitch` instruction is made up of mappings of integer values to bytecode instruction labels (or line numbers). Now the rules for the optimization become more apparent. If the compiler is going to create this `tableswitch` instruction, it needs to know the values of each case statement expression in order to do the right thing. It's fairly easy to mess this up. Let's look at a few ways to do this.

First, we can include a type check in the pattern match. This can be surprising, as you might expect the type check would be superfluous, and not change the compiled code. Let's take our original function and add a type check for `Int` on one of the case statements.

```
def notOptimised(x: Int) = x match {
    case 1 => "One"
    case 2 => "Two!"
    case i: Int => "Other"
  }
```

The difference between this example and the previous one is the type check on the third case statement: `i : Int`. Although the type of the variable is already known to be an `Int`, the compiler will still create a type check in the pattern match and this will prevent it from using a `tableswitch` bytecode. Let's look at the bytecode (shortened to fit here):

```
public java.lang.String notOptimised(int);
  Code:
    0:  iload_1
    1:  iconst_1
    2:  if_icmpne 10
    ...
    10: iload_1
    11: iconst_2
    12: if_icmpne 20
    ...
    20: iload_1
    21: invokestatic #43;
            //Method scala/runtime/BoxesRunTime.boxToInteger:      Runtime
            (I)Ljava/lang/Integer;                                 type
    24: instanceof #85; //class java/lang/Integer                  check
    27: ifeq 33
    30: ldc #87; //String Other
```

```
32: areturn
33: new #89; //class scala/MatchError
...
```
Non-match
exception throwing

The first thing you'll notice is that there's an if_icmpne comparison bytecode instead of the tableswitch. Truncating the output, you'll see that the method *is* compiled as a sequence of such comparison bytecodes. We also find that there's a MatchError constructed on line 33. The truncated section is the remaining bytecode to throw the error. The compiler has inferred that our match was not complete, so it created a default case that will result in a runtime error.

> **ON PRIMITIVES AND TYPE CHECKING** In the preceding example on lines 21 and 24, you may have noticed that our argument, an Int, is boxed to perform an instanceof bytecode. The instanceof bytecode is how the JVM performs typechecks for classes, traits, and objects. But an integer is a primitive on the JVM, so to perform a type check, Scala must "box" the integer primitive into an object form of that integer. This is Scala's standard mechanism for checking the type of any primitive on the JVM; therefore, try not to let any extraneous type checks in your code.

As you can see, it was fairly easy to construct a case where we thought the compiler would optimize our code, and yet it could not. A simple solution to this problem is to annotate your expressions so the compiler will warn you if it can't make an optimization.

As of Scala 2.8.0, the compiler currently provides two annotations that can be used to prevent compilation if an optimization isn't applied. These are the @tailrec and @switch annotations, which you can apply to the expression you want optimized. Let's look at the following listing to see how the switch annotation could have helped us earlier:

Listing 3.18 Using the @switch annotation

```
import annotation.switch
def notOptimised3(x: Int) =
  (x: @switch) match {
    case 1 => "One"
    case 2 => "Two!"
    case i: Int => "Other"
  }
```
Annotated
match
expression

```
<console>:6: error: could not emit switch for @switch annotated match
       def notOptimised3(x : Int) = (x : @switch) match {
```

The first thing you'll notice is the funny (x : @switch) syntax. Scala allows annotations to be ascribed to type expressions. This tells the compiler to know that we expect the switch optimization to be performed, among other things. You could also fully ascribe the type by writing (x: Int @switch); however, adding the annotation is fine.

The compiler has given us the warning statement we desired. We're unable to compile because our pattern match can't be optimized. The merits of using a `tableswitch` are debatable, and not nearly as universal as the next annotation.

3.5.2 *Using the tail recursion optimization*

The `@tailrec` annotation is used to ensure that tail call optimization (usually abbreviated TCO) can be applied to a method. Tail call optimization is the conversion of a recursive function that calls itself as the last statement into something that won't absorb stack space but rather execute similarly to a traditional `while` or `for` loop. The JVM doesn't support TCO natively, so tail recursive methods will need to rely on the Scala compiler performing the optimization.

Rule 8   **Annotate tail recursion**

Tail recursion is easy to mix up in Scala. By annotating tail recursive methods, we can guarantee expected runtime performance.

To optimize tail calls, the Scala compiler requires the following:

- The method must be final or private: It can't be polymorphic.
- The method must have its return type annotated.
- The method must call itself as the "end" of one of its branches.

Let's see if we can create a good tail recursive method. My first tail recursive function was working with a tree structure, so let's do the same: Implementing a breadth first search algorithm using tail recursion.

The breadth first search algorithm is a way to inspect a graph or tree such that you inspect the top-level elements, then the nearest neighbors of those elements, and then the nearest neighbors of the nearest neighbors, and so on, until you find the node you're looking for. Let's first decide what the function should look like:

```
case class Node(name: String, edges: List[Node] = Nil)

def search(start: Node, predicate: Node => Boolean): Option[Node] = {
  error("write me")
}
```

The first thing we do is define a `Node` class that allows us to construct a graph or tree. This class is pretty simple and doesn't allow the creation cycles, but it's a good starting point for defining the algorithm. Next is the definition of the `search` method. It takes in a starting point, a `Node`, and a predicate that will return `true` when the correct node is found. The algorithm itself is fairly simple and involves maintaining a queue of nodes to inspect a mechanism to determine if a node has already been seen.

Let's create a helper function that will use tail recursion and search for the node. This function should take the queue of nodes to inspect and a set of nodes that have already been visited. The search method can then call this helper function, passing in `List(start)` for the initial queue of nodes and an empty set for the list of visited nodes.

```scala
def search(start: Node, p: Node => Boolean) = {
  def loop(nodeQueue: List[Node], visited: Set[Node]): Option[Node] =
    nodeQueue match {
      case head :: tail if p(head) =>
        Some(head)
      case head :: tail if !visited.contains(head) =>
        loop(tail ++ head.edges, visited + head)
      case head :: tail =>
        loop(tail, visited)
      case Nil =>
        None
    }
  loop(List(start), Set())
}
```

The help method, called `loop`, is implemented with a pattern match. The first case pops the first element from the queue of nodes to inspect. It then checks to see if this is the node we are looking for and returns it. The next case statement also pops the first element from the work queue and checks to see if it hasn't already been visited. If it hasn't, the node is added to the list of visited nodes and its edges are added to the end of the work queue of nodes. The next case statement is hit when a node has already been visited. This case will continue the algorithm with the rest of the nodes in the queue. The last case statement is hit if the queue is empty. In that case, None is returned indicating no Node was found.

The interesting part of this algorithm is what the compiler does to it. Let's look at the bytecode for the `loop` helper method for any sort of function call. We find none, so the tail call optimization must have kicked in for this method. Let's check for any kind of branching in the method to see what happened. Three `goto` bytecodes and one return bytecode exist:

```
private final scala.Option loop$1(scala.collection.immutable.List,
    scala.collection.immutable.Set, scala.Function1);
  Code:
  0:    aload_1
  ...
  61:   invokespecial  #97;
    //Method scala/Some."<init>":(Ljava/lang/Object;)V
  64:   goto  221
  ...
  150: astore_2
  151: astore_1
  152: goto 0
  ...
  186: astore_1
  187: goto 0
  ...
  218: getstatic #158; //Field scala/None$.MODULE$:Lscala/None$;
  221: areturn
  ...
```

Line 61 shows the byte code constructing a new Some object and then jumping to line 221. Line 221 is our return bytecode for the method. Immediately before line 221 is a getstatic operation that retrieves a reference to the None object. Finally, lines 152 and 187 both have goto instructions that return to line 0. These lines are the final bytecodes in each of our case statements. Lines 61, 64, and 221 correspond to the Some(head) call in our first case statement. Lines 218 and 221 correspond to returning None in which case our work queue is empty. Lines 150, 151, and 152 correspond to updating the current work queue and visited lists, using the astore bytecodes, and then jumping back into the algorithm. Finally, lines 186 and 187 correspond to updating the workQueue and jumping back to the start of the algorithm. The compiler has converted the tail recursion into a while loop.

This technique of converting a tail recursive function into a while loop can help prevent stack overflow issues at runtime for many recursive algorithms. It's perhaps the most important optimization to require of the compiler when writing code. No one wants an unexpected stack overflow in production code! So, once again requiring the optimization is as simple as annotating the tail recursive method with @tailrec. Let's take a look:

```
def search(start: Node, p: Node => Boolean) = {
  @tailrec
  def loop(nodeQueue: List[Node], visited: Set[Node]): Option[Node] =
    nodeQueue match {
      case head :: tail if p(head) =>
        Some(head)
      case head :: tail if !visited.contains(head) =>
        loop(tail ++ head.edges, visited + head)
      case head :: tail =>
        loop(tail, visited)
      case Nil =>
        None

    }
  loop(List(start), Set())
}
```

Great! Now you can ensure that expected optimizations appear in programs when needed. Remember that these annotations aren't asking the compiler to provide an optimization, but rather requiring that the compile do so or issue a warning.

In the switch example, if the compiler had been unable to provide a tableswitch instruction, the code would still have failed to compile. This doesn't indicate that the code would have performed slowly. In fact, with only two case statements, it would possibly be slower to use a tableswitch bytecode. Therefore, make sure you use these annotations only when you require an optimization.

Unlike the switch optimization, it's always a good idea to annotate tail recursion.

3.6   *Summary*

In this chapter, you've learned or refreshed your memory on coding conventions, their utility, and why you should look at them with fresh eyes when coming to Scala. This is a modern programming language, with an interesting twist to C style languages. As such, Scala requires adjustments to syntax and coding styles. Users of Scala should make sure to:

- Keep opening braces on the same line
- Dangle operators or use parentheses
- Use meaningful names
- Consistently name parameters
- Always mark methods with override

These rules should help you avoid simple syntax-related programming errors and be productive in your efforts.

With Scala, the syntax was designed in a "scalable" way. This means that if you attempt to write concise code and run into issues, try to use the less concise, more formal syntax until you resolve the issue. This graceful degradation is helpful in practice as it lets users "grow" into their understanding of the syntax rules. Syntax is something that shouldn't get in the way of development but instead become a vehicle for programmers to encode their thoughts into programs. Therefore, know the syntax and how to avoid compilation or runtime problems from poor use of the language.

Now that we've looked at how to use Scala syntax, it's time to dig into some of its more advanced features, starting with its object orientation.

Utilizing
object orientation

4

Scala is a rich object-oriented language. In Scala, every value is an object. Even operators are method calls against the class of an object. Scala offers mixin inheritance through the use of traits. Objects are core to everything in Scala, and understanding the details of how they work is important for using Scala.

Object, class, and traits are used to define public APIs for libraries. The initialization, comparison, and composition of objects are the bread and butter of Scala development. Initialization is important because of mixin inheritance and the way objects get instantiated in various locations. Comparing two objects for equality is critical and can be made trickier when inheritance gets in the mix. Finally, composition of functionality is how code reuse is accomplished, and Scala provides a few new ways to compose objects.

4.1 Limit code inside an object or trait's body to initialization logic

In Scala, the code inside an `object`, `trait` or `class`'s body is the constructor.

A common starting point for most developers learning Scala is the standard "Hello, World" program. You'll see many examples on the internet with the following code:

Listing 4.1   Poor Hello World! example in Scala

```
object Test extends Application {
  println("Hello, World!")
}
```

Although elegant, this code sample is misleading in its simplicity. The `Application` trait uses a nifty trick to simplify creating a new application but comes with a price. Let's look at a simplified version of the `Application` trait in the following listing.

Listing 4.2   `Application` trait

```
trait Application {
  def main(args: Array[String]): Unit = {}
}
```

That's it. That one empty method is all that's needed for the `Application` trait. Why does this work? Let's dig into the bytecode.

When compiling traits, Scala creates an interface/implementation pair of classes. The interface is for JVM interoperability and the implementation is a set of static methods that can be used by classes implementing the trait. When compiling the `Test` object, a main method is created that forwards to the `Application` implementation class. Although this method is empty, the logic inside the `Test` object is placed in the `Test` object's constructor. Next, Scala creates "static forwarders" for the object. One of these static forwarder methods will be the main method, in the signature the JVM expects. The static forwarder will call the method on the singleton instance of the `Test` object. This instance is constructed in a static initialization block. And finally, we get to the issue. Code inside a static initialization block isn't eligible for HotSpot optimization. In fact, in older versions of the JVM, methods called from a static initialization block wouldn't be optimized either. In the most recent benchmarks, this has been corrected, such that only the static block itself isn't optimized.

Scala 2.9 provides a better solution: the `DelayedInit` trait.

4.1.1 Delayed construction

Scala 2.9 provides a new mechanism for dealing with constructors. `DelayedInit` is a marker trait for the compiler. When implementing a class that extends `DelayedInit`, the entire constructor is wrapped into a function and passed to the `delayedInit` method. Let's a look at the `DelayedInit` trait.

```
trait DelayedInit {
  def delayedInit(x: => Unit): Unit
}
```

The trait has one method, `delayedInit`. As stated before, this method has a function object passed to it. This function contains all the regular constructor logic, which provides a clean solution to the `Application` trait. Let's implement your own to demonstrate the `DelayedInit` behavior.

```scala
trait App extends DelayedInit {
  var x: Option[Function0[Unit]] = None
  override def delayedInit(cons: => Unit) {
    x = Some(() => cons)
  }
  def main(args: Array[String]): Unit =
    x.foreach(_())
}
```

The new `App` trait extends `DelayedInit`. It defines an `Option` x containing the constructor behavior. The `delayedInit` method is overridden to store the constructor logic in the x variable. The `main` method is defined so that it will execute the constructor logic stored in the x variable. Now that the trait is created, let's try it in the REPL.

```scala
scala> val x = new App { println("Now I'm initialized") }
x: java.lang.Object with App = $anon$1@2013b9fb

scala> x.main(Array())
Now I'm initialized
```

The first line creates a new anonymous subclass of the `App` trait. This subclass prints the string `"Now I'm initialized"` in its constructor. The string isn't printed to the console during construction. The next line calls the main method on the `App` trait. This calls the delayed constructor, and the string `"Now I'm initialized"` is printed.

The `DelayedInit` trait can be dangerous because it delays the construction of the object until a later time; methods that expect a fully initialized object may fail subtly at runtime. The `DelayedInit` trait is ideal for situations where object construction and initialization are delayed. For example, in the Spring bean container, objects are constructed and then properties are injected before the object is considered complete. The `DelayedInit` trait could be used to delay the full construction of an object until after all properties have been injected. A similar mechanism could be used for objects created in Android.

The `DelayedInit` trait solves the problem where construction and initialization of objects are required, due to external constraints, to happen at different times. This separation isn't recommended in practice but sometimes is necessary. Another initialization problem exists in Scala, and this occurs with multiple inheritance.

4.1.2   *And then there's multiple inheritance*

Scala traits provide the means to declare abstract values and define concrete values that rely on the abstract. For example, let's create a trait that stores property values from a config file.

```scala
trait Property {
  val name: String
```

```
    override val toString = "Property(" + name + ")"
}
```

The `Property` trait defines an abstract member name which stores the current name of the `Property`. The `toString` method is overridden to create a string using the `name` member. Let's instantiate an instance of this trait.

```
scala> val x = new Property { override val name = "HI" }
x: java.lang.Object with Property = Property(null)
```

Rule 9 | **Avoid abstract val in traits**

Using abstract values in traits requires special care with object initialization. While early initializer blocks can solve this, `lazy val` can be a simpler solution. Even better is to avoid these dependencies by using constructor parameters and abstract classes.

The val x is defined as an anonymous subclass of the `Property` trait. The name is overridden to be the string `"HI"`. But when the REPL prints the value of `toString`, it shows the value `null` for name. This is due to order of initialization. The base trait, `Property`, is initialized first during construction. When the `toString` method looks for the value of `name`, it hasn't been initialized yet, so it finds the value `null`. After this, the anonymous subclass is constructed and the `name` property is initialized.

Two ways to solve the problem exist. The first is to define the `toString` method as lazy. Although this delays when the `toString` method will look for the value of the name property, it doesn't guarantee that the initialization order is correct. The better solution is to use early member definitions.

Scala 2.8.0 reworked the initialization order of traits. Part of this was the creation of early member definitions. This is done by creating what looks like an anonymous class definition before mixing in a trait. Here's an example:

```
scala> class X extends { val name = "HI" } with Property
defined class X

scala> new X
res2: X = Property(HI)
```

The class X is defined such that it extends the `Property` trait. But before the `Property` trait is an anonymous block containing the early member definition. This is a block containing a definition of the val `name`. When constructing the class X, the `toString` method correctly displays the name HI. A second way to declare early initializers exists.

```
scala> new { val name = "HI2" } with Property
res3: java.lang.Object with Property{
  val name: java.lang.String("HI2")} = Property(HI2)
```

The next line constructs a new anonymous `Property`. The anonymous block after the new keyword is the early member definition. This defines the members that should be initialized before the `Property` trait's constructor is initialized. The REPL prints the correct `toString` from the `Property` value.

Early member definitions solve issues that occur when a trait defines an abstract value and relies on it in other concrete values. We usually avoid this situation due to issues from previous versions of Scala. For any complicated trait hierarchies, early member initializations provide a more elegant solution to the problem. Because the members that need early initialization can be buried behind several layers of inheritance, it's important to document these throughout a type hierarchy.

Scala makes multiple inheritance simpler and provides mechanisms for dealing with the complicated situation. Early member definitions are one such way. Some things can be done to help prevent issues in the future such as providing empty implementations for abstract methods.

4.2 *Provide empty implementations for abstract methods on traits*

One of the first things I tried to do when first toying with the Scala language was use traits for a kind of "mixin inheritance." The problem I was trying to solve involved modeling a real-world situation. I needed to be able to create managed objects, including physical servers, network switches, and so on. The system needed to emulate the real world and create realistic-looking data that would be fed through our application's processing stream. We used this simulation shown in the following figure 4.1 to test "maximum throughput" of the software.

We want this system to model real-world entities as best as possible. We also want the ability to mix in different behaviors to our entities, where certain base traits could provide default behavior. Starting out, we want to model network switches and network servers, including Windows and Linux servers, along with some form of agent that runs on these services and provides additional functionality. Let's create a simple base class for a `SimulationEntity`.

Listing 4.3 `SimulationEntity` class

```scala
trait SimulationEntity {
  def handleMessage(msg: SimulationMessage,
                    ctx: SimulationContext): Unit
}
```

This is a simple trait that contains a `handleMessage` method. This method takes in a message and a context and performs some behavior. The design of the simulation is such that each entity will communicate through a simulation context via messages.

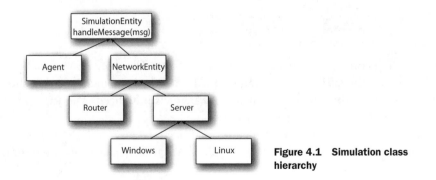

Figure 4.1 Simulation class hierarchy

When an entity receives a message, it updates its current state and sends messages appropriate to that state. The context can also be used to schedule behavior for later in the simulation. We're off to a great start. Let's define a simple `NetworkEntity` trait with simple `NetworkEntity` behavior. Remember that in a chain-of-command pattern, we want to define a base set of functionality and defer the rest to a parent class.

Listing 4.4 `NetworkEntity` **trait**

```scala
trait NetworkEntity {
  def getMacAddress(ip: String) : String
  def hasIpAddress(addr: String) : Boolean

  def handleMessage(msg: SimulationMessage, ctx: Simulation): Unit =
    msg match {
      case PingRequest(ip, sender) if hasIpAddress(ip) =>
        ctx respond (sender, PingResponse(getMacAddress(ip)))
      case _ =>
        super.handleMessage(msg)          ◁──┐ Message may or
    }                                          │ may not point to an
}                                              │ implementation function.
```

Scala traits have a handy property of not defining their super class until after they have been mixed in and initialized. This means that an implementer of a trait doesn't necessarily know which type `super` will be until a process called linearization occurs.

Class linearization

Linearization is the process of specifying a linear ordering to the superclasses of a given class. In Scala, this ordering changes for each subclass and is reconstructed for classes in the hierarchy. This means that two subclasses of some common parent could have different linearizations and therefore different behaviors.

Because of linearization, the `NetworkEntity` trait could be using `super` correctly, or it might not, as the compilation output implies:

```
simulation.scala:21: error: method handleMessage in trait
SimulationEntity is accessed from super.
It may not be abstract unless it's
overridden by a member declared `abstract' and `override'
    case _ => super.handleMessage(msg, ctx)
                    ^

one error found
```

To make this work properly, the Scala compiler must know that no matter what, we can safely call `super.handleMessage`. This means we have to do one of two things: define a self-type or make the abstract method have a default "do nothing" implementation that would get called. The self-type approach could work, but it limits how your trait could be mixed in. We would be defining an alternative "base" that the trait had to be mixed into. This base would then need to have some kind of implementation for `handleMessage`. This provides too much restriction for the aims of the application.

The right way to approach this is to implement the method in the `Simulation-Entity` trait. This gives all our mixed-in traits the ability to delegate to super, which is a common theme when using traits as mixins. You must select some point in an object hierarchy where traits may start being mixed in. In our simulation, we desire to start directly at the top with `SimulationEntity`. But if you're attempting to use traits with a Java hierarchy, this might not be the case. You may desire to start mixing into some lower-level abstraction. In the case of Java Swing, you could start your trait mixin classes with a `javax.swing.JComponent` rather than something lower, like a `java.awt.Component`. The point is that you need to select the right location to ensure that your mixin-delegate behavior will work correctly.

Sometimes with real-life libraries you can't find default behaviors to delegate into. In this case, you might think that you could provide your own "empty implementation" trait. Let's see if we can do that on your network simulation example. Let's define your classes like so:

Listing 4.5 Empty implementation trait attempt

```scala
trait MixableParent extends SimulationEntity {          ◁┐ Trait that
   override def handleMessage(msg : SimulationMessage,      should enable
     ctx: SimulationContext): Unit = {}                     mixin behavior
}

trait NetworkEntity extends MixableParent {             ◁┐ Mixable
   def getMacAddress(ip: String): String                    behavior for
   def hasIpAddress(addr: String): Boolean                  network devices

   override def handleMessage(msg: SimulationMessage,
     ctx: SimulationContext): Unit = msg match {
       case PingRequest(ip, sender) if hasIpAddress(ip) =>
         ctx respond (sender, PingResponse(getMacAddress(ip), this))
       case _ =>
         super.handleMessage(msg, ctx)
     }
}
                                                           ┐ Sample
                                                             entity used
class Router extends SimulationEntity {                 ◁┘ for testing
   override def handleMessage(msg: SimulationMessage,
     ctx: SimulationContext): Unit = msg match {
       case Test(x) => println("YAY! " + x)
       case _ =>
   }
}
```

This code looks like a perfectly reasonable class hierarchy and compiles correctly, but it doesn't work in practice. The reason is that the linearization of a concrete entity (`Router` in this case) doesn't work with the `MixableParent` trait; things aren't ordered as we'd like. The issue arises when we try to create a `Router with NetworkEntity` class. This class compiles fine but fails to handle the `Test` message at runtime, because this is how the linearization works. The following figure 4.2 shows the class hierarchy for a `Router with NetworkEntity` class and numbering classes/traits in their linearization order. This order determines what super means for each trait in the hierarchy.

As you can see, the MixableParent class is being called directly after NetworkEntity but before Router. This means that the behavior in NetworkEntity is never called because the MixableParent doesn't call its super! Therefore, we have to find a way of getting MixableParent earlier in the linearization. Because things linearize right to left in Scala, we want to try creating a MixableParent with Router with NetworkEntity. That first requires turning the Router class into a trait. This might not be feasible in real life, but let's continue the exercise. We'll see what this looks like in a Scala REPL session:

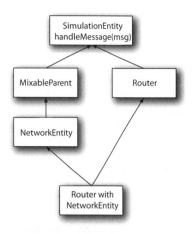

Figure 4.2 Linearization of Router with NetworkEntity

> **Rule 10**
>
> **Provide empty implementations for abstract methods on composable traits**
>
> In Scala, trait linearization means that super calls within a trait may be different depending on how an object is linearized. To provide full flexibility, each composable trait should be able to call a super method, even in that super method doesn't do anything.

Listing 4.6   REPL session with simulation classes

```
$ scala -cp .
...

scala> val rtr = new MixableParent with Router with
     |    DummyNetworkEntity

rtr: java.lang.Object with MixableParent with Router with
  DummyNetworkEntity = $anon$1@169a1c5

scala> rtr.handleMessage(Test(5), null)
YAY! 5

scala> val ctx = new SimulationContext {
     |    override def respond(entity: SimulationEntity,
     |                    msg: SimulationMessage) : Unit = {
     |       println("Sending " + msg + " to " + entity)
     |    }
     | }
ctx: java.lang.Object with SimulationContext = $anon$1@13306ad

scala> rtr.handleMessage(PingRequest("HAI", rtr),ctx)
  Sending PingResponse(HAI,line2$object$$iw$$iw$$anon$1@169a1c5) to
  line2$object$$iw$$iw$$anon$1@169a1c5
```

rtr defined with correct linearization of behavior ◁

Behavior defined in Router shows up correctly ◁

Behavior defined in NetworkEntity shows up correctly ◁

As you can see, the behavior is now correct, but it isn't quite intuitive that you have to use the MixableParent first in every entity creation. Also, the Router trait suffers from the same issues as MixableParent. It doesn't delegate to its parent class! This is okay because Router is an entity that other behavior is mixed into, but in some cases this would be unacceptable. Also, there are cases where you can't convert your classes into traits.

When creating a hierarchy of mixable behaviors via trait, you need to ensure the following:

- You have a mixin point that traits can assume as a parent.
- Your mixable traits delegate to their parent in meaningful ways
- You provide default implementations for chain-of-command style methods at your mixin point.

4.3   Composition can include inheritance

An aphorism among the Java community is "favor composition over inheritance." This simple advice means that it's usually best in object-oriented Java to create new classes that "contain" other classes, rather than inherit from them. This allows the new class to use features/functionality of several other classes, whereas inheritance is limited to one class. This advice also has other benefits, including creating more self-contained "do one thing well" classes. Interestingly, Scala blurs this aphorism with its addition of traits.

Scala traits are composable in flexible ways. You can decide the ordering of poly-morphic behavior by adjusting the order trait inheritance is declared. Multiple traits can also be inherited. These features combine to make traits a viable mechanism of composing functionality. Trait composability isn't all roses; there are still some issues that aren't addressed. Let's look at the issues associated with composing behavior via inheritance in Java in table 4.1. Let's look at the complaints associated with compos-ing behavior via inheritance in Java and see how they stack up against Scala. I refer to composing behavior via inheritance as "inheritance-composition" and classes/traits that can do this as "inheritance-composable." Composition that's done via members of an object I'll refer to as "member-composition" and classes/traits that can do this as "member-composable."

Scala traits immediately solve the problem of having to reimplement behavior in subclasses. They also use a clever trick to support multiple-inheritance on the JVM, making them "inheritance-composable" with more than one parent's behavior. Scala traits still suffer from two major issues, breaking encapsulation and needing access to a constructor. Let's look at how critical breaking encapsulation is.

Table 4.1   Issues with inheritance versus object composition

Issue	Java interfaces	Java abstract classes	Scala traits
Reimplement behavior in subclasses	X		
Can only compose with parent behavior		X	
Breaks encapsulation	X	X	X
Need to call a constructor to compose	X	X	X

Scala traits break encapsulation when used for composable behaviors. Let's see what the impact of this would be. Suppose we have a class that represents a data access service in the system. This class has a set of query-like methods that look for data and return it. Suppose also that we want to provide a logging ability so we can do postmortem analysis on a system if it runs into an issue. Let's see how this would look with classic composition techniques:

Listing 4.7 Composition of `Logger` and `DataAccess` classes

```
trait Logger {
  def log(category: String, msg: String): Unit = {
      println(msg)
  }
}

trait DataAccess {
  val logger = new Logger                             Logger exists
                                                      as internal
  def query[A](in: String): A = {                     variable
    logger.log("QUERY", in)
    ...
  }
}
```

Notice how the `DataAccess` class uses the `Logger` class. The current method of composition means that the `DataAccess` class must be able to instantiate the `Logger` class. An alternative would be to pass a logger into the constructor of the `DataAccess` class. In either case, the `DataAccess` trait contains all logging behavior. One point about the preceding implementation is that the logging behavior is nested in your `DataAccess` class. If we instead wanted to also have the ability to use `DataAccess` with *no* `Logger`, then we need to create a third entity that composes behavior from the first two. It would look something like this:

Listing 4.8 Composition of `Logger` and `DataAccess` into third class

```
trait Logger {
  def log(category: String, msg: String) : Unit = {
      println(msg)
  }
}

trait DataAccess {
  def query[A](in: String) : A = {
    ...
  }
}

trait LoggedDataAccess {
  val logger = new Logger
  val dao = new DataAccess

  def query[A](in: String) : A = {
    logger.log("QUERY", in)
```

```
      dao.query(in)
   }
}
```

Now we have standalone classes `Logger` and `DataAccess` that are minimal in implementation. We've composed their behavior into the third `LoggedDataAccess` class. This implementation has all the benefits of `DataAccess` and `Logger` being encapsulated and doing only one thing. The `LoggedDataAccess` class aggregates the two, providing mixed behavior. The issue here is that `LoggedDataAccess` doesn't implement the `DataAccess` interface. These two types can't be used interchangeably in client code via polymorphism. Let's see what this would look like with pure inheritance:

> **Listing 4.9 Inheritance-based composition of `Logger` and `DataAccess`**

```
trait Logger {
  def log(category: String, msg: String) : Unit = {
      println(msg)
  }
}

trait DataAccess {
   def query[A](in: String): A = {
     ...
   }
}

trait LoggedDataAccess extends DataAccess with Logger {
    def query[A](in: String): A = {
       log("QUERY", in)
       super.query(in)
    }
}
```

Notice how the `LoggedDataAccess` class is now polymorphic on `DataAccess` *and* `Logger`. This means you could use the new class where you would expect to find a `DataAccess` or `Logger` class, so this class is better for later composition. Something is still strange here: `LoggedDataAccess` is also a `Logger`. This seems an odd dichotomy to have for a `DataAccess` class. In this simple example, it seems `Logger` would be an ideal candidate for member-composition into the `LoggedDataAccess` class.

4.3.1 Member composition by inheritance

Another way to design these two classes (outlined in "Scalable Component Abstractions" by Oderksy and colleagues) involves inheritance-composition and member-composition. To start, let's create a `Logger` trait hierarchy. The hierarchy will have three logger types, one for local logging, one for remote logging, and one that performs no logging.

Listing 4.10 Logger hierarchy

```scala
trait Logger {
  def log(category: String, msg: String): Unit = {
      println(msg)
  }
}

trait RemoteLogger extends Logger {
  val socket = ...
  def log(category: String, msg: String): Unit = {
    //Send over socket
  }
}

trait NullLogger extends Logger {
    def log(category: String, msg: String): Unit = {}
}
```

The next thing we do is create what I'll call an abstract member-composition class. This abstract class defines an overridable member. We can then create subclasses matching all the existing Logger subclasses.

Listing 4.11 Abstract member-composition trait HasLogger

```scala
trait HasLogger {
  val logger: Logger = new Logger
}

trait HasRemoteLogger extends HasLogger {
  override val logger: Logger = new RemoteLogger {}
}

trait HasNullLogger extends HasLogger {
  override val logger: Logger = new NullLogger {}
}
```

The HasLogger trait does one thing: contains a logger member. This class can be subclassed by other classes who want to use a Logger. It gives a real "is-a" relationship to make inheritance worthwhile to Logger users. "Why the indirection?" you may be asking yourself. The answer comes with the ability to override members as you would methods in Scala. This allows you to create classes that extend HasLogger and then mixin the other HasLogger traits later for different behavior. In the following listing, let's look at using the HasLogger trait to implement our DataAccess class.

Listing 4.12 DataAccess class with HasLogger trait

```scala
trait DataAccess extends HasLogger {

  def query[A](in: String) : A = {
    logger.log("QUERY", in)
    ...
  }
}
```

Now for the real fun. Let's write a unit test for the `DataAccess` class. In the unit test, we don't want to be logging output; we want to test the behavior of the function. To do so, we want to use the `NullLogger` implementation. Let's look at a specification test for `DataAccess`:

Listing 4.13 Specification test for `DataAccess`

```
object DataAccessSpec extends Specification {
  "A DataAccess Service" should {
    "return queried data" in {
      val service = new DataAccess with HasNullLogger
      service.query("find mah datah!") must notBe(null)
    }
  }
}
```

◁─ **Mixing new logger behavior to DataAccess**

We now have the ability to change the composition of the `DataAccess` class when we instantiate it. As you can see, we gain the benefits of member-composition and inheritance composition at the cost of more legwork. Let's see if Scala has something that could reduce this legwork.

NOTE A trait containing multiple abstract members is sometimes called an *environment*. This is because the trait contains the environment needed for another class to function.

4.3.2 *Classic constructors with a twist*

In the case of classic Java-like inheritance, we can try to compose using constructor arguments. This reduces the number of parent classes to one, as only abstract/concrete classes can have arguments, and they can only be singly inherited. But Scala has two features that will help you out:

- Named and default parameters
- Promote constructor arguments to members

In the following listing, let's recreate the `DataAccess` class, but this time as a full up class where the logger is a constructor argument. Let's also define a default argument for logger. We'll promote this argument to be an immutable member on the `Data-Access` class.

Listing 4.14 `DataAccess` as a class with default arguments

```
class DataAccess(val logger: Logger = new Logger {}) {

  def query[A](in: String) : A = {
    logger.log("QUERY", in)
    ...
  }
}
```

This class is simple. It defaults to a particular logger at instantiation time and lets you supply your own (via constructor) if desired. The real fun comes when we want to extend this class, provide users with a mechanism to supply a logger to the subclass and use the same default as the `DataAccess` class. To do so, we'll have to understand how the compiler collects default arguments.

When a method has default arguments, the compiler generates a static method for obtaining the default. Then when user code calls a method, if it doesn't supply an argument, the compiler calls the static method for the default and supplies the argument. In the case of a constructor, these arguments get placed on the companion object for the class. If there's no companion object, one will be generated. The companion object will have methods for generating each argument. These argument-generating methods use a form of name mangling so the compiler can deterministically call the correct one. The mangling format is method name followed by argument number, all separated with $. Let's look at what a subclass of `DataAccess` would have to look like for our requirements:

Listing 4.15 Inheritance with default arguments

```scala
class DoubleDataAccess(
    logger: Logger = DataAccess.`init$default$1`
) extends DataAccess(logger) {
  ...
}
```

You'll notice two things in this code. First, the constructor is pickled with a method name of `init`. This is because in the JVM bytecode, constructors are called <init>. The second is the use of the backtick (`) operator. In Scala, this method is used to denote "I'm going to use an identifier here with potentially nonstandard characters that could cause parsing issues." This is handy when calling methods defined in other languages that have different reserved words and identifiers.

We've finally created a method of simplifying composition using constructor arguments. The method certainly suffers from ugliness when trying to also include inheritance in your classes. Let's look at the pros and cons of each compositional method in the following table:

Table 4.2 Pros/Cons of compositional methods

Method	Pros	Cons
Member composition	▪ Standard Java practice	▪ No polymorphism ▪ Inflexible
Inheritance composition	▪ Polymorphism	▪ Violation of encapsulation
Abstract member composition	▪ Most flexible	▪ Code bloat—especially setting up parallel class hierarchies
Composition using constructor with default arguments	▪ Reduction in code size	▪ Doesn't work well with inheritance

Many "new" methods of doing object composition are possible within Scala. I recommend picking something you're comfortable with. When it comes to inheritance, I prefer "is-a" or "acts-as-a" relationships for parents. If there's no "is-a" or "acts-as-a" relationship and you still need to use inheritance-composition, use the abstract member composition pattern. If you have single-class hierarchies and no "is-a" relationships, your best option is composition using constructors with default arguments. Scala provides the tools you need to solve the problem you have at hand. Make sure you understand it fully before deciding on an object-composition strategy.

In section 11.3.2, we show an alternative means of composing objects using a functional approach. Although the concepts behind this approach are advanced, the approach offers a good middle ground between using constructors with default arguments and abstract member composition.

4.4   *Promote abstract interface into its own trait*

> **Rule II**
>
> **Put the abstract interface into its own trait**
>
> It's possible to mix implementation and interface with traits, but it is still a good idea to provide a pure abstract interface. This can be used by either Scala or Java libraries. It can then be extended by a trait which fills in the implementation details.

Modern object-oriented design promotes the use of abstract types to declare interfaces. In Java, these use the interface keywords and can't include implementation. In C++ the same could be accomplished by using all pure virtual functions. A common pitfall among new Scala developers was also an issue with C++: With the new power of traits, it can be tempting to put method implementations into traits. Be careful when doing so! Scala's traits do the most to impact binary compatibility of libraries. In the following listing, let's look at a simple Scala trait and a class that uses this trait to see how it compiles:

Listing 4.16   Simple Scala trait and implementation class

```
trait Foo {
  def someMethod(): Int = 5
}
class Main() extends Foo{
}
```

The following listing shows the `javap` output for the `Main` class:

Listing 4.17   `javap` disassembly of `Main` class

```
public class Main extends java.lang.Object
  implements Foo,scala.ScalaObject{
public Main();
  Code:
   0: aload_0
   1: invokespecial #10; //Method java/lang/Object."<init>":()V
   4: aload_0
```

```
5: invokestatic #16; //Method Foo$class.$init$:(LFoo;)V
8: return
public int $tag()    throws java.rmi.RemoteException;
  Code:
  0: aload_0
  1: invokestatic #23;
     //Method scala/ScalaObject$class.$tag:(Lscala/ScalaObject;)I
  4: ireturn
public int someMethod();
  Code:
  0: aload_0
  1: invokestatic #30; //
    Method Foo$class.someMethod:(LFoo;)I
  4: ireturn

}
```

← Delegating construction initializer

Delegate method calls static implementation ←

As you can see, with some adjustment to reading JVM bytecode, the Main class is given a delegate class from the compiler. One obvious issue with binary compatibility is that if the Foo trait is given another method, the Main class won't be given a delegate method without recompiling it. The JVM does something funny, though. It will allow you to link (think binary compatibility) even if a class doesn't fully implement an interface. It errors out only when someone tries to use a method on the interface that's unimplemented. Let's take it for a test toast in the following listing. We'll change the Foo trait without modifying the Main class.

Listing 4.18 Modified Foo trait

```
trait Foo {
  def someMethod(): Int = 5
  def newMethod() = "HAI"
}
```

As you can see, we've added the newMethod method. We should still be able to use the compiled Main to instantiate a Foo at runtime. Here's what it looks like:

Listing 4.19 ScalaMain testing class

```
object ScalaMain {
   def main(args : Array[String]) {
      val foo: Foo = new Main();
      println(foo.someMethod());
      println(foo.newMethod());
   }
}
```

You'll notice we're making a new Main object and coercing its type to be a Foo. The most interesting piece of this class is that it compiles and runs. Let's look at its output.

```
java -cp /usr/share/java/scala-library.jar:. ScalaMain
5
Exception in thread "main" java.lang.AbstractMethodError:
```

```
Main.newMethod()Ljava/lang/String;
at ScalaMain$.main(ScalaMain.scala:7)
at ScalaMain.main(ScalaMain.scala)
```

Notice that the classes link fine; it even runs the first method call! The issue comes when calling the new method from the `Foo` trait. This finally causes an `Abstract-MethodError` to be thrown, the closest we get to a linking error. The confusing part to a Scala newcomer is that the trait provides a default implementation! Well, if we want to call the default implementation, we can do so at runtime. Let's look at the modified `ScalaMain` in the following listing:

Listing 4.20   Modified `ScalaMain` testing class

```
object ScalaMain {
   def main(args: Array[String]) {
      val foo: Foo = new Main()
      println(foo.someMethod())

      val clazz = java.lang.Class.forName("Foo$class")
      val method = clazz.getMethod("newMethod", Array(classOf[Foo]): _*)
      println(method.invoke(null, foo));
   }
}
```

You'll see we're looking up and using the new method via reflection. Here's the run-time output:

```
java -cp /usr/share/java/scala-library.jar:. ScalaMain
5
HAI
```

This points out an interesting side of the JVM/Scala's design; methods added to traits can cause unexpected runtime behavior. Therefore it's usually safe to recompile all downstream users, to be on the safe side. The implementation details of traits can throw off new users, who expect new methods with implementations to automatically link with precompiled classes. Not only that, but adding new methods to traits will also not break binary compatibility unless someone calls the new method!

4.4.1   Interfaces you can talk to

When creating two different "parts" of a software program, it's helpful to create a completely abstract interface between them that they can use to talk to each other. See figure 4.3. This middle piece should be relatively stable, compared to the others, and have as few dependencies as possible. One thing you may have noticed from earlier is that Scala's traits compile with a dependency on the `ScalaObject` trait. It's possible to remove this dependency, something that's handy if the two pieces of your software wanted to use differing Scala-library versions.

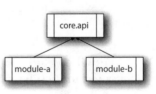

Figure 4.3   Abstract interface between software modules.

The key to this interaction is that each module depends on the common interface code and no artifacts from each other. This strategy is most effective when there are different developers on module A and module B, such that they evolve at different rates. Preventing any kind of dependencies between the modules allows the new module systems, such as OSGi, to dynamically reload module B without reloading module A so long as the appropriate framework hooks are in place and all communications between the modules A and B happen via the core-api module.

To create a trait that compiles to a pure abstract interface, similar to a Java interface don't define any methods. Look at the `PureAbstract` trait in the following listing:

Listing 4.21 PureAbstract trait

```
trait PureAbstract {
    def myAbstractMethod(): Unit
}
```

Now let's look at the `javap` disassembled code:

```
javap -c PureAbstract
Compiled from "PureAbstract.scala"
public interface PureAbstract{
  public abstract void myAbstractMethod();
}
```

You'll notice the `PureAbstract` trait doesn't have a dependency on `ScalaObject`. This is a handy method of creating abstract interfaces when needed; it becomes important when used with module systems like OSGi. In fact, this situation is similar to the one faced when interfacing two C++ libraries using C interfaces.

4.4.2 Learning from the past

Although this rule may seem contradictory to the "Provide empty implementations for abstract methods," the two are used to solve differing problems. Use this rule when trying to create separation between modules, and provide implementations for abstract methods when creating a library of traits you intend users to extend via mixins. Pure abstract traits also help explicitly identify a minimum interface. A dichotomy of thought exists here. Some designers prefer "rich" APIs, and others prefer "thin," where a thin API would be the minimum necessary to implement a piece of functionality, and a rich API would contain a lot of extra helper methods to ease usage.

Scala traits bring the power to add lots of helper methods, something lacking in Java's interfaces. This kind of power was common in C++, which also suffered many more issues with binary compatibility. In C++, binary compatibility issues forced the creation of a pure "C" integration layer for libraries. This layer wrapped a rich C++ hierarchy inside the library. Clients of the library would then implement wrappers around the C layer, converting back from classless world to OO and providing the "rich" API. In my experience, these classes usually were thin wrappers around the C layer and mostly lived in header files, such that users of the library could gain binary compatibility without having to write their own wrapper.

In Scala, we can provide our rich interface via a simple delegate trait and some mixins. The "thin" interface should be something that we can reasonably expect someone to implement completely. This way the users of the "abstract interface" can grow their rich interface as needed for their project, assuming the "thin" interface is complete.

When you have two pieces of software that will be interacting but were developed by diverse or disparate teams, you should promote abstract interfaces into their own traits and lock those traits down as best as possible for the life of that project. When the abstract interface needs to be modified, all dependent modules should be upgraded against the changed traits to ensure proper runtime linkage.

4.5　*Provide return types in your public APIs*

Rule 12

Provide return types for public APIs

Scala can infer return types to methods. However, for a human reading a nontrivial method implementation, infering the return type can be troubling. In addition, letting Scala infer the return type can allow implementation details to slip past an interface. It's best to explicitly document and enforce return types in public APIs.

Imagine you're developing a messaging library. This library contains a `Message-Dispatcher` interface that users of your library can use to send messages. A `Factory` method also takes various configuration parameters and returns a `MessageDispatcher`. As a library designer, we decide that we want to rework existing implementation to create different `MessageDispatcher` implementations based on the parameters to the `Factory` method. Let's start with a `MessageDispatcher` trait in the following listing:

Listing 4.22　`MessageDispatcher` trait

```
trait MessageDispatcher[-T] {
  def sendMessage(msg: T) : Unit
}
```

The trait is rather simple; it provides a mechanism to send messages. Now let's create the factory and an implementation class:

Listing 4.23　`MessageDispatcher` factory and implementation class

```
class ActorDispatcher[-T, U <: OutputChannel[T]](receiver: U)
 extends MessageDispatcher[T] {
  override def sendMessage(msg: T) {
    receiver ! msg
  }
}

object MyFactory {
  def createDispatcher(a: OutputChannel[Any]) =
    new ActorDispatcher(actor)
}
```

The code is pretty standard. The actor dispatcher will transmit messages to an actor in the Scala actors library. We'll discuss that library in depth later. For now, we'll focus on the createDispatcher factory method. This method looks standard but has one issue: The return type isn't a MessageDispatcher but an ActorDispatcher. This means we've leaked our abstraction. See the javap output for proof:

```
public final class MyFactory$ extends java.lang.Object
  implements scala.ScalaObject{
    public static final MyFactory$ MODULE$;
    public static {};
    public ActorDispatcher createDispatcher(java.lang.Object);
}
```

We've leaked the ActorDispatcher class in the public API. This may be okay in a small project, but it lends itself to issues if others rely on receiving ActorDispatcher instances from this method instead of a MessageDispatcher. We can easily change this by refactoring your API slightly to return more than one type. Let's create a Null-Dispatcher that doesn't send messages. We also change the createDispatcher method to take in any type of object and return appropriate dispatchers for each. If we don't have a useful dispatcher, we'll use the NullDispatcher.

> **Listing 4.24 MessageDispatcher factory with two implementation classes**

```
object NullDispatcher
    extends MessageDispatcher[Any] {
  override def sendMessage(msg: Any) : Unit = {}
}

object MyFactory {
    def createDispatcher(a: Any) = {
      a match {
        case actor: OutputChannel[Any] => new ActorDispatcher(actor)
        case _ => NullDispatcher
      }
    }
}
```

This slight change has made the compiler reinfer a different return type. We can see proof of this in the new javap output:

```
public final class MyFactory$ extends java.lang.Object
    implements scala.ScalaObject{
    public static final MyFactory$ MODULE$;
    public static {};
    public MessageDispatcher createDispatcher(java.lang.Object);
}
```

The resulting API has inferred MessageDispatcher as the return type. This could silently break code that was relying on receiving an ActorDispatcher. It's easy enough to annotate the return type for a public API. Modify the createDispatcher method as follows:

```
object MyFactory {
    def createDispatcher(a: Any): MessageDispatcher[Any] = {
      a match {
        case actor: OutputChannel[Any] => new ActorDispatcher(actor)
        case _ => NullDispatcher
      }
    }
}
```

Now the return type is locked to MessageDispatcher[Any] and anything that violates this will cause a compiler warning, rather than breaking client code.

To help avoid confusion or leaking implementation details, it's best to provide explicit return types on public methods in your API. This can also help speed compilation slightly, as the type inferences don't need to figure out a return type, and it gives a chance for your implicit conversions to kick in, coercing things to the desired type. The only time it would be okay to not specify return types is in the case of sealed single-class hierarchy, a private method, or when overriding a method in a parent that explicitly declares a return type. Ironically, when coding in a functional style, you find that you tend not to use inheritance as much as you would think. I find this rule generally applies to my domain model and perhaps my UI library, but not the more functional aspects of my code.

4.6 *Summary*

Scala's object system is powerful and elegant. The body of code in a class definition defines the constructor of a class. For top-level objects, this means that code in the body should avoid expensive operations and other non-construction behavior. Scala also allows mixin inheritance. But when defining methods, only methods marked with override can override an existing implementation in the hierarchy. Adding override can help ease mixin inheritance and avoid method typos. Mixin inheritance also provides a new way to compose software. Mixins can mark objects as *having* a value and allow new values to be mixed in via inheritance. This technique provides the most flexibility when *pure abstract interfaces* are used for the API systems. Finally, type inference can change an API as the object model expands. For public methods, it's best to explicitly annotate return types on critical interfaces. This leads to the best use of objects in Scala.

Using implicits to write expressive code

In this chapter

- Introduction to implicits
- Mechanics of the implicit resolution system
- Using implicits to enhance classes
- Using implicits to enforce scope rules

The implicit system in Scala allows the compiler to adjust code using a well-defined lookup mechanism. A programmer in Scala can leave out information that the compiler will attempt to infer at compile time. The Scala compiler can infer one of two situations:

- A method call or constructor with a missing parameter.
- Missing conversion from one type to another type. This also applies to method calls on an object that would require a conversion.

In both of these situations, the compiler follows a set of rules to resolve missing data and allow the code to compile. When the programmer leaves out parameters, it's incredibly useful and is done in advanced Scala libraries. When the compiler converts types to ensure that an expression compiles is more dangerous and is the cause of controversy.

The implicit system is one of the greatest assets of the Scala programming language. Using it wisely and conservatively can drastically reduce the size of your code base. It can also be used to elegantly enforce design considerations. Let's look at implicit parameters in Scala.

5.1   Introduction to implicits

Scala provides an implicit keyword that can be used in two ways: method or variable definitions, and method parameter lists. If this keyword is used on method or variable definitions, it tells the compiler that those methods or variable definitions can be used during implicit resolution. Implicit resolution is when the compiler determines that a piece of information is missing in code, and it must be looked up. The implicit keyword can also be used at the beginning of a method parameter list. This tells the compiler that the parameter list might be missing, in which case the compiler should resolve the parameters via implicit resolution.

Let's look at using the implicit resolution mechanism to resolve a missing parameter list:

```
scala> def findAnInt(implicit x : Int) = x
findAnInt: (implicit x: Int)Int
```

The findAnInt method declares a single parameter x of type Int. This function will return any value that's passed into it. The parameter list is marked with implicit, which means that we don't need to use it. If it's left off, the compiler will look for a variable of type Int in the implicit scope. Let's look at the following example:

```
scala> findAnInt
<console>:7: error: could not find implicit value for parameter x: Int
       findAnInt
       ^
```

The findAnInt method is called without specifying any argument list. The compiler complains that it can't find an implicit value for the x parameter. We'll provide one, as follows:

```
scala> implicit val test = 5
test: Int = 5
```

The test value is defined with the implicit keyword. This marks it as available for implicit resolution. Since this is in the REPL, the test value will be available in the implicit scope for the rest of the REPL session. Here's what happens when we can findAnInt:

```
scala> findAnInt
res3: Int = 5
```

The call to findAnInt succeeds and returns the value of the test value. The compiler was able to successfully complete the function call. We can still provide the parameter if desired.

```
scala> findAnInt(2)
res4: Int = 2
```

This method call passes a parameter with a value of 2. Because the method call is complete, the compiler doesn't need to look up a value using implicits. Remember this, as implicit method parameters can still be explicitly provided. This utility will be discussed further in section 5.6.

To understand how the compiler determines if a variable is available for implicit resolution, it's important to dig into how the compiler deals with identifiers and scope.

5.1.1 Identifiers: A digression

Before delving into the implicit resolution mechanism, it's important to understand how the compiler resolves identifiers within a particular scope. This section references chapter 2 of the Scala Language Specification (SLS), I highly recommend reading through the SLS after you have an understanding of the basics. Identifiers play a crucial role in the selection of implicits, so let's dig into the nuts and bolts of identifiers in Scala.

Scala defines the term *entity* to mean types, values, methods, or classes. These are the things we use to build our programs. We refer to them using identifiers, or names. In Scala this is called a *binding*. For example, in the following code:

```
class Foo {
  def val x = 5
}
```

the Foo class itself is an entity, a class containing an x method. But we've given this class the name Foo, which is the binding. If we declare this class locally within the REPL, we can instantiate it using the name Foo because it's locally bound.

```
scala> val y = new Foo
y: Foo = Foo@33262bf4
```

Here we can construct a new variable, named y, of type Foo using the name Foo. Again, this is because the class Foo was defined locally within the REPL and the name Foo was bound locally. Let's complicate things by placing Foo in a package.

```
package test;

class Foo {
  val x = 5
}
```

The Foo class is now a member of the package test. If we try to access it with the name Foo, it will fail on the REPL:

```
scala> new Foo
<console>:7: error: not found: type Foo
       new Foo
```

Trying to call new Foo fails because the name Foo isn't bound in our scope. The Foo class is now in the test package. To access it, we must either use the name test.Foo or create a binding of the name `Foo` to the `test.Foo` class in the current scope. For the latter, Scala provides the `import` keyword:

```
scala> import test.Foo
import test.Foo

scala> new Foo
res3: test.Foo = test.Foo@60e1e567
```

The `import` statement takes `test.Foo` entity and binds it in the local scope with the name `Foo`. This allows us to construct a new `test.Foo` instance by calling `new Foo`. This concept should be familiar from Java's `import` statement or C++'s `using` statement. In Scala, things are a bit more flexible.

The `import` statement can be used anywhere in the source file and it will only create a binding in the local scope. This feature allows us to control where imported names are used within our file. This feature can also be used to limit the scope of implicits views or variables. We'll cover this aspect in more detail in section 5.4.

Scala is also more flexible in binding entities with arbitrary names. In Java or C#, one can only bring the name bound in some other scope, or package, into the current one. For example, the `test.Foo` class could only be imported locally with the name `Foo`. The Scala `import` statement can give arbitrary names to imported entities using the `{OriginalBinding=>NewBinding}` syntax. Let's import our `test.Foo` entity with a different name:

```
scala> import test.{Foo=>Bar}
import test.{Foo=>Bar}

scala> new Bar
res1: test.Foo = test.Foo@596b753
```

The first `import` statement binds the `test.Foo` class to the current scope using the name `Bar`. The next line constructs a new instance of `test.Foo` by calling `new Bar`. You can use this renaming to avoid conflicts in classes imported from different packages. A good example is with `java.util.List` and `scala.List`. To avoid confusion within Scala, it's common to see `import java.util.{List=>JList}` in code that interacts with Java.

> **RENAMING PACKAGES**   Scala's import statement can also be used to alter the names of packages. This can be handy when interacting with Java libraries. For example, when using the `java.io` package, I frequently do the following:
> ```
> import java.{io=>jio}
> def someMethod( input : jio.InputStream ) = ...
> ```

Binding entities allows us to name them within a particular scope. But it's important to understand what constitutes a scope and what bindings are found in a scope.

5.1.2 *Scope and bindings*

A scope is a lexical boundary in which bindings are available. A scope could be anything from the body of a class to the body of a method to an anonymous block. As a general rule, anytime you use the `{}` characters you're creating a new scope.

In Scala, scopes can be nested. This means I can construct a new scope inside another scope. When creating a new scope, the bindings from the outer scope are still available. This allows us to do the following:

```
class Foo(x : Int) {
  def tmp = {
    x
  }
}
```

The Foo class is defined with the constructor parameter x. We then define the tmp method with a nested scope. We can still access the constructor parameter inside this scope with the name x. This nested scope has access to bindings in its parent scope, however we can create new bindings that shadow the parent. In this case, the tmp method can create a new binding called x that does not refer to the constructor parameter x. Let's take a look:

```
scala> class Foo(x : Int) {
     |     def tmp = {
     |       val x = 2
     |       x
     |     }
     | }
defined class Foo
```

The Foo class is defined the same as before, but the tmp method defines a variable named x in the nested scope. This binding *shadows* the constructor parameter x. Shadowing means that the local binding is visible and the constructor parameter is no longer accessible, at least using the name x. In Scala, bindings of higher precedence shadow bindings of lower precedence within the same scope. Also, bindings of higher or the same precedence shadow bindings in an outer scope.

Scala defines the following precedence on bindings:

1 Definitions and declarations that are local, inherited, or made available by a package clause in the same source file where the definition occurs have highest precedence.

2 Explicit imports have next highest precedence.

3 Wildcard imports (import foo._) have next highest precedence.

4 Definitions made available by a package clause not in the source file where the definition occurs have lowest precedence.

Let's look at an example of this precedence. First, let's define a test package and an

---

Bindings and Shadowing

In Scala, a binding shadows bindings of lower precedence within the same scope. A binding shadows bindings of the same or lower precedence in an outer scope. This is what allows us to write:

```
class Foo(x : Int) {
  def tmp = {
  val x = 2
  x
  }
}
```

And have calls to tmp return the value 2.

object x within it in a source file called `externalbindings.scala`, as shown in the following listing:

Listing 5.1   externalbindings.scala

```
package test;

object x {
  override def toString = "Externally bound x object in package test"
}
```

This file defines a package `test` with the x object inside it. The x object overrides the `toString` method so we can easily call `toString` on it. This means that for the purposes of our test, the x object should have the lowest binding precedence with binding rules. Now, let's create a file that will test the binding rules:

Listing 5.2   Implicit binding test file

```
package test;

object Test {
  def main(args : Array[String]) : Unit = {
    testSamePackage()
    testWildcardImport()
    testExplicitImport()
    testInlineDefinition()
  }
  ...
}
```

First, we declare the contents of the file to be in the same test package as our earlier definition. Next, we define a main method that will call four testing methods, one for each binding precedence rule. Let's fill the first one in now:

```
def testSamePackage() {
  println(x)
}
```

This method calls `println` on an entity called x. Because the `Test` object is defined within the `test` package, the x object created earlier is available and used for this method. To prove this, look at the output of this method:

```
scala> test.Test.testSamePackage()
Externally bound x object in package test
```

Calling the `testSamePackage` method produces the string we defined for the object x. Now let's see what happens if we add a `Wildcard` import:

Listing 5.3   Wildcard imports

```
object Wildcard {
  def x = "Wildcard Import x"
}

def testWildcardImport() {
```

```
  import Wildcard._
  println(x)
}
```

The `Wildcard` object is a nested object used to contain the x entity so that it can later be imported. The entity x is defined as a method that returns the string `"Wildcard Import x"`. The `testWildcardImport` method first calls `import Wildcard._`. This is a wildcard import that will bind all the names/entities from the `Wildcard` object into the current scope. Because wildcard imports have higher precedence than resources made available from the same package but in a different source file, the `Wildcard.x` entity will be used instead of the `test.x` entity. We see this when we run the `test-WildcardImport` function:

```
scala> test.Test.testWildcardImport()
Wildcard Import x
```

When calling the `testWildcardImport` method, the string `Wildcard Import x` is returned—exactly what we expect from the binding precedence. Things get more interesting when we add explicit imports.

Listing 5.4   Explicit imports

```
object Explicit {
  def x = "Explicit Import x"
}

def testExplicitImport() {
  import Explicit.x
  import Wildcard._
  println(x)
}
```

Once again, the `Explicit` object is used to create a new namespace for another x entity. The `testExplicitImport` method first imports this entity directly and then uses the wildcard import against the `Wildcard` object. Although the wildcard import is after the explicit import, the binding precedence rules kick in and the method will use the x binding from the `Explicit` object. Let's take a look:

```
scala> test.Test.testExplicitImport()
Explicit Import x
```

As expected, the returned string is the one from `Explicit.x`. This precedence rule is important when dealing with implicit resolution, but we'll get to that in section 5.1.3.

The final precedence rule to test is for local declarations. Let's modify the `test-ExplicitImport` method to define a local binding for the name x:

Listing 5.5   Inline definitions

```
def testInlineDefinition() {
    val x = "Inline definition x"
    import Explicit.x
    import Wildcard._
    println(x)
  }
```

The first line in the `testInlineDefinition` method declares a local variable named x. The next two lines explicitly import and implicitly import x bindings from the `Explicit` and `Wildcard` objects, as we saw earlier. Finally, we call `println(x)` and see which binding is selected.

```
scala> test.Test.testInlineDefinition()
Inline definition x
```

Again, even though the import statements come after the `val x` statement, the local variable is chosen based on the binding priorities.

Non-shadowing bindings

It's possible to have two bindings available for the same name. In this case, the compiler will warn you that the name is ambiguous. Here's an example directly from the Scala Language Specification:

```
scala> {
 | val x = 1;
 | {
 | import test.x;
 | x
 | }
 | }
 <console>:11: error: reference to x is ambiguous; it is both defined in
            value res7 and imported subsequently by import test.x
  x
  ^
```

In this example, the name x is bound in an outer scope. The name x is also imported from the test package in a nested scope. Neither of these bindings shadows the other. The value x from the outer scope isn't eligible to shadow within the nested scope, and the imported value x doesn't have high enough precedence to shadow.

Why all the emphasis on name resolution within the compiler? Implicit resolution is intimately tied to name resolution, so these intricate rules become important when using implicits. Let's look at the compiler's implicit resolution scheme.

5.1.3   *Implicit resolution*

The Scala Language Specification declares two rules for looking up entities marked as implicit:

- The implicit entity binding is available at the lookup site with no prefix—that is, not as `foo.x` but only x.
- If there are no available entities from this rule, then all `implicit` members on objects belong to the implicit scope of an implicit parameter's type.

The first rule is intimately tied to the binding rules of the previous section. The second rule is a bit more complex and we'll look into it in section 5.1.4.

First, let's look at our earlier example of implicit resolution:

```
scala> def findAnInt(implicit x : Int) = x
findAnInt: (implicit x: Int)Int

scala> implicit val test = 5
test: Int = 5
```

The findAnInt method is declared with an implicit parameter list of a single integer. The next line defines a val test with the implicit marker. This makes the identifier, test, available on the local scope with no prefix. If we were to write test in the REPL, it would return the value 5. When we write this method call, findAnInt, the compiler will rewrite it as findAnInt(test). This lookup uses the binding rules we examined earlier.

The second rule for implicit lookup is used when the compiler can't find any available implicits using the first rule. In this case, the compiler will look for implicits defined within any object in the *implicit scope* of the type it's looking for. The implicit scope of a type is defined as all companion modules that are associated with that type. This means that if the compiler is looking for a parameter to the method def foo(implicit param : Foo), that parameter will need to conform to the type Foo. If no value of type Foo is found using the first rule, then the compiler will use the *implicit scope* of Foo. The implicit scope of Foo would consist of the companion object to Foo.

Let's look at the following listing:

Listing 5.6 Companion object and implicit lookup

```
scala> object holder {
     | trait Foo
     | object Foo {
     |   implicit val x = new Foo {
     |     override def toString = "Companion Foo"
     |   }
     | }
     | }
defined module holder

scala> import holder.Foo
import holder.Foo

scala> def method(implicit foo : Foo) = println(foo)
method: (implicit foo: holder.Foo)Unit

scala> method
Companion Foo
```

The holder object is used so we can define a trait and companion object within the REPL, as described in section 2.1.2. Inside, we define a trait Foo and companion object Foo. The companion object Foo defines a member x of type Foo that's available for implicit resolution. Next we import the Foo type from the holder object into the current scope. This step isn't necessary, it's done to simplify the method definition. Next is the definition of method. The method takes an implicit parameter of type Foo.

When called with no argument lists, the compiler will use the `implicit val x` defined on the companion.

Because the implicit scope is looked at second, we can use the implicit scope to store default implicits while allowing users to import their own overrides as necessary. We'll investigate this a bit further in section 7.2.

As stated previously, the implicit scope of a type `T` is the set of companion objects for all types associated with the type `T`—that is, there's a set of types that are associated with `T`. All of the companion objects for these types are searched during implicit resolution. The Scala Language Specification defines association as any class that's a base class of some *part* of type `T`. The parts of type `T` are:

- The subtypes of `T` are all parts of `T`. If type `T` is defined as `A` with `B` with `C`, then `A`, `B`, and `C` are all parts of the type `T` and their companion objects will be searched during implicit resolution for type `T`.
- If `T` is parameterized, then all type parameters and their parts are included in the parts of type `T`. For example, an implicit search for the type `List[String]` would look in `List`'s companion object and `String`'s companion object.
- If `T` is a singleton type `T`, then the parts of the type `p` are included in the parts of type `T`. This means that if the type `T` lives inside an object, then the object itself is inspected for implicits. Singleton types are covered in more detail in section 6.1.1.
- If `T` is a type projection `S#T`, then the parts of `S` are included in the parts of type `T`. This means that if type `T` lives in a class or trait, then the class or trait's companion objects are inspected for implicits. Type projections are covered in more detail in section 6.1.1.

The implicit scope of a type includes many different locations and grants a lot of flexibility in providing handy implicit resolution.

Let's look at a few of the more interesting cases of implicit scope.

IMPLICIT SCOPE VIA TYPE PARAMETERS

The Scala language defines the implicit scope of a type to include the companion objects of all types or subtypes included in the type's parameters. This means, for example, that we can provide an implicit value for `List[Foo]` by including it in the type `Foo`'s companion object. Here's an example:

```scala
scala> object holder {
     |    trait Foo
     |    object Foo {
     |      implicit val list = List(new Foo{})
     |    }
     | }
defined module holder

scala> implicitly[List[holder.Foo]]
res0: List[holder.Foo] = List(holder$Foo$$anon$1@2ed4a1d3)
```

The `holder` object is used, again, to create companion objects in the REPL. The `holder` object contains a trait `Foo` and its companion object. The companion object contains an implicit definition of a `List[Foo]` type. The next line calls Scala's implicitly function. We can use this function to look up a type using the current implicit scope. The `implicitly` function is defined as `def implicitly[T](implicit arg : T) = arg`. It uses the type parameter `T` to allow us to reuse it for every type we're looking for. We'll cover type parameters in more detail in section 6.2. The call to `implicitly` for the type `List[holder.Foo]` returns the implicit list defined within `Foo`'s companion object.

This mechanism is used to implement *type traits* sometimes called *type classes*. Type traits describe generic interfaces using type parameters such that implementations can be created for any type. For example, we can define a `BinaryFormat[T]` type trait. This trait can be implemented for a given type to describe how it should be serialized into a binary format. Here's an example interface:

```
trait BinaryFormat[T] {
  def asBinary(entity: T) : Array[Bytes]
}
```

The `BinaryFormat` trait defines one method, `asBinary`. This method takes in an instance of the type parameter and returns an array of bytes representing that parameter. Code that needs to serialize objects to disk can now attempt to find a `Binary-Format` type trait via implicits. We can provide an implementation for our type `Foo` by providing an `implicit` in `Foo`'s companion object, as follows:

```
trait Foo {}
object Foo {
  implicit lazy val binaryFormat = new BinaryFormat[Foo] {
    def asBinary(entity: Foo) = "serializedFoo".toBytes
  }
}
```

The `Foo` trait is defined as an empty trait. Its companion object is defined with an `implicit val` that holds the implementation of the `BinaryFormat`. Now, when code that requires a `BinaryFormat` sees the type `Foo`, it will be able to find the `Binary-Format` implicitly. The details of this mechanism and design techniques are discussed in detail in section 7.2.

Implicit lookup from type parameters enables elegant type trait programming. Nested types provides another great means to supply implicit arguments.

IMPLICIT SCOPE VIA NESTING

Implicit scope also includes companion objects from outer scopes if a type is defined in an inner scope. This allows us to provide a set of handy implicits for a type in the outer scope. Let's look at an example.

```
scala> object Foo {
     | trait Bar
     | implicit def newBar = new Bar {
     |   override def toString = "Implicit Bar"
```

```
  | }
  | }
defined module Foo

scala> implicitly[Foo.Bar]
res0: Foo.Bar = Implicit Bar
```

The object `Foo` is the outer type. Inside is defined the trait `Bar`. The `Foo` object also defines an implicit method that creates an instance of the `Bar` trait. When calling `implicitly[Foo.Bar]`, the implicit value is found from a search of the `Foo` outer class. This technique is similar to placing implicits directly in a companion object. Defining implicits for nested types is convenient when the outer scope contains several subtypes. We can use this technique in situations where we can't create an implicit on a companion object.

Scala objects can't have companion objects for implicits. Because of this, implicits associated with the object's type, that are desired on the implicit scope of that object's type, must be provided from an outer scope. Here's an example:

```
scala> object Foo {
  |     object Bar { override def toString = "Bar" }
  |     implicit def b : Bar.type = Bar
  | }
defined module Foo

scala> implicitly[Foo.Bar.type]
res1: Foo.Bar.type = Bar
```

The object `Bar` is nested inside the object `Foo`. The object `Foo` also defines an implicit that returns `Bar.type`. Now, when calling `implicitly[Foo.Bar.type]`, the object `Bar` is returned. This mechanism allows defining an implicit for objects.

An additional case of nesting that may surprise those not used to it is the case of package objects. As of Scala 2.8, objects can be defined as package objects. A package object is an object defined using the `package` keyword. It's convention in Scala to locate all package objects in a file called `package.scala` in a directory corresponding to the package name.

Any class that's defined within a package is nested inside the package. Any implicits defined on a package object will be on the implicit scope for all types defined inside the package. This provides a handy location to store implicits rather than defining companion objects for every type in a package, as shown in the following example:

```
package object foo {
  implicit def foo = new Foo
}

package foo {
  class Foo {
    override def toString = "FOO!"
  }
}
```

The package object foo is declared with a single implicit that returns a new instance of the Foo class. Next, the class Foo is defined within the package foo. In Scala, packages can be defined in multiple files and the types defined in each source file is aggregated to create the complete package. There can only be one package object defined in all source files for any given package. The Foo class has an overridden toString method that will print the string "Foo!". Let's compile the foo package and use it in the REPL, as follows:

```
scala> implicitly[foo.Foo]
res0: foo.Foo = FOO!
```

Without importing the package object or its members, the compiler can find the implicit for the foo.Foo object. It's common in Scala to find a set of implicit definitions within the package object for a library. Usually this package object also contains implicit views, a mechanism for converting between types.

5.2   *Enhancing existing classes with implicit views*

An implicit view is an automatic conversion of one type to another to satisfy an expression. An implicit view definition takes the general form: implicit def <myConversion-Name>(<argumentName> : OriginalType) : ViewType. The previous conversion would implicitly convert a value of OriginalType to a value of ViewType if available on the implicit scope.

Let's look at a simple example attempting to convert an integer to a string:

```
scala> def foo(msg : String) = println(msg)
foo: (msg: String)Unit

scala> foo(5)
<console>:7: error: type mismatch;
 found    : Int(5)
 required: String
       foo(5)
```

The foo method is defined to take a String and print it to the console. The call to foo using the value 5 fails, as there's a type mismatch. An implicit view can make this succeed. Let's define one:

```
scala> implicit def intToString(x : Int) = x.toString
intToString: (x: Int)java.lang.String

scala> foo(5)
5
```

The method intToString is defined using the implicit keyword. It takes a single value of type Int and returns a String. This method is the implicit view, and is commonly referred to as the view Int => String. Now, when calling the foo method with the value 5, it prints the string 5. The compiler detected that the types did not conform and that there was a single implicit view that could correct the situation.

Implicit views are used in two situations:

- If an expression doesn't meet the type expected by the compiler, the compiler will look for an implicit view that would make it meet the expected type. An example of this would be passing a value of type `Int` to a function that expects a `String` would require an implicit view of `String => Int` in scope.

- Given a selection `e.t`, where selection means a member access, such that e's type doesn't have a member `t`, the compiler will look for an implicit view that will apply to `e` and whose resulting type contains a member `t`. If we try to call method `foo` on a `String`, then the compiler will look for an implicit view from `String` that can be used to make the expression compile. The expression `"foo".foo()` would require an implicit view like the following: `implicit def stringToFoo(x : String) = new { def foo() : Unit = println("foo") }`.

The implicit scope used for implicit views is the same as for implicit parameters. But when the compiler is looking for type associations, it uses the type it's attempting to convert from, not the type it's attempting to convert to. Let's look at an example:

```scala
scala> object test {
     |     trait Foo
     |     trait Bar
     |     object Foo {
     |        implicit def fooToBar(foo : Foo) = new Bar {}
     |     }
     | }
defined module test

scala> import test._
import test._
```

The `test` object is a scoping object used so we can create a companion object in the REPL. This contains the `Foo` and `Bar` traits as well as a companion object to `Foo`. The companion object to `Foo` contains an implicit view from `Foo` to `Bar`. Remember that when the compiler is looking for implicit views, the type it's converting *from* defines the implicit scope. This means the implicit views defined in `Foo`'s companion object will be inspected only when attempting to convert an expression of type `Foo` to some other expression. Let's try this out by defining a method that expects the type `Bar`.

```scala
scala> def bar(x : Bar) = println("bar")
bar: (x: test.Bar)Unit
```

The bar method takes a `bar` and prints the string bar. Let's try to call it with a value of `foo` and see what happens:

```scala
scala> val x = new Foo {}
x: java.lang.Object with test.Foo = $anon$1@15e565bd

scala> bar(x)
bar
```

The x value is of type `Foo`. The expression `bar(x)` triggers the compiler to look for an implicit view. Because the type of x is `Foo`, the compiler look in associated types of `Foo` for implicit views. Finding the `fooToBar` view, the compiler inserts the necessary transformation and the method compiles successfully.

This style of implicits allows us to adapt libraries to other libraries, or add our own convenience methods to types. It's a common practice in Scala to adapt Java libraries so that they work well with the Scala standard library. For example, the standard library defines a `scala.collection.JavaConversions` module that helps the Java collections library interoperate with the Scala collections library. This module is a set of implicit views that can be imported into the current scope to allow automatic conversion between Java collections and Scala collections and to "add" methods to the Java collections. Adapting Java libraries, or third party libraries, into your project using implicit views is a common idiom in Scala. Let's look at an example.

We'd like to write a wrapper around the `java.security` package for easier usage from Scala. Specifically, we want to simplify the task of running privileged code using `java.security.AccessController`. The `AccessController` class provides the static method `doPrivileged`, which allows us to run code in a privileged permission state. The `doPrivileged` method has two variants, one that grants the current context's permissions to the privileged code and one that takes an `AccessControlContext` containing the privileges to grant the privileged code. The `doPrivileged` method takes an argument of type `PrivilegedExceptionAction` which is a trait that defines one method: `run`. The trait is similar to Scala's `Function0` trait, and we'd like to be able to use an anonymous function when calling the `doPrivileged` method.

Let's create an implicit view from a `Function0` type to a `doPrivileged` method:

```
object ScalaSecurityImplicits {
  implicit def functionToPrivilegedAction[A](func : Function0[A]) =
    new PrivilegedAction[A] {
      override def run() = func()
    }
}
```

This defines an object `ScalaSecurityImplicits` which contains the implicit view. The implicit view `functionToPrivilegedAction` takes a `Function0` and returns a new `PrivilegedAction` object such that the `run` method calls the function. Let's use this implicit:

```
scala> import ScalaSecurityImplicits._
import ScalaSecurityImplicits._

scala> AccessController.doPrivileged( () =>
     | println("This is privileged"))
This is privileged
```

The first statement imports the implicit view into scope. Next, the call to `doPrivileged` passed the anonymous function `() => println("this is privileged")`. Again, the compiler sees that the anonymous function doesn't match the expected type. The compiler then looks and finds the implicit view defined and imported from `Scala-SecurityImplicits`. This technique can also be used when wrapping Java objects with Scala objects

It's common to write a wrapper class for existing Java libraries that add more advanced Scala idioms. Scala implicits can be used to convert from the original type into the wrapped type and vice versa. For example, let's look at adding some convenience methods onto the java.io.File class.

We'd like to provide a convenience notation for java.io.File so that the / operator can be used to create new file objects. Let's create the wrapper class that will provide the / operator:

```
class FileWrapper(val file: java.io.File) {
    def /(next : String) = new FileWrapper(new java.io.File(file, next))
    override def toString = file.getCanonicalPath
}
```

The class FileWrapper takes a java.io.File in its constructor. It provides one new method / that takes a string and returns a new FileWrapper object. The newly returned FileWrapper object points to a file with the name specified to the / method inside the directory of the original file. For example, if the original FileWrapper, called file, pointed at the /tmp directory, then expression file / "mylog.txt" will return a FileWrapper object that points at the /tmp/mylog.txt file. We'd like to use implicits to automatically convert between java.io.File and FileWrapper, so let's add an implicit view to FileWrapper's companion object:

```
object FileWrapper {
  implicit def wrap(file : java.io.File)  = new FileWrapper(file)
}
```

The FileWrapper companion object defines one method, wrap, which takes a java.io.File and returns a new FileWrapper. Let's look at an example usage in the REPL:

```
scala> import FileWrapper.wrap
import FileWrapper.wrap

scala> val cur = new java.io.File(".")
cur: java.io.File = .

scala> cur / "temp.txt"
res0: FileWrapper = .../temp.txt
```

The first line imports the implicit view into scope. The next line creates a new java.io.File object with the string ".". This string denotes that the file object should point to the current directory. The last line calls the / method against a java.io.File. The compiler doesn't find this method on a standard java.io.File and looks for an implicit view that would enable this line to compile. Finding the wrap method in scope, the compiler wraps the java.io.File into a FileWrapper and calls the / method. The resulting FileWrapper object is returned.

This mechanism is a great way to append methods onto existing Java classes, or any library. We have the performance overhead of the wrapper object instantiation, but the HotSpot optimizer may mitigate this. I say "may" here because there's no guarantee that the HotSpot optimizer will remove the wrapper allocation, but in some microbenchmarks this will occur. Again, it's best to profile an application to determine critical regions rather than assuming `HotSpot` will take care of allocations.

One issue with the `FileWrapper` is that calling its `/` method will return another `FileWrapper` object This means we can't pass the result directly into a method that expects a vanilla `java.io.File`. The `/` method could change to instead return a `java.io.File` object, but Scala also provides another solution. When passing a `File-Wrapper` to a method that expects a `java.io.File` type, the compiler will begin a search for a valid implicit view. As stated earlier, this search will include the companion object for the `FileWrapper` type itself. Let's add an unwrap implicit view to the companion object and see if this works:

```
object FileWrapper {
  implicit def wrap(file : java.io.File) = new FileWrapper(file)
  implicit def unwrap(wrapper : FileWrapper) = wrapper.file
}
```

The `FileWrapper` companion object now contains two methods: `wrap` and `unwrap`. The `unwrap` method takes an instance of `FileWrapper` and returns the wrapped `java.io.File` type. We'll test this out in the REPL:

```
scala> import test.FileWrapper.wrap
import test.FileWrapper.wrap

scala> val cur = new java.io.File(".")
cur: java.io.File = .

scala> def useFile(file : java.io.File) = println(file.getCanonicalPath)
useFile: (file: java.io.File)Unit

scala> useFile(cur / "temp.txt")
/home/jsuereth/projects/book/scala-in-depth/chapter5/wrappers/temp.txt
```

The first line imports the `wrap` implicit view. The next line construct a `java.io.File` object pointing to the current directory. The third line defines a `useFile` method. This method expects an input of type `java.io.File` and will print the path to the file. The last line calls the `useFile` method with the expression: `cur / "temp.txt"`. Again, the compile sees the `/` method call and looks for an implicit view to resolve the expression. The resulting type of the expression is a `FileWrapper`, but the `useFile` method requires a `java.io.File`. The compiler performs another implicit lookup using the type `Function1[java.io.File, FileWrapper]`. This search finds the `unwrap` implicit view on `FileWrapper`'s companion object. The types are now satisfied and the compiler has completed the expression. The runtime evaluation yields the correct string.

Notice that utilizing the `unwrap` implicit view doesn't require an import, as needed for the `wrap` method. This is because the `wrap` implicit view was used when the compile did not know the required type to satisfy the `cur / "temp.txt"` expression; therefore it looked for only local implicits, as `java.io.File` has no companion object. This feature allows us to provide a wrapper object with additional functionality and near-invisible conversions to and from the wrapper.

Take care when providing additional functionality to existing classes using implicit views. This mechanism makes it much harder to determine if there's a name conflict across differing implicit views of a type. It also has a performance penalty that may not be mitigated by the HotSpot optimizer. Finally, for folks not using a modern Scala IDE, it can be difficult to determine which implicit views are providing methods used in a block of code.

Rule 13

Avoid implicit views

Implicit views are the most abused feature in Scala. While they seem like a good idea in a lot of situations, Scala provides better alternatives in most cases. Using too many implicit views can greatly increase the ramp-up time of new developers on a code base. While useful, they should be limited to situations where they are the right solution.

Scala implicit views provide users with the flexibility to adapt an API to their needs. Using wrappers and companion object implicit views can drastically ease the pain of integrating libraries with varied but similar interfaces or can allow developers to add functionality to older libraries. Implicit views are a key component in writing expressive Scala code, and should be handled with care.

Implicits also have an interesting interaction with another Scala feature—default parameters.

5.3   *Utilize implicit parameters with defaults*

Implicit arguments provide a great mechanism to ensure that users don't have to specify redundant arguments. They also work well with default parameters. In the event that no parameter is specified and no implicit value is found using implicit resolution, the default parameter is used. This allows us to create default parameters that remove redundant ones while still allowing users to provide different parameters.

For example, let's implement a set of methods designed to perform matrix calculations. These methods will utilize threads to parallelize work when performing calculations on matrices. But as a library designer, we don't know where these methods will be called. They may be operating within a context where threading isn't allowed, or they may already have their own work queue set up. We want to allow users to tell us how to use threads in their context but provide a default for everyone else.

Let's start by defining the Matrix class:

Listing 5.7   Simple Matrix class

```scala
class Matrix(private val repr : Array[Array[Double]]) {
  def row(idx : Int) : Seq[Double] = {
    repr(idx)
  }
  def col(idx : Int) : Seq[Double] = {
    repr.foldLeft(ArrayBuffer[Double]()) {
      (buffer, currentRow) =>
        buffer.append(currentRow(idx))
        buffer
    } toArray
```

```
  }
  lazy val rowRank = repr.size
  lazy val colRank = if(rowRank > 0) repr(0).size else 0
  override def toString = "Matrix" + repr.foldLeft(") {
    (msg, row) => msg + row.mkString("\n|", " | ", "|")
  }
}
```

The `Matrix` class takes an array of double values and provides two similar methods: `row` and `col`. These methods take an index and return an array of the values for a given matrix row or column respectively. The `Matrix` class also provides `rowRank` and `colRank` values which return the number of rows and columns in the matrix respectively. Finally the `toString` method is overridden to create a prettier output of the matrix.

The `Matrix` class is complete and ready for a parallel multiplication algorithm. Let's start by creating an interface we can use in our library for threading:

```
trait ThreadStrategy {
  def execute[A](func : Function0[A]) : Function0[A]
}
```

The `ThreadStrategy` interface defines one method, `execute`. This method takes a function that returns a value of type `A`. It also returns a function that returns a value of type `A`. The returned function should return the same value as the passed-in function, but could block the current thread until the function is calculated on its desired thread. Let's implement our matrix calculation service using this `ThreadStrategy` interface:

```
object MatrixUtils {
  def  multiply(a: Matrix,
               b: Matrix)(
               implicit threading: ThreadStrategy): MatrixN = {
    ...
  }
}
```

The `MatrixUtils` object contains the method `multiply`. The method takes two `Matrix` classes, assumed to have the correct dimensions, and will return a new matrix that's the multiplication of the passed-in matrices. `Matrix` multiplication involves multiplying the elements in `Matrix` a's rows by the elements in `Matrix` b's columns and adding the results. This multiplication and summation is done for every element in the resulting matrix. A simple way to parallelize this is to compute each element of the result matrix on a separate thread. The algorithm for the `MatrixUtils.multiply` method is simple:

- Create a buffer to hold results.
- Create a closure that will compute a single value for a row/column pair and place it in the buffer.
- Send the closures created to the `ThreadStrategy` provided.

- Call the functions returned from `ThreadStrategy` to ensure they have completed.
- Wrap the buffer in a `Matrix` class and return it.

Let's start with creating the buffer:

```
def  multiply(a: Matrix,
              b: Matrix)(
              implicit threading : ThreadStrategy): Matrix = {
    assert(a.colRank == b.rowRank)
    val buffer = new Array[Array[Double]](a.rowRank)
    for ( i <- 0 until a.rowRank ) {
      buffer(i) = new Array[Double](b.colRank)
    }
    ...
 }
```

The initial assert statement is used to ensure that the `Matrix` objects passed in are compatible for multiplication. By definition, the number of columns in `Matrix` a must equal the number of rows in `Matrix` b. We then construct an array of arrays to use as the buffer. The resulting matrix will have the same number of rows as `Matrix` a and the same number of columns as `Matrix` b. Now that the buffer is ready, let's create a set of closures in the following listing that will compute the values and place them in the buffer:

Listing 5.8   `Matrix` multiplication

```
def  multiply(a: Matrix,
              b: Matrix)(
              implicit threading : ThreadStrategy) : Matrix = {
    ...
    def computeValue(row : Int, col : Int) : Unit = {
       val pairwiseElements =
         a.row(row).zip(b.col(col))
       val products =
         for((x,y) <- pairwiseElements)
         yield x*y
       val result = products.sum
       buffer(row)(col) = result
    }
...
```

The `computeValue` helper method takes a row and a column attribute and computes the value in the buffer at that row and column. The first step is matching the elements of the row of a with the elements of the column of b in a pairwise fashion. Scala provides the `zip` function which, given two collections, will match their elements. Next, the `paired` elements are multiplied to create a list of the products of each element. The final calculation takes a sum of all the products. This final value is placed into the correct row and column in the buffer. The next step is to take this method and construct a function for every row and column in the resulting matrix and pass these functions to the threading strategy, as follows:

```
val computations = for {
    i <- 0 until a.rowRank
    j <- 0 until b.colRank
} yield threading.execute { () => computeValue(i,j) }
```

This `for` expression loops every row and column in the resulting matrix and passes a function into the `ThreadStrategy` parameter threading. The `()` => syntax is used when creating anonymous function objects that take no arguments, required by the type `Function0`. After farming out the work to threads, the multiply method must ensure that all work is complete before returning results. We do this by calling each method returned from the `ThreadStrategy`.

```
def  multiply(a: Matrix,
              b: Matrix)(
              implicit threading : ThreadStrategy) : Matrix = {
    ...
  computations.foreach(_())
  new Matrix(buffer)
}
```

The last portion of the multiple method ensures all work is completed and returns the result `Matrix` built from the buffer object. Let's test this in the REPL, but first we need to implement the `ThreadStrategy` interface. Let's create a simple version that executes all work on the current thread:

```
object SameThreadStrategy extends ThreadStrategy {
    def execute[A](func : Function0[A]) = func
  }
```

The `SameThreadStrategy` ensures that all passed-in work operates on the calling thread by returning the original function. Let's test out the `multiply` method in the REPL, as follows:

```
scala> implicit val ts = sameThreadStrategy
ts: ThreadStrategy.sameThreadStrategy.type = ...

scala> val x = new Matrix(Array(Array(1,2,3), Array(4,5,6)))
x: library.Matrix =
Matrix
|1.0 | 2.0 | 3.0|
|4.0 | 5.0 | 6.0|

scala> val y = new Matrix(Array(Array(1), Array(1), Array(1)))
y: library.Matrix =
Matrix
|1.0|
|1.0|
|1.0|

scala> MatrixService.multiply(x,y)
res0: library.Matrix =
Matrix
|6.0|
|15.0|
```

The first line is creating an implicit `ThreadStrategy` that will be used for all remaining calculations. We then construct two matrices and multiply the results. The 2 x 3 matrix is multiplied by a 3 x 1 matrix to product a 2 x 1 matrix, as expected. Everything appears to be working correctly with a single thread, so let's create a multithreaded service, as in the following listing:

Listing 5.9   Concurrent strategey

```
import java.util.concurrent.{Callable, Executors}

 object ThreadPoolStrategy extends ThreadStrategy {
   val pool = Executors.newFixedThreadPool(
               java.lang.Runtime.getRuntime.availableProcessors)
   def execute[A](func : Function0[A] ) = {
     val future = pool.submit(new Callable[A] {
       def call() : A = {
         Console.println("Executing function on thread: " +
                        Thread.currentThread.getName)
         func()
       }
     })
     () => future.get()
   }
 }
```

The first thing the `ThreadPoolStrategy` implementation does is create a pool of threads using Java's `java.util.concurrent.Executors` library. The thread pool is constructed with the number of threads equal to the number of available processors. The execute method takes the passed-in function and creates an anonymous `Callable` instance. The `Callable` interface is used in Java's concurrent library to pass work into the thread pool. This returns a `Future` that can be used to determine when the passed-in work is completed. The last line of execute returns an anonymous closure that will call get on future. This call blocks until the original function executes and returns the value returned by the function. Also, every time a function is executed inside the `Callable`, it will print a message informing which thread it's executing on. Let's try this out in the REPL:

```
scala> implicit val ts = ThreadPoolStrategy
ts: ThreadStrategy.ThreadPoolStrategy.type = ...

scala> val x = new Matrix(Array(Array(1,2,3), Array(4,5,6)))
x: library.Matrix =
Matrix
|1.0 | 2.0 | 3.0|
|4.0 | 5.0 | 6.0|

scala> val y = new Matrix(Array(Array(1), Array(1), Array(1)))
y: library.Matrix =
Matrix
|1.0|
|1.0|
|1.0|

scala> MatrixUtils.multiply(x,y)
```

```
Executing function on thread: pool-2-thread-1
Executing function on thread: pool-2-thread-2
res0: library.Matrix =
Matrix
|6.0|
|15.0|
```

The first line creates an implicit `ThreadPoolStrategy` that will be used for all remaining calculations within the REPL session. Again, the x and y variables are created as 2 x 3 and 3 x 1 matrices, respectively. But the `MatrixService.multiply` now outputs two lines indicating that the calculations for the result matrix are occurring on different threads. The resulting matrix displays the correct values, as before.

Now what if we wanted to provide a default threading strategy for users of the library, and still allow them to override if desired? We can use the default parameter mechanism to provide a default. This will be used if no value is available in the implicit scope, meaning that our users can override the default in a scope by importing or creating their own implicit `ThreadStrategy`. Users can also override the behavior for a single method call by explicitly passing the `ThreadStrategy`. Let's modify the signature of `MatrixService.multiply`:

```
def  multiply(a: Matrix, b: Matrix)(
            implicit threading: ThreadStrategy = SameThreadStrategy
          ) : Matrix = {
  ...
}
```

The `multiply` method now defines the `SameThreadStrategy` as the default strategy. Now when we use this library, we don't have to provide our own implicit `Thread-Strategy`:

```
scala> val x = new Matrix(Array(Array(1,2,3), Array(4,5,6)))
x: library.Matrix =
Matrix
|1.0 | 2.0 | 3.0|
|4.0 | 5.0 | 6.0|

scala> val y = new Matrix(Array(Array(1), Array(1), Array(1)))
y: library.Matrix =
Matrix
|1.0|
|1.0|
|1.0|

scala> MatrixService.multiply(x,y)
res0: library.Matrix =
Matrix
|6.0|
|15.0|
```

Unlike normal default parameters, an implicit parameter list with defaults doesn't need to be specified in the method call with an additional `()`. This means we get the elegance of implicit parameters with the utility of default parameters. We can still utilize implicits as normal:

```
scala> implicit val ts = ThreadPoolStrategy
ts: ThreadStrategy.ThreadPoolStrategy.type = ...

scala> MatrixUtils.multiply(x,y)
Executing function on thread: pool-2-thread-1
Executing function on thread: pool-2-thread-2
res1: library.Matrix =
Matrix
|6.0|
|15.0|
```

The first line creates an implicitly available thread strategy. Now when calling the MatrixService.multiply call, the method is using the ThreadPoolStrategy. This allows users of the MatrixService to decide when to parallelize computations performed with the library. They can do this for a particular scope by providing an implicit or for a single method call by explicitly passing the ThreadStrategy.

This technique of creating an implicit value for a scope of computations is a powerful, flexible means of using the strategy pattern. The *strategy pattern* is an idiom where a piece of code needs to perform some operation, but certain behaviors, or execution "strategy," can be swapped into the method. The ThreadPoolStrategy is such a behavior that we're passing into our MatrixUtils library methods. This same ThreadPoolStrategy could be used across different subsections of components in our system. It provides an alternative means of composing behavior than using inheritance, as discussed in section 4.3.

Another good example of implicits with default parameters is reading the lines of a file. In the general case, users don't care if the line endings are \r, \n, or \r\n. However, a complete library would handle all situations. This can be done by providing an implicit argument for the line ending strategy and providing a default value of "don't care."

Implicits provide a great way to reduce boilerplate in code, such as repeated parameters. The most important thing to remember when using them is be careful, which is the topic of the next section.

5.4   *Limiting the scope of implicits*

The most important aspect of dealing with implicits is ensuring that programmers can understand what's happening in a block of code. Programmers can do this by limiting the places they must check to discover available implicits. Let's look at the possible locations of implicits:

- The companion objects of any associated types, including package objects
- The scala.Predef object
- Any imports that are in scope.

As seen in section 1.1.3, Scala will look in the companion objects of associated types for implicits. This behavior is core to the Scala language. Companion and package objects should be considered part of the API of a class. When investigating how to use a new library, check the companion and package objects for implicit conversions that you may use.

> **Rule 14**
>
> **Limit the scope of implicits**
>
> Because implicit conflicts require explicit passing of arguments and conversions, it's best to avoid them. This can be accomplished by limiting the number of implicits that are in scope and providing implicits in a way that they can overridden or hidden.

At the beginning of every compiled Scala file there's an implicit `import scala.Predef._`. The `Predef` object contains many useful transformations, in particular the implicits used to add methods to the `java.lang.String` type so that it can support the methods required by the Scala Language Specification. It also contains implicits that will convert between Java's boxed types and Scala's unified types for primitives. For example, there's an implicit conversion in `scala.Predef` for `java.lang.Integer => scala.Int`. When coding in Scala, it's a good idea to know the implicits are available in the `scala.Predef` object.

The last possible location for implicits are explicit `import` statements within the source code. Imported implicits can be difficult to track down. They're also hard to document when designing a library. Because these are the only form of implicits that require an explicit `import` statement in every source file they're used, they require the most amount of care.

5.4.1 Creating implicits for import

When defining a new implicit view or parameter that's intended to be explicitly imported, you should ensure the following:

- The implicit view or parameter doesn't conflict with any other implicit.
- The implicit view or parameter's name doesn't conflict with anything in the `scala.Predef` object.
- The implicit view or parameter is *discoverable*, which means that users of the library or module should be able to find the location of the implicit and determine its use.

Because Scala uses scope resolution to look up implicits, if there's a naming conflict between two implicit definitions it can cause issues. These conflicts are hard to detect because implicit views and parameters can be defined in any scope and imported. The `scala.Predef` object has its contents implicitly imported into every Scala file so that conflicts become immediately apparent. Let's look at what happens when there's a conflict:

```
object Time {
  case class TimeRange(start : Long, end : Long)
  implicit def longWrapper(start : Long) = new {
    def to(end : Long) = TimeRange(start, end)
  }
}
```

This defines a `Time` object that contains a `TimeRange` class. An implicit conversion on `Long` provides a `to` method. You can use this method to construct time range objects.

This implicit conflicts with `scala.Predef.longWrapper` which, among other things, provides an implicit view that also has a `to` method. This `to` method returns a `Range` object that can be used in `for` expressions. Imagine a scenario where someone is using this `TimeRange` implicit to construct time ranges, and then desires the original implicit defined in `Predef` for a `for` expression. One way to solve this is to import the `Predef` implicit at a higher precedence level in a lower scope where it's needed. This can be confusing, as shown in the following example:

Listing 5.10   Scoped precedence

```
object Test {
  println(1L to 10L)
  import Time._
  println(1L to 10L)
  def x() = {
    import scala.Predef.longWrapper
    println(1L to 10L)
    def y() = {
      import Time.longWrapper
      println(1L to 10L)
    }
    y()
  }
  x()
}
```

The `Test` object is defined and immediately prints the expression `(1L to 10L)`. The `Time` implicits are imported and the expression is again printed. Next, in a lower scope, the `Predef` `longWrapper` is imported and the expression is printed. Finally, in yet a lower scope, the `Time` `longWrapper` is imported and the expression is again printed. The result of this objects construction is:

```
scala> Test
NumericRange(1, 2, 3, 4, 5, 6, 7, 8, 9, 10)
TimeRange(1,10)
NumericRange(1, 2, 3, 4, 5, 6, 7, 8, 9, 10)
TimeRange(1,10)
res0: Test.type = Test$@2d34ab9b
```

The first `NumericRange` result is the expression `(1L to 10L)` before any import statements. The second `TimeRange` result is after the `Time` implicit conversion is imported. The next `NumericRange` result is from the nested scope in method `x()` and the final `TimeRange` result is the result of the statement in the deeply nested `y()` method. If the `Test` object contained a lot of code such that all these scopes were not visible within a single window, it would be hard to figure out what the result of the expression `(1L to 10L)` would return at any particular point. Avoid this kind of confusion. The best way is to avoid conflicts across implicit views, but sometimes this is difficult. In those cases, it's better to pick one conversion to be implicit and use the other explicitly.

Making implicits discoverable also helps make code readable, as it helps a new developer determine what is and should be happening in a block of code. Making implicits discoverable is important when working on a team. Within the Scala community, it's common practice to limit importable implicits into one of two places:

- Package objects
- Singleton objects that have the `postfix Implicits`

Package objects make a great place to store implicits because they're already on the implicit scope for types defined within the package. Users need to investigate the package object for implicits relating to the package. Placing implicit definitions that need explicit import on the package object means that there's a greater chance a user will find the implicits and be aware of them. When providing implicits via package object, make sure to document if they require explicit imports for usage.

A better option to documenting explicit import of implicits is to avoid import statements altogether.

5.4.2 *Implicits without the import tax*

Implicits work well without requiring any sort of import. Their secondary lookup rules, which inspect companion objects of associated types, allow the definition of implicit conversions and values that don't require explicit `import` statements for these implicit values. With some creative definitions, expressive libraries can be defined that make the full use of implicits without requiring any imports. Let's look at an example of this: a library for expressing complex numbers.

Complex numbers are numbers that have a rational and imaginary part to them. The imaginary part is the part multiplied by the square root of -1, also known as i (or j for electrical engineers). This is simple to model using a case class in Scala:

```
package complexmath
case class ComplexNumber(real : Double, imaginary : Double)
```

The `ComplexNumber` class defines a real component of type `Double` called `real`. The `ComplexNumber` class also defines an imaginary component of type `Double` called `imaginary`. This class represents complex numbers using floating point arithmetic for the component parts. Complex numbers allow addition and multiplication. Let's take a look at those methods:

Listing 5.11 `ComplexNumber` class

```
package complexmath

case class ComplexNumber(real : Double, imaginary : Double) {
  def *(other : ComplexNumber) =
    ComplexNumber( (real*other.real) + (imaginary * other.imaginary),
                   (real*other.imaginary) + (imaginary * other.real) )
  def +(other : ComplexNumber) =
    ComplexNumber( real + other.real, imaginary + other.imaginary )
}
```

Addition,+, is defined such that the real/imaginary component of the sum of two complex numbers is the sum of the real/imaginary components of two numbers. Multiplication,*, is more complicated and defined as follows:

- The real component of the product of two complex numbers is the product of their real components added to the product of their imaginary components: `(real*other.real) + (imaginary * other.imaginary)`.
- The imaginary component of the product of two complex numbers is the sum of the product of the real component of one number with the imaginary component of the other number: `(real*other.imaginary) + (imaginary * other.real)`.

The complex number class now supports addition and multiplication. Let's look at the class in action:

```
scala> ComplexNumber(1,0) * ComplexNumber(0,1)
res0: imath.ComplexNumber = ComplexNumber(0.0,1.0)

scala> ComplexNumber(1,0) + ComplexNumber(0,1)
res1: imath.ComplexNumber = ComplexNumber(1.0,1.0)
```

The first line multiplies a real component by an imaginary component and the resulting complex number is imaginary. The second line adds a real component to an imaginary component, resulting in a complex number with both real and imaginary parts. The operators * and + work as desired, but calling the `ComplexNumber` factory method is a bit verbose. This can be simplified using a new notation for complex numbers.

In mathematics, complex numbers are usually represented as a sum of the real and imaginary parts. An example representation of `ComplexNumber(1.0,1.0)` would be `1.0 + 1.0*i`, where i is the symbol for the imaginary number, the square root of -1. This notation would make an ideal syntax for the complex number library. Let's define the symbol i to refer to the square root of -1.

```
package object complexmath {
  val i = ComplexNumber(0.0,1.0)
}
```

This defines the `val i` on the package object for `complexmath`. This places the name i available within the `complexmath` package and allows it to be imported directly. This name can be used to construct complex numbers from their component parts. But a piece is missing, as shown in the following REPL session:

```
scala> i * 1.0
<console>:9: error: type mismatch;
 found    : Double(1.0)
 required: ComplexNumber
       i * 1.0
```

Attempting to multiply the imaginary number i by a `Double` fails because the `Complex-Number` type only defines multiplication on `ComplexNumber` types. In mathematics, real numbers can be multiplied by complex numbers because a real number can be considered a complex number that has no imaginary component. This property can be emulated in Scala using an implicit conversion from `Double` to `ComplexNumber`:

```
package object complexmath {
  implicit def realToComplex(r : Double) = new ComplexNumber(r, 0.0)
  val i = ComplexNumber(0.0, 1.0)
}
```

The `complexmath` package object now contains the definition for the value `i` as well as an implicit conversion from `Double` to `ComplexNumber` called `realToComplex`. We'd like to limit the usage of this implicit conversion so that it's only used when absolutely needed. Let's try using the `complexmath` package without explicitly importing any implicit conversions:

```
scala> import complexmath.i
import complexmath.i

scala> val x = i*5.0 + 1.0
x: complexmath.ComplexNumber = ComplexNumber(1.0,5.0)
```

The `val x` is declared using the expression `i*5 + 1` and has the type `ComplexNumber` with a real component of `1.0` and an imaginary component of `5.0`. The important thing to note here is that only the name `i` is imported from `complexmath`. The rest of the implicit conversions are all trigged from the `i` object when the compiler first sees the expression `i*5`. The value `i` is known to be a `ComplexNumber` and defines a `*` method that takes another `ComplexNumber`. The literal `5.0` isn't of the type `Complex-Number`, but `Double`. The compiler issues an implicit search for the type `Double => complexmath.ComplexNumber`. This search finds the `realToComplex` conversion on the package object and applies it. Next the compiler sees the expression `(... : Complex-Number) + 1.0`. The compiler finds a `+` method defined on `ComplexNumber` that accepts a `ComplexNumber`. The value `1.0` is of type `Double`, not `ComplexNumber` so the compiler issues another implicit search for the type `Double => ComplexNumber`. Again this is found and applied, resulting in the final value for the expression of `Complex-Number(1.0, 5.0)`.

Notice how the value `i` is used to trigger complex arithmetic. Once a complex number is seen, the compiler can accurately find implicits to ensure that expressions are compiled. The syntax is elegant and concise, and no implicit conversions were needed to make this syntax work. The downside is that the value `i` must be used to begin a `ComplexNumber` expression. Let's look at what happens when `i` appears at the end of the expression:

```
scala> val x = 1.0 + 5.0*i
<console>:6: error: overloaded method value * with alternatives:
  (Double)Double <and>
  (Float)Float <and>
  (Long)Long <and>
  (Int)Int <and>
  (Char)Int <and>
  (Short)Int <and>
```

```
        (Byte)Int
 cannot be applied to (complexmath.ComplexNumber)
        val x = 1 + 5*i
```

The compiler complains about the expression because it can't find a + method defined for the type `Double` that takes a `ComplexNumber`. This issue could be solved by importing the implicit view of `Double => ComplexNumber` into scope:

```
scala> import complexmath.realToComplex
import complexmath.realToComplex

scala> val x = 1.0 + 5.0*i
x: complexmath.ComplexNumber = ComplexNumber(1.0,5.0)
```

The `realToComplex` implicit view is imported first. Now the expression `1 + 5*i` evaluates correctly to a `ComplexNumber(1.0, 5.0)`. The downside is that there's now an additional implicit view in scope for the type `Double`. This can cause issues if other implicit views are defined that provide similar methods to `ComplexNumber`. Let's define a new implicit conversion that adds an `imaginary` method to `Double`.

```
scala> implicit def doubleToReal(x : Double) = new {
     |    def real = "For Reals(" + x + ")"
     | }
doubleToReal: (x: Double)java.lang.Object{def real: java.lang.String}

scala> 5.0 real
<console>:10: error: type mismatch;
 found    : Double
 required: ?{val real: ?}
Note that implicit conversions are not applicable
 because they are ambiguous:
 both method doubleToReal in object $iw of type
   (x: Double)java.lang.Object{def real: java.lang.String}
 and method realToComplex in package complexmath of type
   (r: Double)complexmath.ComplexNumber
 are possible conversion functions from
   Double to ?{val real: ?}
       5.0 real
```

The first statement defines an implicit view on the `Double` type that adds a new type containing a `real` method. The `real` method returns a string version of the `Double`. The next statement attempts to call the `real` method and is unable to do so. The compiler complains about finding ambiguous implicit conversions. The issue here is the `ComplexNumber` type also defines a method `real`, and so the implicit conversion from `Double => ComplexNumber` is getting in the way of our `doubleToReal` implicit conversion. This conflict can be avoided by not importing the `Double => ComplexNumber` conversion:

```
scala> import complexmath.i
import complexmath.i

scala> implicit def doubleToReal(x : Double) = new {
     |    def real = "For Reals(" + x + ")"
     | }
```

```
doubleToReal: (x: Double)java.lang.Object{def real: java.lang.String}

scala> 5.0 real
res0: java.lang.String = For Reals(5.0)
```

The example starts a new REPL session that only imports `complexmath.i`. The next statement redefines the `doubleToReal` conversion. Now the expression `5.0 real` successfully compiles because there's no conflict.

You can use this idiom to successfully create expressive code without all the dangers of implicit conflicts. The pattern takes the following form:

- Define the core abstractions for a library, such as the `ComplexNumber` class.
- Define the implicit conversions needed for expressive code in one of the associated types of the conversion. The `Double => ComplexNumber` conversion was created in the `complexmath` package object which is associated with the `ComplexNumber` type and therefore discovered in any implicit lookup involving the `ComplexNumber` type.
- Define an *entry point* into the library such that implicit conversions are disambiguated after the entry point. In the `complexmath` library, the value `i` is the entry point.
- Some situations require an explicit import. In the `complexmath` library, the entry point `i` allows certain types of expressions but not others that intuition would suggest should be there. For example, `(i * 5.0 + 1.0)` is accepted and `(1.0 + 5.0*i)` is rejected. In this situation, it's acceptable to provide implicit conversions that can be imported from a well-known location. In `complexmath`, this location is the package object.

Following these guidelines helps create expressive APIs that are also discoverable.

5.5   *Summary*

In this chapter, we discussed the implicit lookup mechanism of Scala. Scala supports two types of implicits: implicit value and implicit views. Implicit values can be used to provide arguments to method calls. Implicit views can be used to convert between types or to allow method calls against a type to succeed. Both implicit values and implicit views use the same implicit resolution mechanism. Implicit resolution uses a two stage process. The first stage looks for implicits that have no prefix in the current scope. The second stage looks in companion objects of associated types. Implicits provide a powerful way to enhance existing classes. They can also be used with default parameters to reduce the noise for method calls and tie behavior to the scope of an implicit value.

Most importantly, implicits provide a lot of power and should be used responsibly. Limiting the scope of implicits and defining them in well-known or easily discoverable locations is key to success. You can do this by providing unambiguous entry points into implicit conversions and expressive APIs. Implicits also interact with Scala's type system in interesting ways. We'll discuss these in chapter 7, but first let's look at Scala's type system.

The type system

The type system is an important component of the Scala language. It enables lots of rich optimizations and constraints to be used during compilation, which helps runtime speed and prevents programming errors. The type system allows us to create all sorts of interesting walls around ourselves, known as types. These walls help prevent us from accidentally writing improper code. This is done through the compiler tracking information about variables, methods, and classes. The more you know about Scala's type system, the more information you can give the compiler, and the type walls become less restrictive while still providing the same protection.

When using a type system, it's best to think of it as an overprotective father. It will constantly warn you of problems or prevent you from doing things altogether. The better you communicate with the type system, the less restrictive it becomes. But if you attempt to do something deemed inappropriate, the compiler will warn you. The compiler can be a great means of detecting errors if you give it enough information.

In his book *Imperfect C++*, Matthew Wilson uses an analogy of comparing the compiler to a batman. This batman isn't a caped crusader but is instead a good friend who offers advice and supports the programmer. In this chapter, you'll learn the basics of the type system so you can begin to rely on it to catch common programming errors. The next chapter will cover more advanced type system concepts, as well as utilizing implicits with the type system.

This chapter will cover the basics of the type system, touching on definitions and theory. The next chapter covers more practical applications of the type system and the best practices to use when defining constraints. Feel free to skip this information if you're already comfortable with Scala's type system.

Understanding Scala's type system begins in first understanding what a type is and how to create it.

6.1 *Types*

A type is a set of information the compiler knows. This could be anything from "what class was used to instantiate this variable" to "what collection of methods are known to exist on this variable." The user can explicitly provide this information, or the compiler can infer it through inspection of other code. When passing or manipulating variables, this information can be expanded or reduced, depending on how you've written your methods. To begin, let's look at how types are defined in Scala.

> **WHAT IS A TYPE?** A good example is the `String` type. This type includes a method `substring`, among other methods. If the user called a `substring` on a variable of type `String` the compiler would allow the call, because it knows that it would succeed at runtime (move above when passing or manipulating variables).

In Scala, types can be defined in two ways:

- Defining a class, trait or object.
- Directly defining a type using the `type` keyword.

Defining a class, trait, or object automatically creates an associated type for the class, trait, or object. This type can be referred to using the same name as the class or trait. For objects we refer to the type slightly differently due to the potential of classes or traits having the same name as an object. Let's look at defining a few types and referring to them in method arguments:

Listing 6.1 Defining types from class, trait, or object keywords

```
scala> class ClassName
defined class ClassName

scala> trait TraitName
defined trait TraitName

scala> object ObjectName
defined module ObjectName
```

```
scala> def foo(x: ClassName) = x                        ◁── Simple type

foo: (x: ClassName)ClassName

scala> def bar(x: TraitName) = x                        ◁── Refers to a trait
 bar: (x: TraitName)TraitName

scala> def baz(x: ObjectName.type) = x                  ◁── Refers to object's type
 baz: (x: ObjectName.type)object ObjectName
```

As seen in the example, class and trait names can be referenced directly when annotating types within Scala. When referring to an object's type, you need to use the `type`
member of the object. This syntax isn't normally seen in Scala, because if you know an
object's type, you can just as easily access the object directly, rather than ask for it in a
parameter.

Using objects as parameters

Using objects as parameters can greatly help when defining domain specific languages, as you can embed words as objects that become parameters. For example, we could define a simulation DSL as follows:

```
object Now
object simulate {
 def once(behavior : () => Unit) = new {
 def right(now : Now.type) : Unit = ...
 }
}
simulate once { () => someAction() } right Now
```

6.1.1 Types and paths

Types within Scala are referenced relative to a binding or path. As discussed in chapter 5, a binding is the name used to refer to an entity. This name could be imported
from another scope. A path isn't a type; it's a location of sorts where the compiler can
find types. A path could be one of the following:

- An empty path. When a type name is used directly, there's an implicit empty
  path preceding it.
- The path `C.this` where `C` refers to a class. Using the `this` keyword directly in a
  class `C` is shorthand for the full path `C.this`. This path type is useful for referring to identifiers defined on outer classes.
- The path `p.x` where `p` is a path and `x` is a stable identifier of x. A stable identifier is an identifier that the compiler knows for certain will always be accessible
  from the path `p`. For example, the path `scala.Option` refers to the `Option` singleton defined on the package `scala`. It's always known to exist. The formal definition of stable members are packages, objects, or value definitions introduced
  on nonvolatile types. A volatile type is a type where the compiler can't be
  certain its members won't change. An example would be an abstract type
  definition on an abstract class. The type definition could change depending on

the subclass and the compiler doesn't have enough information to compute a stable identifier from this volatile type.

- The path `C.super` or `C.super[P]` where `C` refers to a class and `P` refers to a parent type of class `C`. Using the `super` keyword directly is shorthand for `C.super`. Use this path to disambiguate between identifiers defined on a class and a parent class.

Types within Scala are referred to via two mechanisms: the hash (#) and dot (.) operators. The dot operator can be thought of doing the same for types as it does for members of an object. It refers to a type found on a specific object instance. This is known as a path-dependent type. When a method is defined using the dot operator to a particular type, that type is bound to a specific instance of the object. This means that you can't use a type from a different object, of the same class, to satisfy any type constraints made using the dot operator. The best way to think of this is that there's a path of specific object instances connected by the dot operator. For a variable to match your type, it must follow the same object instance path. You can see an example of this later.

The hash operator (#) is a looser restriction than the dot operator. It's known as a type projection, which is a means of referring to a nested type without requiring a path of object instances. This means that you can reference a nested type as if it weren't nested. You can see an example usage later.

Listing 6.2 Path-dependent types and type projection examples

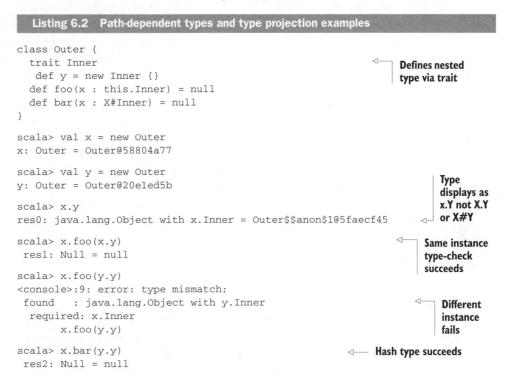

```
class Outer {
  trait Inner                           ◁── Defines nested
   def y = new Inner {}                       type via trait
  def foo(x : this.Inner) = null
  def bar(x : X#Inner) = null
}

scala> val x = new Outer
x: Outer = Outer@58804a77

scala> val y = new Outer
y: Outer = Outer@20e1ed5b                    Type
                                             displays as
scala> x.y                                   x.Y not X.Y
res0: java.lang.Object with x.Inner = Outer$$anon$1@5faecf45  ◁─  or X#Y

scala> x.foo(x.y)                     ◁── Same instance
 res1: Null = null                        type-check
                                          succeeds
scala> x.foo(y.y)
<console>:9: error: type mismatch;
 found    : java.lang.Object with y.Inner
   required: x.Inner                        ◁── Different
       x.foo(y.y)                               instance
                                               fails
scala> x.bar(y.y)                     ◁── Hash type succeeds
 res2: Null = null
```

In the preceding example, the `Outer` class defines a nested trait `Inner` along with two methods that use the `Inner` type. Method `foo` uses a path dependent type and method `bar` uses a type projection. Variables x and y are constructed as two different instances of the `Outer` class. The reference to the y member of an instance of `Outer` displays its type, `java.lang.Object with x.Y` when we type this into the REPL. This type displays with the *variable instance* of `Outer`, which is x. This is what we meant earlier by our path. To access the correct type `Y`, you must travel the path through the x variable. If we call the `foo` method on x using the `Inner` instance from the same x variable, then the call is successful. But using the `Inner` instance from the y variable causes the compiler to complain with a type error. The type error explicitly states that it's expecting the `Inner` type to come from the same instance as the method call—the x instance.

The bar method was defined using a type projection. The instance restriction isn't in place as it was for the `foo` method. When calling the bar method on the x instance using the `inner` type from the y instance, the call succeeds. This shows that although path-dependent types (`foo.Bar`) require the `Bar` instances to be generated from the same `foo` instance, type projections (`Foo#Bar`) match any `Bar` instances generated from any `Foo` instances. Both path-dependent and type projection rules apply to all nested types, including those created using the `type` keyword.

> **PATH-DEPENDENT TYPES VERSUS TYPE PROJECTS**   All path-dependent types are type projections. A path-dependent type `foo.Bar` is rewritten as `foo.type#Bar` by the compiler. The expression foo.type refers to the singleton type of Foo. This singleton type can only be satisfied by the entity referenced by the name foo. The path-dependent type (`foo.Bar`) requires the `Bar` instances to be generated from the same `foo` instance, while a type projection `Foo#Bar` would match any `Bar` instances generated from any `Foo` instances, not necessarily the entity referred to by the name Foo.
>
> In Scala, all type references can be written as projects against named entities. The type `scala.String` is shorthand for `scala.type#String` where the name `scala` refers to the package `scala` and the type `String` is defined by the `String` class on the `scala` package.
>
> There can be some confusion when using path-dependent types for classes that have companion objects. For example, if the trait `bar.Foo` has a companion object `bar.Foo`, then the type `bar.Foo` (`bar.type#Foo`) would refer to the trait's type and the type `bar.Foo.type` would refer to the companion object's type.

6.1.2   *The type keyword*

Scala also allows types to be constructed using the `type` keyword. This can be used to create both concrete and abstract types. Concrete types are created by referring to existing types, or through structural types which we'll discuss later. Abstract types are created as place holders that you can later refine in a subclass. This allows a significant level of abstraction and type safety within programs. We'll discuss this more later, but for now let's create our own types.

The `type` keyword can only define types within some sort of context, specifically within a class, trait, or object, or within subcontext of one of these. The syntax of the `type` keyword is simple. It consists of the keyword itself, an identifier, and, optionally, a definition or constraint for the type. If a definition is provided, the type is concrete. If no constraints or assignments are provided, the type is considered abstract. We'll get into type constraints a little later; for now let's look at the syntax for the `type` keyword:

```
type AbstractType
type ConcreteType = SomeFooType
type ConcreteType2 = SomeFooType with SomeBarType
```

Notice that concrete types can be defined through combining other types. This new type is referred to as a *compound type*. The new type is satisfied only if an instance meets all the requirements of both original types. The compiler will ensure that these types are compatible before allowing the combination.

As an analogy, think of the initial two types as a bucket of toys. Each toy in a given bucket is equivalent to a member on the original type. When you create a compound type of two types using the `with` keyword, you're taking two buckets, from two of your friends, and placing all their toys into one larger, compound bucket. When you're combining the buckets, you notice that one friend may have a cooler version of a particular toy, such as the latest Ninja Turtle action figure, while the other friend, not as wealthy, has a ninja turtle that's bright yellow and has teeth marks. In this case, you pick the coolest toy and leave it in the bucket. Given a sufficient definition of cool, this is how type unions work in Scala. For Scala, cool refers to type refinement. A type is more refined if Scala knows more about it. You may also have situations where you discover that both friends have broken or incomplete toys. In this case, you would take pieces from each toy and attempt to construct the full toy. For the most part, this analogy holds for compound types. It's a simple combination of all the members from the original types, with various override rules. Type unions are even easier to understand when looking at them through the lens of structural types.

6.1.3 *Structural types*

In Scala, a structural type is created using the `type` keyword and defining what method signatures and variable signatures you expect on the desired type. This allows a developer to define an abstract interface without requiring users to extend some trait or class to meet this interface. One common usage of structural typing is in the use of resource management code.

Rule 15 | **Avoid structural types**

Structural types are usually implemented with reflection. Reflection isn't always available on every platform and it can lead to performance issues. It's best to provide named interfaces rather than use structural types in the general case. However for nonperformance sensitive situations, they can be very useful.

Some of the most annoying bugs, in my experience, are resource-related. We must always ensure that something acquired is released, and something created is eventually destroyed. As such, there's a lot of boilerplate code common when using resources. I would love to avoid boilerplate code in Scala, so let's see if structural types can come to the rescue. Let's define a simple function that will ensure that a resource is closed after some block of code is executed. There's no formal definition for what a resource is, so we'll try to define it as anything that has a close method.

Listing 6.3   Resource handling utility

```
object Resources {                                          Define type
  type Resource = {
    def close() : Unit                              Require close method
  }
  def closeResource(r : Resource) = r.close()       Using method on type
}

scala> Resources.close(System.in)
Exception in thread "main" java.io.IOException:        System.in closed!
    Stream is Closed
```

The first thing we do is define a structural type for resources. We define a type of the name Resource and assign it to an anonymous, or structural, resource definition. The resource definition is a block that encloses a bunch of abstract methods or members. In this case, we define the Resource type to have one member, named close. Finally, in the closeResource method, you can see that we can accept a method parameter using the structural type and call the close member we defined in definition. Then we attempt to use our method against System.in, which has a close method. You can tell the call succeeds by the exception that's thrown. In general, you shouldn't close the master input or output streams when running inside the interpreter! But it does show that structural types have the nice feature of working against any object. This is nice for dealing with libraries or classes we don't directly control.

Structural typing also works within nested types and with nested types. We can nest types within the anonymous structural block. Let's try implementing a simple nested abstract type and see if we can create a method that uses this type.

Listing 6.4   Nested structural typing

```
scala> type T = {
     |    type X = Int                                Nested type alias
     |    def x : X
     |    type Y                                     Nested abstract type
     |    def y : Y
     | }
defined type alias T
scala> object Foo {                                      Concrete type
     | type X = Int
     | def x : X = 5
     | type Y = String
     | def y : Y = "Hello, World!"
```

```
  |  }
defined module Foo

scala> def test(t : T) = t.x                              ⟵── Unstable type
 <console>:7: error: illegal dependent method type
        def test(t : T) = t.x
                ^
```

We start by declaring a structural type T. This type contains two nested types: X and Y. X is defined to be equivalent to Int, while Y is left abstract. We then implement a real object Foo that meets this structural type. Now we try to create a test method that should return the result of calling the x method on an instance of type T. We expect this to return an integer, as the x method on T returns the X type, and this is aliased to Int. But the definition of the call fails. Why? Scala doesn't allow a method to be defined such that the types used are path-dependent on other arguments to the method. In this case, the return value of test would be dependent on the argument to test. We can prove this by writing out the expected return type explicitly:

```
scala> def test(t : T) : t.X = t.x
<console>:7: error: illegal dependent
```

Therefore, the compiler inferred the path-dependent type here. If instead of using a path-dependent type, we wanted the type project against X we can modify our code. The compiler won't automatically infer this for us, because the inference engine tries to find the most specific type it can. In this case, t.X is inferred, which is illegal. T#X, on the other hand, is valid in this context, and it's also known to be an Int by the compiler. Let's see what signature the compiler creates for something returning the type T#X.

```
scala> def test(t : T) : T#X = t.x
test: (t: T)Int

scala> test(Foo)
res2: Int = 5
```

As you can see, the method is defined to return an Int, and works correctly against our Foo object. What does this code look like if we have it use the abstract type Y instead? The compiler can make no assumptions about the type Y, so it only allows you to treat it as the absolute minimum type, or Any. Let's create a method that returns a T#Y type to see what it looks like:

```
scala> def test2(t :T) : T#Y = t.y
test2: (t: T)AnyRef{
  type X = Int;
  def x: this.X;
  type Y;
  def y: this.Y}#Y
```

The return type of the test2 method is AnyRef{type X = Int; def x: this.X; typeY; def y: this.Y}#Y. The rather verbose signature shows you how far the compiler goes into enforcing the type of the return. Because T#Y isn't easily equivalent to another type, the compiler must drag all the information about T around with the type T#Y. Because a type projection isn't tied to a particular instance, the compiler can be sure that two type projections are compatible. As a quick aside, notice the types of the x and y methods.

The x and y methods have return values that are path-dependent on this. When we defined the x method, we specified only a type of X, and yet the compiler turned the type into this.X. Because the X type is defined within the structural type T, you can refer to it via the identifier X; it refers to the path-dependent type this.X. Understanding when you've created a path-dependent type and when it's acceptable to refer to these types is important.

When you reference one type defined inside another, you have a path-dependent type. Using a path-dependent type inside a block of code is perfectly acceptable. The compiler can ensure that the nested types refer to the exact object instance through examining the code. But to escape a path-dependent type outside this original scope, the compiler needs some way of ensuring the path is the same instance. This can sometimes boil down to using objects and vals instead of classes and defs.

Listing 6.5   Path-dependent and structural types

```
object Foo {
  type T = {                                          Nested type
    type U                                            definitions
    def bar : U
  }
  val baz : T = new {                                 Stable reference
    type U = String                                   to T instance
    def bar : U = "Hello World!"
  }
}

scala> def test(f : Foo.baz.U) = f                    Argument
  test: (f: Foo.baz.U)Foo.baz.U                       type is stable

scala> test(Foo.baz.bar)
res0: Foo.baz.U = Hello World!
```

First we set up the nested types T and U. These are nested on the singleton Foo. We then create an instance of type Foo.T labeled baz. Being a val member, the compiler knows that this instance is unchanging throughout the lifetime of the program and is therefore stable. Finally, we create a method that takes the type Foo.baz.U as an argument. We accept this because the path-dependent type U is defined on a path known to be stable:Foo.baz. When running into path-dependent type issues, we can fix things by finding a way for the compiler to know that a type is stable—that the type will also be well defined. This can usually be accomplished by utilizing some stable reference path.

Let's look at a more in-depth example of path-dependent types by designing an Observable trait that you can use as a generic mechanism to watch for changes or notify others of a change. The Observable trait should provide two public methods: one that allows observers to subscribe and another that unsubscribes an observer. Observers should be able to subscribe to an Observable instance by providing a simple function callback. The subscription method should return a handle so that an observer can unsubscribe from change events on the observer at a future date. With path-dependent types, we can enforce that this handle is valid only with the originating `Observable` instance. Let's look at the public interface on `Observable`:

```
trait Observable {
  type Handle
  def observe(callback: this.type => Unit): Handle = {
    val handle = createHandle(callback)
    callbacks += (handle -> callback)
    handle
  }

  def unobserve(handle: Handle) : Unit = {
    callbacks -= handle
  }

  protected def createHandle(callback: this.type => Unit): Handle

  protected def notifyListeners() : Unit =
    for(callback <- callbacks.values) callback(this)
}
```

The first thing to notice is the abstract `Handle` type. We'll use this type to refer to registered observer callback functions. The `observe` method is defined to take a function of type `this.type => Unit` and return a handle. Let's look at the callback type. The callback is a function that takes something of `this.type` and returns a `Unit`. The type `this.type` is a mechanism in Scala to refer to the type of the current object. This is similar to calling `Foo.type` for a Scala `object` with one major difference. Unlike directly referencing the current type of the object, `this.type` changes with inheritance. In a later example, we'll show how a subclass of `Observable` will require callbacks to take their specific type as their parameter.

The unobserve function takes in a handle that was previously assigned to a callback and removes that observer. This handle type is path-dependent and must come from the current object. This means even if the same callback is registered to different `Observable` instances, their handles can't be interchanged.

The next thing to notice is that we use a function here that isn't yet defined: `createHandle`. This method should be able to construct handles to callbacks when they're registered in an `observe` method. I've purposely left this abstract so that implementers of the observable pattern can determine their own mechanism for differentiating callbacks with handles. Let's try to implement a default implementation for handles.

```
trait DefaultHandles extends Observable {
  type Handle = (this.type => Unit)
  protected def createHandle(callback: this.type => Unit): Handle =
    callback
}
```

The `DefaultHandles` trait extends `Observable` and provides a simple implementation of `Handle`: It defines the `Handle` type to be the same type as the callbacks. This means that whatever equality and hashing are defined on the callback objects themselves will be used in the `Observable` trait to store and look up observers. In the case of Scala's `Function` object equality and hash code are instance-based, as is the default for any user-defined object. Now that there's an implementation for the handles, let's define an observable object.

Let's create a `IntHolder` class that will hold an integer. The `IntHolder` will notify observers every time its internal value changes. The `IntHolder` class should also allow a mechanism to get the currently held integer and set the integer:

```
class IntStore(private var value: Int)
    extends Observable with DefaultHandles {
  def get : Int = value
  def set(newValue : Int) : Unit = {
    value = newValue
    notifyListeners()
  }

  override def toString : String = "IntStore(" + value + ")"
}
```

The `IntStore` class extends the `Observable` trait from the previous lines of code and mixes in the `DefaultHandles` implementation for handles. The `get` method returns the value stored in the `IntStore`. The `set` method assigns the new value and then notifies observers of the change. The `toString` method has also been overridden to provide a nicer printed form. Let's take a look at this class in action:

```
scala> val x = new IntStore(5)
x: IntStore = IntStore(5)

scala> val handle = x.observe(println)
handle: (x.type) => Unit = <function1>

scala> x.set(2)
IntStore(2)

scala> x.unobserve(handle)

scala> x.set(4)
```

The x variable is constructed as an `IntStore` with an initial value of 5. Next an observer is registered that will print the `IntStore` to the console on changes. The handle to this observer is saved in the `handle` val. Notice that the type of the handle uses a path-dependent `x.type`. Next, the value stored in x is changed to 2. The observer is notified and `IntStore(2)` is printed on the console. Next the `handle` variable is used to remove the observer. Now, when the value stored in x is changed to 4, the new value isn't printed to the console. The observer functionality is working as desired.

What happens if we construct multiple `IntStore` instances and attempt to register the same callback to both? If it's the same callback, using the `DefaultHandles` trait means that the two handles should be equal. Let's try to do this in the REPL:

```
scala> val x = new IntStore(5)
x: IntStore = IntStore(5)

scala> val y = new IntStore(2)
y: IntStore[Int] = IntStore(2)
```

```
scala> y.unobserve(handle1)
<console>:10: error: type mismatch;
 found    : (x.type) => Unit
 required: (y.type) => Unit
        y.unobserve(handle1)
              ^
```

First we create separate instances, x and y of `IntStore`. Next we need to create a call-back we can use on both observers. Let's use the same `println` method as before:

```
scala> val callback = println(_ : Any)
callback: (Any) => Unit = <function1>
```

Now let's register the callback on both the x and y variable instances and check to see if the handles are equal:

```
scala> val handle1 = x.observe(callback)
handle1: (x.type) => Unit = <function1>

scala> val handle2 = y.observe(callback)
handle2: (y.type) => Unit = <function1>

scala> handle1 == handle2
res3: Boolean = true
```

The result is that the handle objects are exactly the same. Note that the == method does a runtime check of equality and works on any two types. This means that theoretically the handle from y could be used to remove the observer on x. Let's look at what happens when attempting this on the REPL:

```
scala> y.unobserve(handle1)
<console>:10: error: type mismatch;
 found    : (x.type) => Unit
 required: (y.type) => Unit
        y.unobserve(handle1)
              ^
```

The compiler won't allow this usage. The path-dependent typing restricts our handles from being generated from the same method. Even though the handles are equal at runtime, the type system has prevented us from using the wrong handle to unregister an observer. This is important because the type of the Handle could change in the future. If we implemented the Handle type differently in the future, then code that relied on handles being interchangeable between IntStores would be broken. Luckily the compiler enforces the correct behavior here.

Path-dependent types have other uses, but this should give you a good idea of their use and utility. What if, in the Observable example, we had wanted to include some kind of restriction on the Handle type? This is where we can use type constraints.

6.2 *Type constraints*

Type constraints are rules associated with a type that must be met for a variable to match the given type. A type can be defined with multiple constraints at once. Each of these constraints must be satisfied when the compiler is type checking expressions. Type constraints take the following two forms:

- Lower bounds (subtype restrictions)
- Upper bounds (supertype restrictions, also known as `Conformance` relations)

Lower bound restrictions can be thought of as super-restrictions. This is where the type selected must be equal to or a supertype of the lower bound restriction. Let's look at an example using Scala's collection hierarchy.

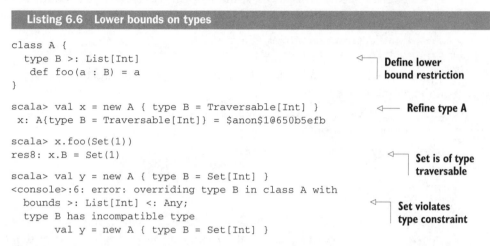

Listing 6.6   Lower bounds on types

```
class A {
  type B >: List[Int]                                     Define lower
  def foo(a : B) = a                                      bound restriction
}

scala> val x = new A { type B = Traversable[Int] }        Refine type A
 x: A{type B = Traversable[Int]} = $anon$1@650b5efb

scala> x.foo(Set(1))
res8: x.B = Set(1)                                        Set is of type
                                                          traversable

scala> val y = new A { type B = Set[Int] }
<console>:6: error: overriding type B in class A with     Set violates
  bounds >: List[Int] <: Any;                             type constraint
  type B has incompatible type
      val y = new A { type B = Set[Int] }
```

The first thing we do is define type `B` inside class `A` to have a lower bound of `List[Int]`. Then we instantiate a variable x as an anonymous subclass of A, such that type B is stabilized at `Traversable[Int]`. This doesn't issue any warning, because `Traversable` is a parent class of `List`. The interesting piece here is that we can call our `foo` method with a `Set` class. A `Set` isn't a supertype of the `List` class; it's a subtype of `Traversable`! Just because the type restriction on type `B` requires it to be a superclass of `List` doesn't mean that arguments matching against type `B` need to be within `List`'s hierarchy. They only need to match against the concrete form of type B, which is `Traversable`. What we can't do is create a subclass of A where the type B is assigned as a `Set[Int]`; a `Set` could be polymorphically referred to as `Iterable` or `Traversable`.

Because Scala is a polymorphic object-oriented language, it's important to understand the difference between the compile-time type constraints and runtime type constraints. In this instance, we are enforcing that type B's compile-time type information must come from a superclass of `List` or `List` itself. Polymorphism means that an object of class Set, which subclasses `Traversable`, can be used when the compile-time type requires a `Traversable`. When doing so, we aren't throwing away any behavior of the object; we're merely dropping some of our compile-time knowledge of the type. It's important to remember this when using with lower bound constraints.

Upper bound restrictions are far more common in Scala. An upper bound restriction states that any type selected must be equal to or a lower than the upper bound type. In the case of a class or trait, this means that any selected type must subclass from the class or trait upper bound. In the case of structural types, it means that whatever type is selected must meet the structural type, but can have more information. Let's define an upper bound restriction.

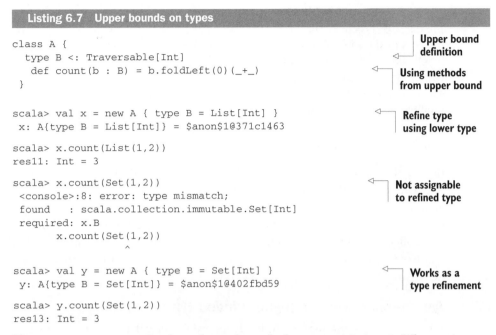

Listing 6.7 Upper bounds on types

```
class A {
  type B <: Traversable[Int]                      Upper bound
  def count(b : B) = b.foldLeft(0)(_+_)           definition
}                                                 Using methods
                                                  from upper bound

scala> val x = new A { type B = List[Int] }       Refine type
x: A{type B = List[Int]} = $anon$1@371c1463       using lower type

scala> x.count(List(1,2))
res11: Int = 3

scala> x.count(Set(1,2))                          Not assignable
  <console>:8: error: type mismatch;              to refined type
  found   : scala.collection.immutable.Set[Int]
  required: x.B
        x.count(Set(1,2))
                ^

scala> val y = new A { type B = Set[Int] }        Works as a
y: A{type B = Set[Int]} = $anon$1@402fbd59        type refinement

scala> y.count(Set(1,2))
res13: Int = 3
```

First we create a type B that has a lower bound of Traversable[Int]. When we use an unrefined type B, we can use any method defined in Traversable[Int] because we know that any type satisfying B's type restriction needs to extend Traversable[Int]. Later we can refine type B to be a List[Int], and everything works great. Once refined, we can't pass other subtypes of Traversable[Int], such as a Set[Int]. The parameters to the count method must satisfy the refined type B. We can also create another refinement of type B that's a Set[Int], and this will accept Set[Int] arguments. As you can see, upper bounds work the opposite way from lower bounds. Another nice aspect of upper bounds is that you can utilize methods on the upper bound without knowing the full type refinement.

MAXIMUM UPPER AND LOWER BOUNDS In Scala, all types have a maximum upper bound of Any and lower bound of Nothing. If the compiler ever warns about incompatible type signatures that include Nothing or Any, without your code referring to them, it's a good bet that you have an unbounded type somewhere the compiler is trying to infer.

An interesting side note about Scala is that all types have an upper bound of Any and a lower bound of Nothing. This is because all types in Scala descend from Any, while all types are extended by Nothing. If the compiler ever warns about incompatible type signatures that include Nothing or Any, without you having specified them, it's a good bet that you have an unbounded type somewhere the compiler is trying to infer. The usual cause of this is trying to combine incompatible types, or you have a missing upper or lower bound on a generic type.

Rule 16

AVOID USELESS <: CONSTRAINTS

In Scala, expressions are polymorphic. If a method accepts an argument of type `Any`, it can be passed an expression of type `Int`. When enforcing type constraints on method parameters it may not be necessary to use a type constraint but instead accept the subtype. For example:

```
def sum[T <: List[Int]](t: T) = t.foldLeft(0)(_+_)
```

The sum method has a redundant type constraint. Because the type `T` doesn't occur in the resulting value, the method could be written as

```
def sum(t: List[Int]) = t.foldLeft(0)(_+_)
```

without any changes to the meaning.

Bounded types are immensely useful in Scala. They help us define generic methods that can retain whatever specialized types they're called with. They help design generic classes that can interoperate with all sorts of code. The standard collection library uses them extensively to enable all sorts of powerful combinations of methods. The collections, and other higher-kinded types, benefit greatly from using both upper and lower bounds in code. To understand how and when to use them, we must first delve into type parameters and higher-kinded types.

6.3   *Type parameters and higher-kinded types*

Type parameters and higher-kinded types are the bread and butter of the type system. A type parameter is a type definition that's taken in as a parameter when calling a method, constructing a type, or extending a type. Higher-kinded types are those that accept other types and construct a new type. Just as parameters are key to constructing and combining methods, type parameters are the key to constructing and combining types.

6.3.1   *Type parameter constraints*

Type parameters are defined within brackets (`[]`) before any normal parameters are defined. Normal parameters can then use the types named as parameters. Let's look at a simple method defined using type parameters in figure 6.1:

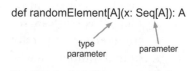

Figure 6.1   Defining type parameters on a method

This is the definition of a `randomElement` method. The method takes a type parameter `A`. This type parameter is then used in the method parameter list. The `randomElement` method takes a `List` of some element type, named `A`, and returns an instance of that element type. When calling the method, we can specify the type parameter as we wish:

```
scala> randomElement[Int](List(1,2,3))
res0: Int = 3

scala> randomElement[Int](List("1", "2", "3"))
<console>:7: error: type mismatch;
 found    : java.lang.String("1")
```

```
      required: Int
          randomElement[Int](List("1", "2", "3"))
                           ^
scala> randomElement[String](List("1", "2", "3"))
res1: String = 2
```

You can see that when we specify `Int` for the type parameter, the method will accept lists of integers but not lists of strings. But we can specify `String` as a type parameter and allow lists of strings but not lists of integers. In the case of methods, we can even leave off the type parameter, and the compiler will infer one for us if it can:

```
scala> randomElement[String](List("1", "2", "3"))
res1: String = 2
```

This inference is pretty powerful. If there are several arguments to a function, the compiler will attempt to infer a type parameter that matches all the arguments. Scala's `List.apply` is a parameterized method. Let's look at this type inference in action.

```
scala> List(1.0, "String")
res7: List[Any] = List(1.0, String)

scala> List("String", Seq(1))
res8: List[java.lang.Object] = List(String, List(1))
```

When passed an integer and a string, the parameter to `List` is inferred as `Any`. This is the lowest possible type that both parameters will conform to. `Any` also happens to be the top type, the one that all values conform to. If we choose different parameters, say a `String` and a `Seq`, the compiler infers a lower type, that of `java.lang .Object`, otherwise known in Scala as `AnyRef`.

The compiler's goal, and yours as well, is to preserve as much type information as possible. This is easier to accomplish using type constraints on type parameters.

It's possible to specify constraints in line with type parameters. These constraints ensure that any type used to satisfy the parameter needs to abide by the constraints. Specifying lower bound constraints also allows you to utilize members defined on the lower bound. Upper bound constraints don't imply what members might be on a type but are useful when combining several parameterized types.

Type parameters are like method parameters except that they parameterize things at compilation time. It's important to remember that all type programming is enforced during compilation and all type information must be known at compile time to be useful.

Type parameters also make possible the creation of higher-kinded types.

6.3.2 *Higher-kinded types*

Higher-kinded types are those that use other types to construct a new type. This is similar to how higher-order functions are those that take other functions as parameters. A higher-kinded type can have one or more other types as parameters. In Scala, you can do this using the `type` keyword. Here's an example of a higher-kinded type.

```
type Callback[T] = Function1[T, Unit]
```

The type definition declares a higher-kinded type called `Callback`. The `Callback` type takes a type parameter and constructs a new `Function1` type. The type `Callback` isn't a complete type until it's parameterized.

> **TYPE CONSTRUCTORS**   Higher-kinded types are also called *type constructors* because they're used to construct types. Higher-kinded types can be used to make a complex type—for example, `M[N[T, X], Y]` look like a simpler type, such as `F[X]`.

The `Callback` type can be used to simplify the signature for functions that take a single parameter and return no value. Let's look at an example:

```
scala> val x : Callback[Int] = y => println(y + 2)
x: (Int) => Unit = <function1>

scala> x(1)
3
```

This first statement constructs a `Callback[Int]` named x that takes an integer, adds it with the value 2 and prints the result. The type `Callback[Int]` is converted by the compiler into the full type `(Int) => Unit`. The next statement calls the function defined by x with the value 1.

Higher-kinded types are used to simplify type signatures for complex types. They can also be used to make complex types fit the simpler type signature on a method. Here's an example:

```
scala> def foo[M[_]](f : M[Int]) = f
foo: [M[_]](f: M[Int])M[Int]

scala> foo[Callback](x)
res4: Function1[Int, Unit] = <function1>
```

The `foo` method is defined as taking a type `M` that's parameterized by an unknown type. The `_` keyword is used as a placeholder for an unknown, existential type. Existential types are covered in more detail in section 6.5. The next statement calls the method `foo` with a type parameter of `Callback` and an argument of x, defined in the earlier example. This would not work with the `Function1` type directly.

```
scala> foo[Function1](x)
<console>:9: error: Function1 takes two type parameters, expected: one
       foo[Function1](x)
```

The `foo` method can't be called directly with the `Function1` type because `Function1` takes two type parameters and the `foo` method expects a type with only one type parameter.

Higher-kinded types are used to simplify type definitions or to make complex types conform to simple type parameters. Variance is an additional complication to parameterized types and higher-kinded types.

Type lambdas

Scala supports a limited version of *type lambdas*. A type lambda, similar to a function lambda, is a notation where you can define a higher-kinded type directly within the parameter of a function. For the `foo` method, we can use a type lambda rather than define the `Callback` type. Here's an example:

```
scala> foo[({type X[Y] = Function1[Y, Unit]})#X]( (x : Int) => println(x) )
res7: (Int) => Unit = <function1>
```

The type lambda is the expression `({type X[Y] = Function1[Y, Unit]})#X`. The type `X` is defined inside parentheses and braces. This constructs an anonymous path containing the type `X`. It then uses type projection (`#`) to access the type from the anonymous path. The type `X` remains hidden behind the anonymous path, and the expression is a valid type parameter, as it refers to a type.

Type lambdas were discovered and popularized by Jason Zaugg, one of the core contributors to the Scalaz framework.

6.4   *Variance*

Variance refers to the ability of type parameters to change or vary on higher-kinded types, like `T[A]`. Variance is a way of declaring how type parameters can be changed to create conformant types. A higher-kinded type `T[A]` is said to conform to `T[B]` if you can assign `T[B]` to `T[A]` without causing any errors. The rules of variance govern the type conformance of types with parameters. Variance takes three forms: invariance, covariance, and contravariance.

Rule 17   **Mutable classes must be invariant**

It's impossible, and unsafe, to define them otherwise. If we want to make use of covariance or contravariance, stick to immutable classes, or expose your mutable class in an immutable interface.

Invariance refers to the unchanging nature of a higher-kinded type parameter. A higher-kinded type that's invariant implies that for any types T, A, and B if `T[A]` conforms to `T[B]` then A must be the equivalent type of B. You can't change the type parameter of T. Invariance is the default for any higher-kinded type parameter.

Covariance refers to the ability to substitute a type parameter with its parent type: For any types T, A and B if `T[A]` conforms to `T[B]` then A <: B. Figure 6.2 demonstrates a covariant relationship. The arrows in the diagram represent type conformance. The `Mammal` and `Cat` relationship is such that the `Cat` type conforms to the `Mammal` type; if a method requires something of type `Mammal`, a value of type `Cat` could be used. If a type `T` were defined as covariant, then the type `T[Cat]` would conform to the type `T[Mammal]`: A method requiring a `T[Mammal]` would accept a value of type `T[Cat]`.

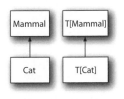

Figure 6.2   Covariance

Notice that the direction of conformance arrows is the same. The conformance of T is the same (co-) as the conformance of its type parameters.

The easiest example of this is a list, which is higher-kinded on the type of its elements. You could have a list of strings or a list of integers. Because Any is a supertype of String, we can use a list of strings where a list of Any is expected.

Creating a Covariant parameter is as easy as adding a + symbol before the type parameter. Let's create a covariant type in the REPL and try out the type conformance it creates.

Listing 6.8   Covariance example

```
scala> class T[+A] {}                          Type-parameter
 defined class T                               A is covariant

scala> val x = new T[AnyRef]
x: T[AnyRef] = T@11e55d39
                                               Upcast AnyRef
scala> val y : T[Any] = x                      to Any
 y: T[Any] = T@11e55d39

scala> val z : T[String] = x                   Downcast
 <console>:7: error: type mismatch;            AnyRef to
 found    : T[AnyRef]                           String
 required: T[String]
       val z : T[String] = x
```

First we construct a higher-kinded class T that takes a covariant parameter A. Next we create a new value with the type parameter bound to AnyRef. Now, if we try to assign our T[AnyRef] to a variable of type T[Any], the call succeeds. This is because Any is the parent type of AnyRef, and our covariant constraint is satisfied. But when we attempt to assign a value of type T[AnyRef] to a variable of type T[String], the assignment will fail.

The compiler has checks in place to ensure that a covariant annotation doesn't violate a few key rules. In particular, the compiler tracks the usage of a higher-kinded type and ensures that if it's covariant, that it occurs only in covariant positions in the compiler. The same is true for contravariance. We'll cover the rules for determining variance positions soon, but for now, we'll look at what happens if we violate one of our variance positions:

```
scala> trait T[+A] {
     | def thisWillNotWork(a : A) = a
     | }
<console>:6: error: covariant type A occurs in
  contravariant position in type A of value a
       def thisWillNotWork(a : A) = a
```

As you can see, the compiler gives us a nice message that we've used our type parameter A in a position that's contravariant, when the type parameter is covariant. We'll cover the rules shortly, but for now it's important to know that full knowledge of the rules isn't needed to utilize variance correctly if you have a basic understanding of the concept. You can reason in your head whether a type should be covariant or contravariant and then let the compiler tell you when you've misplaced your types. You can use tricks to avoid placing types in contravariant positions when you require covariance, but first let's look at contravariance.

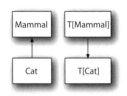

Contravariance is the opposite of covariance. For any types T, A and B, if `T[A]` conforms to `T[B]` then `A >: B`. Figure 6.3 shows the same conformance relationship between `Mammal`

Figure 6.3   Contravariance

and `Cat` types. If the type `T` is defined as contravariant, then a method expecting a type of `T[Cat]` would accept a value of type `T[Mammal]`. Notice that the direction of the conformance relationship is opposite (contra-) that of the Mammal–Cat relationship.

Contravariance can be harder to reason through but makes sense in the context of a `Function` object. A `Function` object is covariant on the return type and contravariant on the argument type. Intuitively this makes sense. You can take the return value of a function and cast it to any supertype of that return value. As for arguments, you can pass any subtype of the argument type. You should be able to take a function of `Any => String` and cast it to a `String => Any` but not vice versa. Let's look at performing this cast using raw methods:

Listing 6.9   Implicit variance of methods

```
scala> def foo(x : Any) : String = "Hello, I received a " + x
foo: (x: Any)String

scala> def bar(x : String) : Any = foo(x)
bar: (x: String)Any

scala> bar("test")
res0: Any = Hello, I received a test

scala> foo("test")
res1: String = Hello, I received a test
```

First we create a `foo` method of type `Any => String`. Next we define `bar` a method of type `String => Any`. As you can see, we can implement `bar` in terms of `foo`, and both calls to `bar` and `foo` with strings return the same value, as the functions are implemented the same. They do require differing types. We can't pass an `Int` variable to the `bar` method, as it will fail to compile, but we can pass that `Int` variable to the `foo` method. Now if we want to construct an object that represents a function, we'd like this same behavior—that is, we'd like to be able to cast the function object as flexibly as possible. Let's begin by defining our function object.

Listing 6.10   First attempt at defining a function object

```
scala> trait Function[Arg,Return]
defined trait Function

scala> val x = new Function[Any,String] {}
x: java.lang.Object with Function[Any,String] = $anon$1@39fba2af
```

```
scala> val y : Function[String,Any] = x
<console>:7: error: type mismatch;
 found    : java.lang.Object with Function[Any,String]
 required: Function[String,Any]
       val y : Function[String,Any] = x
                                      ^

scala> val y : Function[Any,Any] = x
<console>:7: error: type mismatch;
 found    : java.lang.Object with Function[Any,String]
 required: Function[Any,Any]
       val y : Function[Any,Any] = x
```

First we create our Function trait. The first type parameter is for the argument to the function and the second is for the return type. We then construct a new value with an argument of type Any and a return value of type String. If we attempt to cast this to a Function[String,Any] (a function that takes a String and returns an Any), the call fails. This happens because we haven't defined any variance annotations. Let's first declare our return value as covariant. Return values are actual values, and we know that we can always take a variable and cast it to a supertype.

Listing 6.11 Function object with only covariance

```
scala> trait Function[Arg,+Return]
defined trait Function

scala> val x = new Function[Any,String] {}
x: java.lang.Object with Function[Any,String] = $anon$1@3c56b64c

scala> val y : Function[String,Any] = x
<console>:7: error: type mismatch;
 found    : java.lang.Object with Function[Any,String]
 required: Function[String,Any]
       val y : Function[String,Any] = x
                                      ^

scala> val y : Function[Any,Any] = x
y: Function[Any,Any] = $anon$1@3c56b64c
```

Once again, we declare our Function trait; but this time we declare the return value type covariant. We construct a new value of the Function trait, and again attempt to cast it. The cast still fails due to type mismatch. But we're able to cast our return value type from String to Any. Let's use contravariance on the argument value:

Listing 6.12 Function with covariance and contravariance

```
scala> trait Function[-Arg,+Return]
defined trait Function

scala> val x = new Function[Any,String] {}
x: java.lang.Object with Function[Any,String] = $anon$1@69adff28

scala> val y : Function[String,Any] = x
y: Function[String,Any] = $anon$1@69adff28
```

Once again we construct a Function trait, only this time the argument type is contravariant and the return type is covariant. We instantiate an instance of the trait and attempt our cast, which succeeds! Let's extend our trait to include a real implementation and ensure things work appropriately:

Listing 6.13   Complete function example

```scala
scala> trait Function[-Arg,+Return] {
     | def apply(arg : Arg) : Return
     | }
defined trait Function

scala> val foo = new Function[Any,String] {
     | override def apply(arg : Any) : String =
     |   "Hello, I received a " + arg
     | }
foo: java.lang.Object with Function[Any,String] = $anon$1@38f0b51d

scala> val bar : Function[String,Any] = foo
bar: Function[String,Any] = $anon$1@38f0b51d

scala> bar("test")
res2: Any = Hello, I received a test
```

We create our Function trait, but this time it has an abstract apply method that will hold the logic of the function object. Now we construct a new function object foo with the same logic as the foo method we had earlier. We attempt to construct a bar Function object using the foo object directly. Notice that no new object is created; we're merely assigning one type to another similar to polymorphically assigning a value of a child class to a reference of the parent class. Now we can call our bar function and receive the expected output.

Congratulations! You're now an initiate of variance annotations. But there are some situations you may encounter when you need to tweak your code for appropriate variance annotations.

6.4.1   *Advanced variance annotations*

When designing a higher-kinded type, at some point you'll you wish it to have a particular variance, and the compiler won't let you do this. When the compiler restricts variance but you know it shouldn't, there's usually a simple transform that can fix your code to compile and keep the type system happy. The easiest example of this is in the collections library.

The Scala collections library provides a mechanism for combining two collections types. It does this through a method called ++. In the actual collections library, the method signature is pretty complicated due to the library's advanced features, so for this example we'll use a simplified version of the ++ signature. Let's attempt to define an abstract List type that can be combined with other lists. We'd like to be able to convert, for example, a list of strings to a list of Any, so we're going to annotate the ItemType parameter as covariant. We'll define our ++ method such that it takes another list of the same ItemType and returns a new list that's the combination of the two lists. Let's take a look at what happens:

Listing 6.14   First attempt at a list interface

```
scala> trait List[+ItemType] {
     | def ++(other : List[ItemType]): List[ItemType]
     | }
<console>:6: error: covariant type ItemType occurs in
    contravariant position in type List[ItemType] of value other
         def ++(other : List[ItemType]): List[ItemType]
```

The compiler is complaining that we're using the ItemType parameter in a contravariant position! This statement is true, but we know that it should be safe to combine two lists of the same type and still be able to cast them up the ItemType hierarchy. Is the compiler too restrictive when it comes to variance? Perhaps, but let's see if we can work around this.

We're going to make the ++ method take a type parameter. We can use this new type parameter in the argument to avoid having ItemType in a contravariant position. The new type parameter should capture the ItemType of the other List. Let's naively use another type parameter

---

Listing 6.15   Naive attempt to work around variance

```
scala> trait List[+ItemType] {
     | def ++[OtherItemType](other: List[OtherItemType]): List[ItemType]
     | }
defined trait List

scala> class EmptyList[ItemType] extends List[ItemType] {
     | def ++[OtherItemType](other: List[OtherItemType]) = other
     | }
<console>:7: error: type mismatch;
 found    : List[OtherItemType]
 required: List[ItemType]
       def ++[OtherItemType](other: List[OtherItemType]) = other
```

Adding the OtherItemType lets the creation of the List trait succeed. Great! Let's see if we can use it. We implement an EmptyList class that's an efficient implementation of a List of no elements. The combination method,++, should return whatever is passed to it, because it's empty. When we define the method, we get a type mismatch. The issue is that OtherItemType and ItemType aren't compatible types! We've enforced nothing about OtherItemType in our ++ method and therefore made it impossible to implement. Well, we know that we need to enforce some kind of type constraint on OtherItemType and that we're combining two lists. We'd like Other-ItemType to be some type that combines well with our list. Because ItemType is covariant, we know that we can cast our current list up the ItemType hierarchy. As such, let's use ItemType as the upper bound constraint on OtherItemType. We'll also need to change the return type of the ++ method to return the OtherItemType, as OtherItem-Type may be higher up the hierarchy than ItemType is. Let's take a look:

Listing 6.16 Appropriately working with variance

```scala
scala> trait List[+ItemType] {
     | def ++[OtherItemType >: ItemType](
     |   other: List[OtherItemType]): List[OtherItemType]
     | }
defined trait List

scala> class EmptyList[ItemType] extends List[ItemType] {
     | def ++[OtherItemType >: ItemType](
     |   other: List[OtherItemType]) = other
     | }
defined class EmptyList
```

Our new definition of empty list succeeds. Let's take it for a test drive through the REPL and ensure that combining empty lists of various types returns the types we desire.

Listing 6.17 Ensuring the correct type changes

```scala
scala> val strings = new EmptyList[String]
strings: EmptyList[String] = EmptyList@2cfa930d

scala> val ints = new EmptyList[Int]
ints: EmptyList[Int] = EmptyList@58e5ebd

scala> val anys = new EmptyList[Any]
anys: EmptyList[Any] = EmptyList@65685e30

scala> val anyrefs = new EmptyList[AnyRef]
anyrefs: EmptyList[AnyRef] = EmptyList@1d8806f7

scala> strings ++ ints
res3: List[Any] = EmptyList@58e5ebd

scala> strings ++ anys
res4: List[Any] = EmptyList@65685e30

scala> strings ++ anyrefs
res5: List[AnyRef] = EmptyList@1d8806f7

scala> strings ++ strings
res6: List[String] = EmptyList@2cfa930d
```

First we declare our variables. These are lists of String, Int, Any, and AnyRef. Now let's combine lists and see what happens. First we try to combine our list of Strings and Ints. You can see that the compiler infers Any as a common superclass to String and Int and gives you a list of Any. This is exactly what we wanted! Next we combine our list of strings with a list of anys and we get another list of anys. Once again, this is as we desired. If we combine the list of strings with a list of AnyRefs, the compiler infers AnyRef as the lowest possible type, and we retain a small amount of type information. If we combine the list of strings with another list of strings, we'll retain the type of a List[String]. We now have a list interface that's very powerful and type-safe.

> **VARIANCE IS HARD**   In Scala, the choice of making something variant or not is important. The variance annotation can affect a lot of the mechanics in Scala, including type inference. The safest bet when working with variance is to start with everything invariant and mark variance as needed.

In general, when running into covariance or contravariance issues in class methods, its usually the case of introducing a new type parameter and using that for the signature of the method. In fact, the final ++ method definition is far more flexible, and still type-safe; therefore, when you face issues with variance annotations, step back and try to introduce a few new type parameters.

6.5   *Existential types*

Existential types are a means of constructing types where portions of the type signature are existential, where *existential* means that although some real type meets that portion of a type signature, we don't care about the specific type. Existential types were introduced into Scala as a means to interoperate with Java's generic types, so we'll start by looking at a common idiom found in Java programs.

In Java, generic types were added to the language later and done so with backward compatibility in mind. As such, the Java collections API was enhanced to utilize generic types but still supports code that's written without generic types This was done using a combination of erasure and a subdued form of existential types. Scala, seeking to interoperate as closely as possible with Java, also supports existential types for the same reason. Scala's existential types are far more powerful and expressive than Java's, as illustrated next.

Let's look at Java's `List` interface:

```
interface List<E> extends Collection<E> {
  E get(int idx);
  ...
}
```

The interface has a type parameter `E` which is used to specify the type of elements in the list. The `get` method is defined using this type parameter for its return value. This setup should be familiar from the earlier discussion of type parameters. The strangeness begins when we look at the backward compatibility. The older `List` interface in Java was designed without generic types. Code written for this old interface is still compatible with Java Generics. For example:

```
List foo = ...
System.out.println(foo.get(0));
```

The generic parameter for the `List` interface is never specified. Although an experienced Java developer would know that the type returned by the `get` method is `java.lang.Object`, they might not fully understand what's going on. In this example, Java is using existential types when type parameters aren't specified. This means that the only information known about the missing type parameter is that it must be a subtype of or equivalent to `java.lang.Object` because all type parameters in Java are a subtype of or equivalent to java.lang.Object. This allows the older code, where List had no generic type parameter and the get method returned the type Object, to compile directly against the new collections library.

Is creating a list without any type parameters equivalent to creating a List<Object>? The answer is no; they have a subtle difference. When compiling the following code, you'll see unchecked warnings from the compiler:

```
import java.util.*;

class Test {
   public static void main(String[] args) {
      List foo = new ArrayList();
      List<Object> bar = foo;                          Unchecked type
   }                                                    conversion
}
```

When passing the -Xlint flag to javac, the following warning is displayed:

```
es.java:7: warning: [unchecked] unchecked conversion
found    : java.util.List
required: java.util.List<java.lang.Object>
     List<Object> bar = foo;
                        ^
```

```
1 warning
```

Java doesn't consider List and List<Object> the same type, but it will automatically convert between the two. This is done because the practical difference between these two types, in Java, is minimal. In Scala, existential types take on a slightly different flavor. Let's create an existential type in a Java class and see what it looks like in the Scala REPL. First, the Java class:

```
public class Test {
   public static List makeList() {
      return new ArrayList();
   }
}
```

The Test class provides a single makeList method that returns a List with existential type signature. Let's start up the Scala REPL and call this method:

```
scala> Test.makeList()
res0: java.util.List[_] = []
```

The type returned in the REPL is java.util.List[_]. Scala provides a convenience syntax for creating existential types that uses the underscore in the place of a type parameter. We'll cover the full syntax shortly; but this shorthand is more commonly found in production code. This _ can be considered a place holder for a single valid type. The _ is different from closure syntax because it isn't a placeholder for a type argument, but rather is a hole in the type. The compiler isn't sure what the specific type parameter is, but it knows that there is one. You can't substitute a type parameter later; the hole remains.

DEVIATION FROM JAVA   We can't add things to a List[_] unless the compiler can determine that they're of the same type as the list. This means we can't add new values to the list without some form of casting. In Java, this operation would compile and an Unchecked warning would be issued.

Existential types can also have upper and lower bounds in Scala. This can be done by treating the _ as if it were a type parameter. Let's take a look:

```
scala> def foo(x : List[_ >: Int]) = x
foo: (x: List[_ >: Int])List[Any]
```

The foo method is defined to accept a List of some parameter that has a lower bound of Int. This parameter could have any type; the compiler doesn't care which type, as long as it's Int or one of its super types. We can call this method with a value of type String, because Int and String share a parent, Any. Let's look.

```
scala> foo(List("Hi"))
res9: List[Any] = List(Hi)
```

When calling the foo method with a List("Hi") the call succeeds, as expected.

6.5.1   *The formal syntax of existential types*

Scala's formal syntax for existential types uses the forSome keyword. Here's the excerpt explaining the syntax from the Scala Language Specification:

SCALA LANGUAGE SPECIFICATION—EXCERPT FROM SECTION 3.2.10   An existential type has the form T forSome {Q} where Q is a sequence of type declarations.

In the preceding definition, the Q block is a set of type declarations. Type declarations, in the Scala Language Specification could be abstract type statements or abstract val statements. The declarations in the Q block are existential. The compiler knows that there's some type that meets these definitions, but doesn't remember what that type is specifically. The type declared in the T section can then use these existential identifiers directly. This is easiest to see by converting the convenient syntax into the formal syntax. Let's take a look:

```
scala> val y: List[_] = List()
y: List[_] = List()

scala> val x: List[X forSome { type X }] = y
x: List[X forSome { type X }] = List()
```

The y value is constructed having the type List[_]. The x value is constructed to have the type List[X forSome { type X }]. In x value, the type X is existential and acts the same as the _ in the y's type. A more complicated scenario occurs when the existential type has a lower or upper bound restriction. In that case, the entire lower bound or upper bound is translated into the forSome block:

```
scala> val y: List[_ <: AnyRef] = List()
y: List[_ <: AnyRef] = List()
```

```
scala> val x: List[X forSome { type X <: AnyRef }] = y
x: List[X forSome { type X <: AnyRef }] = List()
```

The first value, y, has the type List[_ <: AnyRef]. The existential _ <: AnyRef is translated to type X <: AnyRef in the forSome section. Remember that all type declarations
in the forSome blocks are treated as existential that can be used in the left hand side
type. In this case, the left-hand side type is X. The forSome block could be used for any
kind of type declaration, including values or other existential types.

   And now it's time for a more complex example involving existential types. Remember the Observable trait from the dependent type section? Let's take another look at
the interface for the Observable trait:

```
trait Observable {
  type Handle

  def observe(callback: this.type => Unit) : Handle = ..

  def unobserve(handle: Handle) : Unit = ...

  ...

}
```

Imagine we wanted some generic way to interact with the Handle types that are
returned from this object. You can declare a type that can represent any Handle using
existential types. Let's look at this type:

```
type Ref = x.Handle forSome { val x: Observable }
```

The type is declared with the name Ref. The forSome block contains a val definition.
This means that the value x is existential: the compiler doesn't care *which* Observable
value, only that there is one. On the left-hand side of the type declaration is the path-
dependent type x.Handle. Notice that it isn't possible to create this existential type
using the convenience syntax, as the _ can only stand in for a type declaration.

   Let's create a trait that will track all the handles from Observables using the Ref
type. We'd like this trait to maintain a list of handles such that we can appropriately
clean up the class when needed. This cleanup involves unregistering all observers.
Let's look at the trait:

```
trait Dependencies {
  type Ref = x.Handle forSome { val x : Observable }

  var handles = List[Ref]()

  protected def addHandle(handle: Ref) : Unit = {
    handles :+= handle
  }

  protected def removeDependencies() {
    for(h <- handles) h.remove()
    handles = List()
  }

  protected def observe[T <: Observable](
      obj : T)(handler : T => Unit) : Ref = {
```

```
      val ref = obj.observe(handler)
      addHandle(ref)
      ref
  }
}
```

The trait `Dependencies` redefines the type `Ref` as before. The `handles` member is defined as a `List` of `Ref` types. An `addHandle` method is defined, which takes a handle, the `Ref` type, and adds it to the list of handles. The `removeDependencies` method loops over all registered handles and calls their `remove` method. Finally, the observe method is defined such that it registers a handler with an observable and then registers the `Handle` returned using the `addHandle` method.

You may be wondering how we're able to call remove on the `Handle` type. This is invalid code using the `Observable` trait as defined earlier. The code will work this minor addition to the `Observable` trait:

```
trait Observable {
  type Handle <: {
    def remove() : Unit
  }
  ...
}
```

The `Observable` trait is now defined such that the `Handle` type requires a method `remove() : Unit`. Now you can use the `Dependencies` trait to track handlers registered on observables. Let's look at a REPL session demonstrating this:

```
scala> val x = new VariableStore(12)
x: VariableStore[Int] = VariableStore(12)

scala> val d = new Dependencies {}
d: java.lang.Object with Dependencies = $anon$1@153e6f83

scala> val t = x.observe(println)
t: x.Handle = DefaultHandles$HandleClass@662fe032

scala> d.addHandle(t)

scala> x.set(1)
VariableStore(1)

scala> d.removeDependencies()

scala> x.set(2)
```

The first line creates a new `VariableStore` which is a subclass of `Observable`. The next statement constructs a `Dependencies` object, d, to track registered observable handles. The next two lines register the function `println` with the `Observable`x and add the handle to the `Dependencies` object d. Next, the value inside the `Variable-Store` is changed. This invokes the observers with the current value and the registered observer `println` is called to print `VariableStore(1)` on the console. After this, the `removeDependencies` method is used on the object d to remove all tracked observers.

The next line again changes the value in the `VariableStore` and no values are output on the console.

Existential types provide a convenient syntax to represent these abstract types and interact with them. Although the formal syntax isn't frequently used, this uncommon situation is the most common case where it's needed. It's a great tool to understand and use when running into nested types that seem inexpressible, but it shouldn't be needed in most situations.

6.6 *Summary*

In this chapter, you learned the basic rules governing Scala's type system. We learned how to define types and combine them. We looked at structural typing and how you can use it to emulate duck typing in dynamic languages. We learned how to create generic types using type parameters and how to enforce upper and lower bounds on types. We looked at higher-kinded types and type lambdas and how you can use them to simplify complex types. We also looked into variance and how to create flexible parameterized classes. Finally we explored existential types and how to create truly abstract methods. These basic building blocks of the Scala type system are used to construct advanced models of behavior and interactions within a program. In the next chapter, we use these fundamentals to implement implicit resolution and advanced type system features.

7

Using implicits
and types together

In this chapter

- Introduction to implicit type bounds
- Type classes and their applications
- Type level programming and compile time execution

The type system and the implicit resolution mechanism provide the tools required to write expressive, type-safe software. Implicits can encode types into runtime objects and can enable the creation of type classes that abstract behavior from classes. Implicits can be used to directly encode type constraints and to construct types recursively. Combined with some type constructors and type bounds, implicits and the type system can help you encode complex problems directly into the type system. Most importantly, you can use implicits to preserve type information and delegate behavior to type-specific implementations while preserving an abstract interface. The ultimate goal is the ability to write classes and methods that can be reused anytime they're needed.

To start, let's look at some type bounds that we didn't cover in chapter 6.

7.1   *Context bounds and view bounds*

Scala supports two types of type constraint operators that aren't type constraints but are implicit lookups—context bounds and view bounds. These operators allow us to define an implicit parameter list as type constraints on generic types. This syntax can reduce typing in situations where implicit definitions must be available for lookup but don't need to be directly accessed.

View bounds are used to require an available implicit view for converting one type into another type. Implicit views look like the following:

```
def foo[A <% B](x: A) = x
```

The foo method defines a constraint A <% B. This constraint means that the parameter x is of type A and there must be an implicit conversion function A => B available at any call site. The preceding code can be rewritten as the following:

```
def foo[A](x: A)(implicit $ev0: A => B) = x
```

This foo method is also defined with a type parameter A that has no constraints. Two parameter lists exist: one that accepts an A type and one that requires the implicit conversion function. Although this second form requires more typing, it places a user-defined label on the implicit conversion function.

> **To use implicit type constraints or not**
>
> When should you choose to use view/context bounds vs. directly writing an implicit parameter list? A simple convention is to use view/context bounds in these two scenarios:
>
> - The code within the method doesn't need to access the implicit parameter directly, but relies on the implicit resolution mechanism. In this situation, we must require an implicit parameter be available to call another function that requires that implicit parameter, or the implicit is automatically used. This is most common when using view bounds.
> - The meaning conveyed by the type parameter is more clear using context/view bounds than an implicit parameter list. See section 7.3 on type classes for examples of this scenario.

Context bounds, similar to view bounds, declare that there must be an implicit value available with a given type. Context bounds look like the following:

```
def foo[A : B](x: A) = x
```

The foo method defines a constraint A : B. This constraint means that the parameter x is of type A and there must be an implicit value B[A] available when calling method foo. Context bounds can be rewritten as follows:

```
def foo[A](x: A)(implicit $ev0: B[A]) = x
```

This `foo` method defines two parameter lists, with the implicit parameter list accepting a value of type `B[A]`. The key difference between the two `foo` versions is that this one gives an explicit label to the `B[A]` parameter that can be used within the function.

Context bounds are extremely useful in helping provide implicit values in companion objects. This naturally leads to type classes, shown in section 7.3. Type classes are a means of encoding behavior into a *wrapper* or *accessor* for another type. They are the most common use of context bound constraints.

7.1.1   *When to use implicit type constraints*

Scala's implicit views are often used to enrich existing types, where *enrich* means adding additional behavior that doesn't exist on the raw type (see Odersky's paper "Pimp My Library": http://mng.bz/86Qh). Implicit type constraints are used when we want to enrich an existing type while preserving that type in the type system. For example, let's write a method that will return the first element of a list and the list itself:

```
scala> def first[T](x : Traversable[T]) =
     |    (x.head, x)
first: [T](x: Traversable[T])(T, Traversable[T])

scala> first(Array(1,2))
res0: (Int, Traversable[Int]) = (1,WrappedArray(1, 2))
```

The method defines a type parameter `T` for the element of the collection. It expects a variable of type `Traversable[T]`. It then returns the head of the traversable and the traversable itself. When calling this method with an array, the resulting type is a `Traversable[Int]` and the *runtime* type is `WrappedArray`. This method has lost the original type information about the array.

Context bounds and view bounds allow developers to enforce complex type constraints in a simple fashion. They are best applied when we do not need to access the captured implicit by name, but the method requires the implicit to be available in its scope.

A better polymorphism

One of the key tenants of object-oriented programming is polymorphism: the ability of a complex type to act as a simple type. In the absence of generic types and bounds, polymorphism usually results in a loss of type information. For example, in Java's `java.util.Collections` class, there are two methods: List `synchronizedList(List)` and Collection `synchronizedCollection(Collection)`. In Scala, utilizing some advanced implicit concepts, we can accomplish the same feat with one method: `def synchronizedCollection[A, CC <: Traversable[A] : Manifest](col : CC) : CC`.

One of the biggest benefits of using Scala is the ability to preserve specific types across generic methods. The entire collections API is designed such that methods defined in the lower level types preserve the original types of the collections as much as possible.

For example, a method that works with types that could be serialized but doesn't serialize them might look something like this:

```
def sendMsgToEach[A : Serializable](receivers : Seq[Receiver[A]],
                                    a : A) = {
  receivers foreach (_.send(a))
}
```

The `sendMsgToEach` accepts any type that has a serializable implicit context (that is, the compiler can find the type `Serializable[A]` on the implicit scope—and a sequence of receivers of type a. The method implementation calls `send` on each receiver, passing the message to each. But the implementation of the `send` method on the `Receiver` type would need to use the `Serializable` value, so it's better to explicitly specify the implicit argument list in that method.

Context bound and view bound constraints are used to clarify the intent of an implicit argument. Implicit arguments can be used to capture a relationship from the type system.

7.2   *Capturing types with implicits*

Scala 2.8 formalized the ability to encode type information into implicit parameters. It does this through two mechanisms: `Manifests` and implicit type constraints.

A `Manifest` for a type is generated by the compiler, when needed, with all the known information for that type at that time. `Manifests` were added specifically to handle arrays and were generalized to be useful in other situations where the type must be available at runtime.

Implicit type constraints are direct encoding of supertype and equivalence relationships between types. These can be useful to restrict a generic type further within a method. These constraints are static—that is, they happen at compile time.

The runtime counterpart of a type is the `Manifest`.

7.2.1   *Manifests*

As stated earlier, `Manifests` were first introduced into Scala to help deal with arrays. They capture types for runtime evaluation. In Scala, an array is a class with a parameter. An array of integers has the type `Array[Int]`. On the JVM, however, there are different types of arrays for every primitive type and one for objects. Examples include `int[]`, `double[]`, and `Object[]`. The Java language distinguishes between these types and requires programs to do so as well. Scala allows code to be written for generic `Array[T]` types. But because the underlying implementation must know whether the original array was an `int[]`, a `double[]`, or one of the other array types, Scala needed a way to attach this information to the type so that generic array implementations would know how to treat the array, and so the birth of `Manifests`.

Rule 18 | **Prefer ClassManifest**

`ClassManifest` provides the smallest runtime overhead for the greatest benefit. While `Manifests` are extremely useful, any advanced type checking should still be performed by the compiler and not at runtime. Usually `ClassManifest` is good enough when reified types are required.

You can use `Manifest`s to pass along more specific type information with a generic type parameter. In Scala, all methods involving `Array`s require an appropriate `Manifest` for the array's type parameter. This was done because although Scala treats `Array`s as generic classes, they are encoded differently by type on the JVM. Rather than encode these differently in Scala, for example `int[]` and `double[]`, Scala chose to hide the runtime behavior behind the `Array[T]` class and associated methods. Because different bytecode must be emitted for `Array[Int]` and `Array[Double]`, Scala uses `Manifest`s to carry around the type information about arrays. This is done through `Manifest`s.

Scala provides several types of `Manifest`s:

- *Manifest*—This `Manifest` stores a reflective instance of the class associated with a type `T` as well as `Manifest` values for each of `T`'s type parameters. A reflective instance of a class is a reference to the `java.lang.Class` object for that class. This allows reflective invocations of methods defined on that class.

  A good example is the type `List[Int]`. A `Manifest[List[Int]]` allows access to the `java.lang.Class` for the `scala.List` type. It also contains a `Manifest[Int]` that would allow access to the `java.lang.Class` for the `scala.Int` type.

- *OptManifest*—Require an `OptManifest` for a type makes the `Manifest` requirement optional. If there's one available, then the `OptManifest` instance will be the `Manifest` subclass. If none can be provided, then the instance will be the `NoManifest` class.

- *ClassManifest*—This class is similar to `Manifest` except that it only stores the erased class of a given type. This erased class of a type is associated with the type without any type parameters. For example, the type `List[Int]` would have the erased class `List`.

The `Manifest` class can be expensive to store/compute, as it must have access to the `java.lang.Class` object for every type and type parameter. For a type with a lot of nesting, this can be quite deep, and methods on the `Manifest` may traverse the entire depth. The `ClassManifest` is designed for scenarios where type parameters don't need to be captured. The `OptManifest` is designed for situations where a `Manifest` isn't needed for runtime behavior, but can be used for runtime improvements if it's available.

7.2.2   *Using Manifests*

`Manifest`s are useful in Scala to create abstract methods whose implementations diverge based on the types they work on, but the resulting outputs don't. A good example of this is any method using generic arrays. Because Scala must use different bytecode instructions depending on the runtime array type, it requires a `Class-Manifest` on the `Array` element.

```
scala> def first[A](x : Array[A]) = Array(x(0))
<console>:7: error: could not find implicit value for
```

```
evidence parameter of type scala.reflect.ClassManifest[A]
def first[A](x : Array[A]) = Array(x(0))
```

The first method is defined as taking a generic `Array` of type `A`. It attempts to construct a new array containing only the first element of the old array. But because we haven't captured a `Manifest`, the compiler can't figure out which runtime type the resulting `Array` should have.

```
scala> def first[A : ClassManifest](x : Array[A]) =
     |     Array(x(0))
first: [A](x: Array[A])(implicit evidence$1: ClassManifest[A])Array[A]

scala> first(Array(1,2))
res1: Array[Int] = Array(1)
```

Now the `A` type parameter also captures the implicit `ClassManifest`. When called with an `Array[Int]`, the compiler constructs a `ClassManifest` for the type `Int`, and this is used to construct a runtime array of the appropriate type.

> **CLASSMANIFEST AND ARRAYS** The `ClassManifest` class directly contains a method to construct new arrays of the type it's captured. This could be used directly instead of delegating to Scala's generic `Array` factory method.

Using `Manifests` requires capturing the `Manifest` when a specific type is known before passing to a generic method. If the type of an array were "lost," the array couldn't be passed into the first method.

```
scala> val x : Array[_] = Array(1,2)
x: Array[_] = Array(1, 2)

scala> first(x)
<console>:10: error: could not find implicit value for
  evidence parameter of type ClassManifest[_$1]
        first(x)
```

The value `x` is constructed as an `Array` with existential type. The first method can't be called with the value `x` because a `ClassManifest` can't be found for the array's type. Although this example is contrived, the situation itself occurs when working with Arrays in nested generic code. We solve this by attaching `Manifests` to types all the way down the generic call stack.

> **RUNTIME VERSUS COMPILE TIME** `Manifests` are captured at compile time and encode the type known at *the time of capture*. This type can then be inspected and used at runtime, but the `Manifest` can only capture the type available when the `Manifest` is looked for on the implicit scope.

`Manifests` are useful tools for capturing runtime types, but they can become *viral* in code, needing to be specified in many different methods. Use them with caution and in situations where they're required. Don't use them to enforce type constraints when the type is known by the compiler; instead these can be captured with another implicit at compile time.

7.2.3   *Capturing type constraints*

The intersection of type inference and type constraints sometimes causes issues where you need to use reified type constraints. What are reified type constraints? These are objects whose implicit existence verifies that some type constraint holds true. For example, there's a type called `<:<[A,B]` that, if the compiler can find it on the implicit scope, then it must be true that `A <: B`. The `<:<` class is the reification of the upper bound constraint.

> **WHAT DOES REIFICATION MEAN?**   Think of *reification* as the process of converting some concept in a programming language to a class or object that can be inspected and used at runtime. A `Function` object is a reification of a method. It's an object that you can call methods on at runtime. In this same vein, other things can be *reified*.

Why do we need reified type constraints? Sometimes it can help the type inferencer automatically determine types for a method call. One of the neat aspects of the type inferencing algorithm is that implicits can defer the resolution of types until later in the algorithm. Scala's type inferencer works in a left-to-right fashion across parameter lists. This allows the types inferred from one parameter list to affect the types inferred in the next parameter list.

A great example of this left-to-right inference is with anonymous functions using collections. Let's take a look:

```scala
scala> def foo[A](col: List[A])(f: A => Boolean) = null
foo: [A](col: List[A])(f: (A) => Boolean)Null

scala> foo(List("String"))(_.isEmpty)
res1: Null = null
```

The `foo` method defines two parameter lists with one type parameter: one that takes a list of the unknown parameter and another that takes a function using the unknown parameter. When calling `foo` without a type parameter, the call succeeds because the compiler is able to infer the type parameter `A` as equal to `String`. This type is then used for the second parameter list, where the compiler knows that the `_` should be of type `String`. This doesn't work when we combine the parameter lists into one parameter list.

```scala
scala> def foo[A](col: List[A], f: A => Boolean) = null
foo: [A](col: List[A],f: (A) => Boolean)Null

scala> foo(List("String"), _.isEmpty)
<console>:10: error: missing parameter type for expanded
function ((x$1) => x$1.isEmpty)
       foo(List("String"), _.isEmpty)
```

In this case, the compiler complains about the anonymous function `_.isEmpty` because it has no type. The compiler has not inferred that `A = String` yet, so it can't provide a type for the anonymous function.

This same situation can occur with type parameters. The compiler is unable to infer all the parameters in one parameter list, so the implicit parameter list is used to help the type inferencer.

Let's create a method peek that will return a tuple containing a collection and its first element. This method should be able to handle any collection from the Scala library, and it should retain the original type of the method passed in:

```scala
scala> def peek[A, C <: Traversable[A]](col : C) =
     |    (col.head, col)
foo: [A,C <: Traversable[A]](col: C)(A, C)
```

The method will have two type parameters: one to capture the specific type of the collection, called C, and another to capture the type of elements in the collection, called A. The type parameter C has a constraint that it must be a subtype of Traversable[A], where Traversable is the base type of all collection in Scala. The method returns types A and C, so specific types are preserved. But the type inferencer can't detect the correct types without annotations.

```scala
scala> peek(List(1,2,3))
<console>:7: error: inferred type arguments [Nothing,List[Int]] do
not conform to method peek's type parameter
  bounds [A,C <: Traversable[A]]
        peek(List(1,2,3))
```

The call to peek with a List[Int] type fails because the type inferencer is unable to find both types C and A using only one parameter. To solve this, let's make a new implementation of peek that defers some type inference for the second parameter list:

```scala
scala> def peek[C, A](col: C)(implicit ev: C <:< Traversable[A]) =
     |    (col.head, col)
foo: [C,A](col: C)(implicit ev: <:<[C,Traversable[A]])(A, C)
```

This peek method also has two type parameters but no type constraints on the C parameter. The first argument list is the same as before, but the second argument list takes an implicit value of type C <:< Traversable[A]. This type is taking advantage of Scala's operator notation. Just as methods named after operators can be used in operator notation, so can types with type parameters. The type C <:< Traversable[A] is a shorthand notation for the type <:< [C, Traversable[A]]. The <:< type provides default implicit values in scala.Predef for any two types A and B that have the relationship A <: B. Let's look at the code for the <:< type found in scala.Predef:

> **Listing 7.1 The <:< type**

```scala
sealed abstract class <:<[-From, +To] extends
  (From => To) with Serializable
implicit def conforms[A]: A <:< A = new (A <:< A) {
  def apply(x: A) = x
}
```

The first line declares the <:< class. It extends from Function1 and Serializable. This means that <:< can be used in any context where Java serialization may be used. Next, the conforms method takes a type parameter A and returns a new <:< type such that it converts from type A to A. The trick behind <:< is the variance annotations. Because From is contravariant, if B <: A then <:<[A,A] conforms to the type <:<[B,A] and the compiler will use the implicit value <:<[A,A] to satisfy a lookup for type <:<[B,A].

Now when using the peek method without type parameters, the type inferencer succeeds:

```scala
scala> peek(List(1,2,3))
res0: (Int, List[Int]) = (1,List(1, 2, 3))
```

Calling the peek method with a List[Int] correctly returns an Int and a List[Int] type. Capturing type relationships can also be used to restrict an existing type parameter at a later time.

7.2.4   *Specialized methods*

Sometimes a parameterized class allows methods if the parameter supports a set of features, or extends a class. I call these *specialized methods*—that is, the method is for a specialized subset of a generic class. These methods use the implicit resolution system to enforce the subset of the generic class for which they're defined. For example, the Scala collections have a specialized method sum that works only for numerical types.

Listing 7.2   TraversableOnce.sum method

```scala
def sum[B >: A](implicit num: Numeric[B]): B =
  foldLeft(num.zero)(num.plus)
```

The sum method, defined in TraversableOnce.scala, takes a single type parameter B. This type is any supertype of the type of elements in the collection. The parameter num is an implicit lookup for the Numeric type class. This type class provides the implementation of zero and plus, as well as other methods, for a given type. The sum method uses the methods defined on numeric to fold across the collection and "plus" all the elements together.

This method can be called on any collection whose type supports the Numeric type class. This means that if we desired, we could provide our own type class for types that aren't normally considered numeric. For example, let's use sum on a collection of strings:

```scala
scala> implicit object stringNumeric extends Numeric[String] {
     |    override def plus(x : String, y : String) = x + y
     |    override def zero = "
     |
     |    ... elided other methods ...
     | }
defined module stringNumeric

scala> List("One", "Two", "Three").sum
res2: java.lang.String = OneTwoThree
```

The first REPL line constructs an implicitly available `Numeric[String]` class. The `zero` method is defined to return an empty string and the `plus` method is defined to aggregate two strings together. Next, when calling sum on a `List` of strings, the result is that the strings are all appended together. The `sum` method used the `Numeric` type class we provided for the `String` type.

Methods can also be specialized using the `<:<` and `=:=` classes. For example, a method that compressed a `Set`, if that set was of integers, could be written like this:

```
trait Set[+T] {
  ...
  def compress(implicit ev : T =:= Int) =
    new CompressedIntSet(this)
}
```

The `Set` trait is defined with a type parameter representing the elements contained in the set. The compress function will take the current set and return a compressed version of it. But the only implementation of a compressed set available is the `CompressedIntSet`, is a `Set[Int]` that optimizes storage space using compression techniques. The implicit `ev` parameter is used to ensure that the type of the original set is exactly `Set[Int]` such that a `CompressedIntSet` can be created.

Specialized methods are a great way to provide a rich API and enforce type safety. They help smooth out some rough edges between generalized classes and specific use cases for those generalized classes. In the Scala core library, they're used to support numerical operations within the collection framework. They pair well with type classes, which provide the most flexibility for users of a class.

7.3   *Use type classes*

A type class is a mechanism of ensuring one type conforms to some abstract interface. The type class pattern became popular as a language feature within the Haskell programming language. In Scala, the type class idiom manifests itself through higher-kinded types and implicit resolution. We'll cover the details of defining your own type class, but initially let's look at a motivating example for why you should use type classes.

Let's design a system that synchronizes files and directories between various locations. These files could be local, remote, or located in some kind of version control system. We'd like to design some form of abstraction that can handle synchronizing between all the different location possibilities. Using our object-oriented hats, we start with trying to define an abstract interface that we can use of. Let's call our interface `FileLike`, and define what methods we need for synchronization.

To start, we know that we need a method of determining whether a `FileLike` object is an aggregate of other `FileLike` objects. We'll call this method `isDirectory`. When the `FileLike` object is a directory, we need a mechanism to retrieve the `FileLike` objects it contains. We'll call this method *children*. We need some way of determining if a directory contains a file we see in another directory.

To do this, we'll provide a child method that attempts to discover a `FileObject` contained in the current `FileLike` object with a given relative filename. If there's no object, we'll provide a *null* object. That is, a `FileLike` object that is a placeholder for a real file. We can use the null object to write data into new files. We'd like a mechanism to check whether the `FileLike` object exists, so we'll make a method called `exists`. Finally we need mechanisms to generate content. In the case of directories, we add the `mkdirs` method to create a directory at the path defined by a null `FileLike` object. Next we supply the content and `writeContent` methods as a mechanism to retrieve content from `FileLike` objects and to write content to `FileLike` objects. For now, we'll assume that we always write file contents from one side to another, and there's no optimizations for files that might exist on both sides and be equivalent. Let's look at our interface:

Listing 7.3   Initial `FileLike` interface

```
trait FileLike {
  def name : String
  def exists : Boolean
  def isDirectory : Boolean
  def children : Seq[FileLike]
  def child(name : String) : FileLike
  def mkdirs() : Unit
  def content : InputStream
  def writeContent(otherContent : InputStream) : Unit
}
```

The `FileLike` interface is defined with the methods described earlier. The method `name` returns the relative name of the `FileLike` object. The method `exists` returns whether or not the file has been created on the filesystem. The method `isDirectory` returns whether the class is an aggregate of other files. The `children` method returns a sequence containing all the `FileLike` objects that are contained in the current `FileLike` object, if it is a directory. The `child` method returns a new `FileLike` object for a child file below the current file. This method should throw an exception if the current file isn't a directory. The `mkdirs` method creates directories required to ensure the current file is a directory. The `content` method returns an `InputStream` containing the contents of the file. Finally, the `writeContent` method accepts an `InputStream` and writes the contents to the file.

Now, let's write the synchronizing code.

Listing 7.4   File synchronization using FileLike

```
// Utility to synchronize files
object SynchUtil {

  def synchronize(from : FileLike
                  to : FileLike) : Unit = {

    def synchronizeFile(file1 : FileLike,
                        file2 : FileLike) : Unit = {
```

```
      file2.writeContent(file1.content)
  }

  def synchronizeDirectory(dir1 : FileLike,
                           dir2 : FileLike) : Unit = {
    def findFile(file : FileLike,
                directory : FileLike) : Option[FileLike] =
      (for { file2 <- directory.children
        if file.name == file2.name
      } yield file2).headOption

    for(file1 <- dir1.children) {
      val file2 = findFile(file1, dir2).
            getOrElse(dir2.child(file1.name))
      if(file1.isDirectory) {
        file2.mkdirs()
      }
      synchronize(file2, file1)              ⟵── Synchronize From type
    }
  }

  if(from.isDirectory) {
    synchronizeDirectory(from,to)
  } else {
    synchronizeFile(from,to)
  }
 }
}
```

The synchronize function contains two helper methods, one for directory like objects and another for FileLike objects. The synchronize method then delegates to these two helper functions appropriately. There's only one problem: a subtle bug is in the code! In the synchronizeDirectory helper method, the argument ordering is mixed up when recursively calling the synchronize method! This is the kind of error you can avoid by using the type system more. Let's try to capture the fromFileLike type separate from the toFileLike type. These can ensure the method arguments have the correct order. Let's try it out:

Listing 7.5 Enforcing To/From types with type arguments

```
def synchronize[F <: FileLike,              ⟵── Captures To type
                T <: FileLike](
                from : F,                    ⟵┐ Captures From type
                to : T) : Unit = {

  def synchronizeFile(file1 : F,            ⟵── Enforce type ordering
                      file2 : T) : Unit = {
    file2.writeContent(file1.content)
  }

  def synchronizeDirectory(dir1 : F,        ⟵── Enforce type ordering
                           dir2 : T) : Unit = {
    def findFile(file : FileLike,
                directory : FileLike) : Option[FileLike] =
      (for { file2 <- directory.children
```

```
        if file.name == file2.name
      } yield file2).headOption

    for(file1 <- dir1.children) {
      val file2 = findFile(file1, dir2).
              getOrElse(dir2.child(file1.name))
      if(file1.isDirectory) {
        file2.mkdirs()
      }
      synchronize[F,T](file2, file1)          ◁─── Compilation failure
    }
  }

  if(from.isDirectory) {
    synchronizeDirectory(from,to)
  } else {
    synchronizeFile(from,to)
  }
}
```

The synchronize method now captures the from type in the type parameter F and the to type in the type parameter T. Great! Now there's a compilation failure on the synchronize call. But the exception isn't quite what's desired. In fact, if the arguments are reordered, the exception remains.

```
synchronize.scala:47: error: type mismatch;
 found    : file1.type (with underlying type FileLike)
 required: F
        synchronize[F,T](file1, file2)
                         ^
synchronize.scala:47: error: type mismatch;
 found    : file2.type (with underlying type FileLike)
 required: T
        synchronize[F,T](file1, file2)
```

The compiler is complaining that the types returned from the FileLike.children method are not the captured type F. The FileLike interface doesn't preserve the original type when getting children! One fix would be to modify the FileLike interface to be higher-kinded, and use the type parameter to enforce the static checks. Let's modify the original FileLike interface to take a type parameter:

Listing 7.6　Higher-kinded `FileLike`

```
trait FileLike[T <: FileLike[T]] {           ◁─── Capture subclass type
  def name : String
  def isDirectory : Boolean
  def children : Seq[T]                       ◁─── Returns subclass type
  def child(name : String) : T
  def mkdirs() : Unit
  def content : InputStream
  def writeContent(otherContent : InputStream) : Unit
}
```

This new definition of FileLike uses a recursive type constraint in its type parameter. The captured type T must be a subtype of FileLike. This type T is now returned by the child and children methods. This interface works great for the synchronization method, except it suffers from one problem: the need to create FileLike wrappers for every FileLike object passed to the method. When synchronizing java.io.File and java.net.URL instances, a wrapper must be provided. There's an alternative. Instead of defining the type FileLike[T <: FileLike[T]], we can define File-Like[T]. This new trait would allow interacting with any T as if it were a file and doesn't require any inheritance relationship. This style of trait is called a *type class*.

7.3.1 FileLike as a type class

The type class idiom, as it exists in Scala, takes this form: (1) a type class trait that acts as the accessor or utility library for a given type; (2) an object with the same name as the trait (this object contains all default implementations of the type class trait for various types); and (3) methods with context bounds where the type trait need to be used. Let's look at the type class trait for our file synchronization library:

Listing 7.7 FileLike type class trait

```
trait FileLike[T] {
  def name(file : T) : String
  def isDirectory(file : T) : Boolean
  def children(directory : T) : Seq[T]
  def child(parent : T, name : String) : T
  def mkdirs(file : T) : Unit
  def content(file : T) : InputStream
  def writeContent(file : T, otherContent : InputStream) : Unit
}
```

The FileLike type class trait looks similar to the higher-kinded FileLike trait, except for two key points. First, it doesn't have any restriction on type T. The FileLike type class works for a particular type T and against it. This brings us to the second difference: All the methods take a parameter of type T. The FileLike type class isn't expected to be a wrapper around another class, but instead it's an *accessor* of data or state from another class. It allows us to keep a specific type, while treating it generically. Let's look at what the synchronization method becomes using the FileLike type class trait.

Listing 7.8 Synchronize method using type class

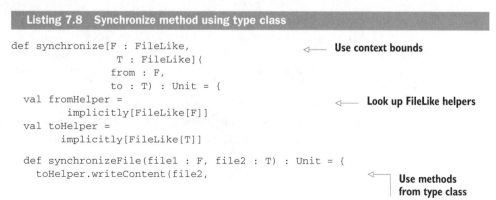

```
def synchronize[F : FileLike,                    ⟵── Use context bounds
                T : FileLike](
                from : F,
                to : T) : Unit = {
  val fromHelper =                               ⟵── Look up FileLike helpers
      implicitly[FileLike[F]]
  val toHelper =
      implicitly[FileLike[T]]

  def synchronizeFile(file1 : F, file2 : T) : Unit = {
    toHelper.writeContent(file2,                 ⟵┐ Use methods
                                                   │ from type class
```

```
          fromHelper.content(file1))
  }

  def synchronizeDirectory(dir1 : F,
                           dir2 : T) : Unit = {
    def findFile(file : F,
                 directory : T) : Option[T] =
      (for { file2 <- toHelper.children(directory)
        if fromHelper.name(file) == toHelper.name(file2)
      } yield file2).headOption

    for(file1 <- fromHelper.children(dir1)) {
      val file2 = findFile(file1, dir2).
              getOrElse(toHelper.child(dir2,
                          fromHelper.name(file1)))
      if(fromHelper.isDirectory(file1)) {
        toHelper.mkdirs(file2)
      }
      synchronize[T,F](file1, file2)
    }
  }

  if(fromHelper.isDirectory(from)) {
    synchronizeDirectory(from,to)
  } else {
    synchronizeFile(from,to)
  }
}
```

Notice the use of the context bounds syntax for `FileLike`. As described in section 7.1, this is equivalent to defining an implicit parameter for the `FileLike` on a given type. The next thing to notice is the `implicitly` method lookup of the `FileLike` parameters. Finally, every call made that utilizes type F or T uses the `FileLike` type class. The synchronize method can now work across many different types. Let's see what happens when we use it on two `java.io.File` objects.

```
scala> synchronize(
     |     new java.io.File("tmp1"),
     |     new java.io.File("tmp2"))
<console>:12: error: could not find implicit value for
evidence parameter of type FileLike[java.io.File]
       synchronize(new java.io.File("tmp1"), new java.io.File("tmp2"))
```

The compiler now complains that there's no implicit value for `FileLike` `[java.io.File]`. This is the error message provided if we attempt to use a type that doesn't have a corresponding type trait in the implicit scope. The error message isn't quite what we want, and may be improved later, but it's important to understand what this message means.

The synchronize method requires a type trait implementation for `java.io.File`. The conventional way to provide default implicit values for a set of types is through a companion object to the type class trait. Let's look at the following listing:

Implicit lookup error messages

As of Scala 2.8.1, type classes may be annotated to provide different error messages if the implicit lookup fails. Here's an example for a `Serializable` type class:

```
scala> @annotation.implicitNotFound(msg =
  | "Cannot find Serializable type class for ${T}")
  | trait Serializable[T]
defined trait Serializable
scala> def foo[X : Serializable](x : X) = x
foo: [X](x: X)(implicit evidence$1: Serializable[X])X
scala> foo(5)
 <console>:11: error: Cannot find Serializable type class for Int foo(5) ^
```

Listing 7.9   Creating default type class implementation for `java.io.File`

```
import java.io.File

object FileLike {
  implicit val ioFileLike = new FileLike[File] {        ◁─┐  Automatic
    override def name(file: File) =                         │  lookup path
        file.getName()
    override def isDirectory(file: File) =
        file.isDirectory()
    override def parent(file : File) =
        file.getParentFile()
    override def children(directory: File) =            ┐  Returns
        directory.listFiles()                        ◁─┘  raw file
     override def child(parent: File, name: String) =
        new java.io.File(parent, name)
    override def mkdirs(file: File) : Unit =
        file.mkdirs()
    override def content(file: File) =
        new FileInputStream(file)
    override def writeContent(file: File, otherContent: InputStream) =
        ...
  }
}
```

Notice that this implementation of `FileLike` is simple. Most methods delegate directly to the underlying implementation. The `writeClient` method is more complex, so you can find the implementation in the source for this book. Now that the implicit `FileLike[java.io.File]` value is in the `FileLike` companion object, anytime the compiler needs to find an implicit value of type `FileLike[java.io.File]`, it'll find one. Remember that the companion object is one of the last places checked for implicit values. This means a user can override the default implementation of `Filelike[java.io.File]` with their own by importing/defining it at the correct location. The type class pattern also provides many benefits.

7.3.2   *The benefits of type classes*

Type classes provide you with four primary benefits:

- *Separation of abstractions*—Type classes create new abstractions and allow other types to adapt, or be adapted, to the abstraction. This is helpful when creating an abstraction that works with preexisting types, and those types can't be changed.
- *Composability*—You can use the context bound syntax to specify multiple types. This means you can easily require the existence of several type classes when writing your methods. This is far more flexible than expected for some abstract interface, or a combination of abstract interfaces. Type classes can also use inheritance to compose two type classes together into one implicit variable that provides both. Sometimes this may make sense, but in general type classes retain the most flexibility by avoiding inheritance.
- *Overridable*—Type classes allow you to override a default implementation through the implicit system. By putting an implicit value higher in the lookup chain, you can completely replace how a type class is implemented. This can be helpful when providing several type classes with various behaviors because the user can select a nondefault type class when needed.
- *Type safety*—You could use several mechanisms, such as reflection, instead of type classes. The primary reason to prefer type classes over these methods is the guaranteed type safety. When requiring a specific behavior using a type class, the compiler will warn if that behavior isn't found, or isn't yet implemented. Although reflection could be used to find methods on any class and call them, its failure occurs at runtime and isn't guaranteed to occur during testing.

Type classes are a powerful design tool and can greatly improve the composability and reusability of methods and abstractions. These abstractions can also compose into higher-level type classes that are combinations of the lower-level ones.

Here's an example:

```
trait Serializable[T] { ... }
object Serializable {
  implicit def tuple2[T,V](implicit t : Serializable[T],
                           v : Serializable[V]) =
    new Serializable[(T,V)] { .. }
}
```

The `Serializable` type class is defined such that it can serialize a given type `T`. A `Serializable` type class for `Tuple2` values can be constructed using the `Serializable` type class against the types of the `Tuple2`. The method `Tuple2` accepts two type parameters, `T` and `V`, as well as implicit `Serializable` type classes associated with these parameters. The `Tuple2` method returns a `Serializable` type class for `(T,V)` tuples. Now any `Tuple2` of types that support the `Serializable` type class also supports the `Serializable` class.

Type classes start to show some of the power and complex constraints that can be encoded into the type system. This can be further extended to encode significantly complex type dependent algorithms and type level programming.

7.4 *Conditional execution using the type system*

There comes a time in an algorithm's life when it needs to do something rather clever. This clever behavior encodes portions of the algorithm into the type system so that it can execute at compile time. An example of this could be a sort algorithm. The sort algorithm can be written against the raw `Iterator` interface. But if I call `sort` against a vector, then I'd like to be able to utilize vector's natural array separation in my sorting algorithm. Traditionally this has been solved with two mechanisms: overloading and overriding.

Using overloading, the `sort` method is implemented in terms of `Iterable` and another is implemented in terms of `Vector`. The downside to overloading is that it prevents you from using named/default parameters, and it can suffer at compile time due to type erasure.

> **TYPE ERASURE** *Type erasure* refers to the runtime encoding of parameterized classes in Scala. The types used in parameters are erased at runtime into a lower type. This means that functions that operate on parameterized types can erase to the same bytecode on the JVM causing conflict. For example:
>
> ```
> def sum(x : List[Int]) : Unit
> ```
>
> and
>
> ```
> def sum(x : List[Double]) : Unit
> ```
>
> have the same runtime encoding `def sum(x : List[_]) : Unit`. The compiler will complain that the overloading isn't allowed. This is one of the reasons to avoid overloading in Scala.

Using overriding, the `sort` method is implemented against a base class. Each subclass that wishes to specialize the `sort` method should override the base class implementation with its own custom `sort` mechanism. In the case of `Iterable` and `Vector`, both would need to define the same sort method. The downside to overriding is that the type signatures must be the same and there must be an inheritance relationship between the classes owning a method.

Overriding seems like a better option than overloading but imposes some strict limitations, especially the inheritance relationship. The inheritance restriction prevents external methods from using overriding behavior, limiting them to overloading and its drawbacks.

The solution is to use the implicit system to associate a type class with the external types. For the `sort` method, it can be modified to accept an implicit parameter of type `Sorter`, where the `Sorter` class contains all the sort logic, as follows:

```
trait Sorter[A,B] {
  def sort(a : A) : B
```

```
}
def sort[A,B](col: A)(implicit val sorter: Sorter[A,B]) =
  sorter.sort(col)
```

The `Sorter` class is defined with a single method `sort`. The `sort` method accepts a value of type `A` and returns type `B`. It's assumed that `A` and `B` are collections types. The `sort` method is constructed such that it accepts a collection of type `A` and an implicit `Sorter` object and sorts the collection.

The sort algorithm selection has been turned into a type system problem. Each algorithm has been converted into a type and the selection has been encoded into the implicit system. This premise can be generalized to encode other types of problems into the type system.

It's simple to encode conditional logic into the type system. This can be done by encoding Boolean types into the type system.

```
sealed trait TBool {
  type If[TrueType <: Up, FalseType <: Up, Up] <: Up
}
```

The `TBool` trait is defined having one type constructor `If`. This type constructor can be considered a method working inside the type system with types as its arguments and types as its results. The `If` type constructor takes three arguments: the type to return if the `TBool` is true, the type to return if the `TBool` is false, and an upper bound for the return values. Now let's encode the true and false types into the type system.

```
class TTrue extends TBool {
  type If[TrueType <: Up, FalseType <: Up, Up] = TrueType
}

class TFalse extends TBool {
  type If[TrueType <: Up, FalseType <: Up, Up] = FalseType
}
```

The `TTrue` type represents true in the type system. Its `If` type constructor is overridden to return the first type passed in. The `TFalse` type represents false in the system. Its `If` type constructor is overridden to return the second type passed in. Let's use these types:

```
scala> type X[T <: TBool] = T#If[String, Int, Any]
defined type alias X

scala> val x : X[TTrue] = 5
<console>:11: error: type mismatch;
 found    : Int(5)
 required: X[booleans.TTrue]
       val x : X[TTrue] = 5
                          ^

scala> val x : X[TTrue] = "Hi"
x: X[booleans.TTrue] = Hi
```

The `X` type constructor is created to accept an encoding Boolean type and return either the type `String` or the type `Int`. In the next line, the value x is defined with a type of X[TTrue], but because the X type constructor is designed to return the type String when passed the TTrue type, compilation fails because the value is of type Int. The next definition of x succeeds because the X type constructor evaluates to String and the value is of type String.

This mechanism of encoding logic into the type system can be useful at times. One example is heterogeneous lists.

7.4.1 *Heterogeneous typed list*

One feature that's lacking in the Scala standard library but that's available in the Meta-Scala library is a heterogeneous typed list—that is, a type-safe list of values with unbounded size. This is similar to Scala's TupleN classes, except that a heterogeneous typed list supports append operations to grow the list with additional types. The key to a type-safe list is encoding all the types of the list into the type system and preserving them throughout the usage of the list.

Here's an example of a heterogeneous list instantiation:

```
scala> val x = "Hello" :: 5 :: false :: HNil
x: HCons[java.lang.String,HCons[Int,HCons[Boolean,HNil]]] =
  Hello :: 5 :: false :: Nil
```

The preceding line constructs a heterogeneous list comprising of a string, an integer, and a Boolean value. HNil is considered the terminating point of the list, similar to Nil for scala.immutable.List. The return type is interesting. It contains each of the types in the list embedded within HCons types, ending with HNil. The structure of the heterogeneous list is shown in the type. It's a linked list of cons cells, holding a single value type and the rest of the list. There's a special list called HNil, which represents the termination of a list or an empty list.

Figure 7.1 is of the heterogeneous list "Hello" :: 5 :: false :: Nil. The HCons rectangles represent each instance of HCons. The HCons cells are links in the linked list. They also carry around the current type of the head and the remaining type of the list. HCons is a linked list both in physical memory and in the type system. The HNil type represents the termination of the list and is similar to using Nil to terminate reference/pointer based linked lists. HNil will also represent empty in the type system.

TYPE LEVEL PROGRAMMING The key to writing programs that partially execute within the type system is to encode all the required information into the type system. This is the same for creating if/else type constructs or heterogeneous lists.

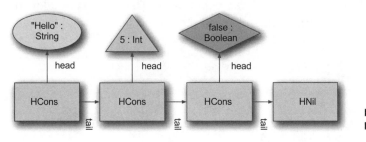

Figure 7.1 Sample heterogeneous list

Let's look at the implementation:

> **Listing 7.10   Basic `HList` implementation**

```
sealed trait HList {}

final case class HCons[H, T <: HList](head : H,          ⟵—— Link type
                                      tail : T)
                             extends HList {
  def ::[T](v : T) = HCons(v,this)
  override def toString = head + " :: " + tail
}
final class HNil extends HList {                          ⟵—— Empty list
  def ::[T](v : T) = HCons(v,this)
  override def toString = "Nil"
}

object HList {
  type ::[H, T <: HList] = HCons[H,T]                     Convenience
  val :: = HCons                                          alias for HCons
  val HNil = new HNil
}
```

This `HList` trait is a marker trait for constructing `HLists`. The `HCons` type encodes a link in a linked list. The value for the head is parameterized and can be any type. The tail is another `HList` but is parameterized as `T`. This is how the type system can capture the complete types of the heterogeneous list. The types are encoded in a linked list of `HCons` types as the values are stored in a linked list of `HCons` values. The `HNil` class also extends `HList` and represents an empty list or the end of list. Finally, the object `HList` is used to provide convenience aliases for the `HCons` and `HNil` types.

> **WHY THE DUPLICATED :: METHOD?**   You may be wondering why, in the simple `HList` implementation, the `::` method is defined in both the `HCons` and `HNil` classes with the same definition. The answer is the full type of the list is required when constructing a new `HCons` cell. If you placed this definition on `HList`, the captured type `T` in any new `HCons` cell would always be only `HList`. This negates the desired effect of preserving the type information in the list. The source code we include in this book, and describe later, has a solution to the problem by using a secondary trait, `HListLike[FullListType]`, that captures the complete type of the current list and defines the `::` method using this type.

The `::` and `HNil` types are encoded as a class with corresponding value because they must be used in type signatures *and* expressions. The class types allow them to be directly referenced in type signatures, and the values allow them to be used as expressions. Let's look at an example:

```
scala> val x : ( String :: Int :: Boolean :: HNil) =
    "Hi" :: 5 :: false :: HNil
x: HList.::[String,HList.::[Int,HList.::[Boolean,HNil]]] =
    Hi :: 5 :: false :: Nil
```

The val x is defined with type String :: Int :: Boolean :: HNil and the expression "Hi" :: 5 :: false :: HNil. If we made HNil an object, the type would instead be String :: Int :: Boolean :: HNil.type.

The HCons class was defined as a case class. Combined with the HNil value, this enables us to extract typed values from a list using pattern matching. Let's pull the values out of the x list constructed earlier:

```
scala> val one :: two :: three :: HNil = x
one: java.lang.String = Hi
two: Int = 5
three: Boolean = false
```

The first line is a pattern match value assignment from list x. The resulting types of one, two, and three are String, Int, and Boolean respectively, and the values are extracted correctly. You can also use this extraction to pull out portions of the list; for example, let's pull the first two elements from the x list:

```
scala> val first :: second :: rest = x
first: String = Hi
second: Int = 5
rest: HList.::[Boolean,HNil] = false :: Nil
```

This line extracts the first and second value into variables called first and second. The rest of the list is placed into a variable called rest. Notice the types of each: first and second have the correct types from the portion of the list, and the rest variables is of type ::[Boolean,HNil] or Boolean :: HNil. This mechanism of extracting typed values from the list is handy, but it'd be nice to have an indexing operation.

The indexing operation can be encoded directly into the type system using functions. Let's take a look at the following listing:

```
scala> def indexAt2of3[A,B,C]( x : (A :: B :: C :: HNil)) =
     |    x match {
     |       case a :: b :: c :: HNil => b
     |    }
indexAt2of3: [A,B,C](x: HList.::[A,HList.::[B,HList.::[C,HNil]]])B

scala> indexAt2of3( 1 :: false :: "Hi" :: HNil )
res5: Boolean = false
```

The indexAt2of3 method takes a heterogeneous list of three elements and returns the second element. The next call shows that the method works and will infer the types from the heterogeneous list.

This direct encoding of indexing operations is less than ideal. An explosion of methods is required to index elements into lists of various sizes. The heterogeneous list would also have support methods like insert into index and remove from index. These operations would have to be duplicated if we used this style of direct encoding. Instead, let's construct a general solution to the problem.

7.4.2   *IndexedView*

Let's construct a type that looks at a particular index and can perform various operations like adding, retrieving, or removing the element at the index. This type is called an `IndexedView` as it represents a view of the heterogeneous list at a given index into the list. To be able to append or remove elements from the list, the view must have access to the types preceding the current index and the types after the current index. The basic trait looks like this:

Listing 7.11   `IndexedView`

```
sealed trait IndexedView {
 type Before <: HList
 type After <: HList
 type At
 def fold[R](f : (Before, At, After) => R) : R
 def get = fold( (_, value, _) => value)
}
```

The `IndexedView` trait defines three abstract types. `Before` is the types of all the elements in the list before the current index. `After` is the types of all elements in the list after the current index. `At` is the type at the current index of the list. The `Indexed-View` trait defines two operations: `fold` and `get`. Fold is used to look at the entire list and return a given value. Fold takes a function that will look at the before, at and after portions of the list. This allows us to use fold to perform operations centered at this current index.

The `get` method is implemented in terms of `fold` to return the value at the current index.

Figure 7.2 shows the `IndexedView` at the third index of heterogeneous list `"Hello"` `:: 5 :: false :: Nil`. At this index, the `Before` type would be `String :: Int ::HNil`. Notice that the `Before` type isn't exactly the same as the previous `HCons` cell, because it's terminated with `HNil` after the previous two types. The important aspect of the `IndexedView` is that it gives us direct access to the type of the current value—that is, we can name the current type using the type parameter `At`. It also preserves the types preceding and following the current type such that we can use them with aggregate functions.

Constructing an `IndexedView` at an index in the list is done recursively. Let's start with the base case of defining an `IndexedView` at the first index of a list.

```
class HListView0[H, T <: HList](val list : H :: T)
    extends IndexedView {
  type Before = HNil
  type After = T
  type At = H
  def fold[R](f : (Before, At, After) => R): R =
    f(HNil, list.head, list.tail)
}
```

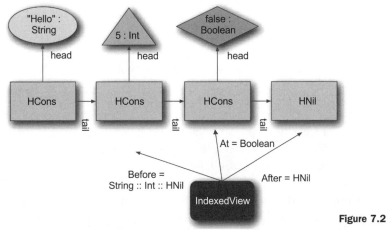

Figure 7.2 IndexedView

IndexedView folds

We can use the fold operation on `IndexedView` to implement many methods that need an index, including `remove`, `append`, and `split`. These methods require a join operation to join two heterogeneous lists. If this `join` method was called `:::`, similar to normal list joins, we could implement these methods on `IndexedView` as:

```
def remove = fold {
  (before, _, after) => before ::: after
}

def insertBefore[B](x : B) = fold {
  (before, current, after) =>
  before ::: (x :: current :: after)
}

def replace[B](x : B) = fold {
  (before, _, after) => before ::: (x :: after)
}

def insertAfter[B](x : B) = fold {
  (before, current, after) => before ::: (current :: x :: after)
}
```

The `:::` method isn't covered in this book and left as an exercise for the reader. For implementation help, see the Meta-Scala library at http://mng.bz/Zw9w.

The class `HListView0` accepts a list of head type H and a tail type of T. The `Before` type is an empty list, as there are no elements before for the first index. The `After` type is the same as the captured type of the list's tail, T. The `At` type is the type of the current head of the list, H. The `fold` method is implemented such that it calls the function f with an empty list, the head and the tail of the list.

The next case of `IndexedView` is the recursive case. Let's create an instance of `IndexedView` that delegates to another `IndexedView`. The idea is that for index N, there are N-1 classes that deconstruct the HList's type to the point where the `HListView0` class can be used. Let's call this recursive class `HListViewN`.

```
final class HListViewN[H, NextIdxView <: IndexedView](
    h : H, next : NextIdxView) extends IndexedView {
  type Before = H :: NextIdxView#Before
  type At = NextIdxView#At
  type After = NextIdxView#After
  def fold[R](f : (Before, At, After) => R) : R =
    next.fold( (before, at, after) =>
      f(HCons(h, before), at, after) )
}
```

The HListViewN class has two type parameters: H and NextIdxView. H is the type at the current head of the list. NextIdxView is the type of the next IndexedView class used to construct an IndexedView. The Before type is the current type parameter H appended to the next indexer's HList. The At type is deferred to the next indexer. The After type is also deferred to the next indexer. The side effect of this is that the At and After types will be determined by an HListView0 and carried down the recursive chain by the HListViewN classes. Finally, the fold operation calls fold on the next IndexedView and wraps the before list with the current value. The HListViewN expands the previous types of an IndexedView.

Figure 7.3 shows the recursive nature of HListViewN. To construct an IndexedView at the third element of an HList requires two HListViewN classes linked to an HListView0 class. The HListView0 class points directly at the cons cell, which holds the third element of the HList. Each instance of the HListViewN class appends one of the previous types of the list to the original HListView0 class. The outer HListViewN class holds the correct types for an IndexedView of the original list at element 2.

One important piece to mention about the HListViewN classes is that they retain references to the elements of the list and recursively rebuild portions of the list in

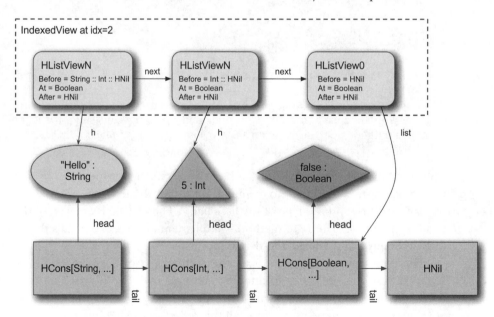

Figure 7.3   Recursive HListViewN

their `fold` method. You can see this in the diagram with the arrows labeled "h". The runtime performance implications are that the farther down a list an index goes, the more recursion required to perform operations.

Now that there's a mechanism to construct `IndexedView` classes at arbitrary depths of the `HList`, there must be a method of constructing these classes. Let's split this process into two. The first will be a mechanism that takes a list and builds a type for the view at index N of that list. The second mechanism is a way of constructing the recursive `IndexedView` types if the final type is known.

For the first mechanism, let's add a type to the `HList` class that will construct an `IndexedView` at a given index value for the current list.

```
sealed trait HList {
  type ViewAt[Idx <: Nat] <: IndexedView
}
```

The `ViewAt` type constructor is defined as constructing a subclass of `IndexedView`. The full value will be assigned in the `HCons` and `HNil` classes respectively. The `ViewAt` type constructor takes a parameter of type `Nat`. `Nat` is a type that we create for this purpose representing natural numbers encoded into the type system. `Nat` is constructed the same way naturally numbers are constructed in mathematical proofs, by building from a starting point.

Listing 7.12 Natural numbers encoded into types

```
sealed trait Nat
object Nat {
  sealed trait _0 extends Nat                           ⊲─── Encoding of 0
   sealed trait Succ[Prev <: Nat] extends Nat
  type _1 = Succ[_0]                                     ⊲─┐ Recursively
   type _2 = Succ[_1]                                      │ created from 0
  ...
  type _22 = Succ[_21]
}
```

The trait `Nat` is used to mark natural number types. The trait `_0` is used to denote the starting point for all natural numbers, zero. The `Succ` trait isn't directly referenced but is used to construct the rest of the natural number set (or at least as many as we wish to type). The types `_1` through `_22` are then defined using the `Succ` trait applied to the previously defined type.

The `Nat` types `_0` through `_22` can now be used to denote indexes into an `HList`. The next step is to use these index values to construct the `IndexedView` type for an `HList` at that index. To do so, let's construct a mechanism to pass type lambdas into natural numbers and build complete types.

```
sealed trait Nat {
  type Expand[NonZero[N <: Nat] <: Up, IfZero <: Up, Up] <: Up
}
```

The `Nat` trait is given a new type called `Expand`. `Expand` takes three type parameters. The first is a type `lambda` that's applied against the previous natural number if the `Nat` isn't _0. The second is the type returned if the natural number is _0. The third type is an upper bound for the first two types to avoid compilation type inference issues. Let's implement this type on the _0 and Succ traits:

```
sealed trait _0 extends Nat {
    type Expand[NonZero[N <: Nat] <: Ret, IfZero <: Ret, Ret] =
      IfZero
}
  sealed trait Succ[Prev <: Nat] extends Nat {
    type Expand[NonZero[N <: Nat] <: Ret, IfZero <: Ret, Ret] =
      NonZero[Prev]
}
```

The _0 trait defines its Expand type to be exactly the second parameter. This is similar to a method call that returns its second parameter. The Succ trait defines its expand method to call the type constructor passed into the first parameter against the previous Nat type. This can be used to recursively build a type by providing a type that uses itself in the NonZero type attribute. Let's use this trick and define the ViewAt type on HList.

```
final case class HCons[H, T <: HList](head: H,
                                      tail: T) extends HList {
    ..
  type ViewAt[N <: Nat] = N#Expand[                        Recursive
    ({ type Z[P <: Nat] = HListViewN[H, T#ViewAt[P]] })#Z,  type
    HListView0[H,T],                                        lambda
    IndexedView]                                            Encoding
}                                                           of 0
```

The ViewAt type is defined as an expansion against the natural number parameter N. The first type parameter to Expand is the recursive type constructor. This type constructor is defined as HListViewN[H, T#ViewAt[P]]. Deconstructing, the type is an HListViewN comprised of the current head type and the tail's ViewAt type applied to the previous natural number (or N-1). Eventually, there will be a ViewAt called for _0 that will return the second parameter, HListView0[H,T]. If a Nat index is passed into the ViewAt type that goes beyond the size of the list, it will fail at compile time with the following message:

```
scala> val x = 5 :: "Hi" :: true :: HNil
x: HCons[Int,HCons[java.lang.String,HCons[Boolean,HNil]]] =
    5 :: Hi :: true :: HNil

scala> type X = x.ViewAt[Nat._11]
<console>:11: error: illegal cyclic reference involving type ViewAt
       type X = x.ViewAt[Nat._11]
```

The compiler will issue an illegal cyclic reference in this instance. Although not exactly the error message desired in this situation, the compiler prevents the invalid index operation.

Now that the indexed type can be constructed for a given index and a given HList, let's encode the construction of the IndexedView into the implicit system. We can do this with a recursive implicit lookup against the constructed IndexedView type.

```
object IndexedView {
  implicit def index0[H, T <: HList](list : H :: T) : HListView0[H,T] =
    new HListView0[H,T](list)
  implicit def indexN[H, T <: HList, Prev <: IndexedView](
      list: (H :: T))(
      implicit indexTail: T => Prev): HListViewN[H,Prev] =
        new HListViewN[H, Prev](list.head, indexTail(list.tail))
}
```

The IndexedView companion object is given two implicit functions: index0 and indexN. The function index0 takes an HList and constructs an indexed view of index _0 on that list. The function indexN takes an HList and an implicit conversion of the tail of the HList into an IndexedView and returns a new IndexedView of the complete list. The type parameters on indexN preserve the types of the head and tail of the list as well as the full type of the IndexedView used against the tail of the list.

Now when the compiler looks for a type Function1[Int :: Boolean :: Nil, HListViewN[Int, HListView0[Boolean, HNil]]], the indexN function will be called with H = Int and T = Boolean :: HNil and Prev = ?. The compiler will then look for an implicit Function1[Boolean :: Nil, ? <: IndexedView]. This is satisfied by the index0 implicit, and the Prev type is filled in as HListView0[Boolean, HNil]. The full implicit value is found, and a constructor of an IndexedView from a HList is available. Now let's write the indexing method itself:

```
trait HCons[H, T <: HList] extends HList {
  type FullType = HCons[H,T]
  def viewAt[Idx <: Nat](
      implicit in: FullType => FullType#ViewAt[Idx]) =
    in(this.asInstanceOf[FullType])
  ...
}
```

The viewAt method is defined as taking a type parameter of the Nat index and an implicit function that constructs the IndexedView from the current list. Now the heterogeneous lists support indexing.

```
scala> val x = 5 :: "Hi" :: true :: HNil
x: HCons[Int,HCons[java.lang.String,HCons[Boolean,HNil]]] =
    5 :: Hi :: true :: HNil

scala> x.viewAt[Nat._1].get
res3: java.lang.String = Hi
```

The first line in the example constructs a heterogeneous list and the second shows how to use a natural number to index into the list (assuming _0 is the first element of the list).

The heterogeneous list demonstrates the power of Scala's type system. It encodes an arbitrary sequence of types and allows type-safe indexing of this sequence. Most type-level programming problems within Scala can be handled using the mechanisms seen with heterogeneous lists, in particular:

- Divide and Conquer: Use recursion to loop over types
- Encode Boolean and integer logic into types
- Use implicit lookup to construct recursive types or return types

This type-level programming is the most advanced usage of the Scala type system that may be required for general development. The simple build tool (SBT) is used to build Scala code that utilizes a different form of the HList presented earlier. Although HLists are complicated, the SBT tool introduces them in a way that's simple and elegant for the user. It's worth going to http://mng.bz/Cdgl and reading how they're used.

7.5   *Summary*

In this chapter, you learned the advanced techniques for utilizing Scala's type system. Implicits allow the capturing of runtime and compile time type constraints. You can use type classes as a general purpose abstraction to associate types with functionality. They are one of the most powerful forms of abstraction within Scala. Finally, we explored in depth the conditional execution and type level programming. This advanced technique tends to be used in core libraries and not as much in user code.

The main theme in all of these sections is that Scala allows developers to preserve type information while writing low-level generic functions. The more type information that can be preserved, the more errors the compiler can catch. For example, the synchronize method defined in section 7.3 was able to prevent accidental argument reversal by capturing the from and to types. The HList class allows developers to create arbitrarily long typed lists of elements that can be modified directly rather than passing around a List[Any] and having to determine the types of each element at runtime. This also prevents users from placing the wrong type at a given index.

Writing low-level generic functions is also important. The less a method or class assumes about its arguments or types, the more flexible it is and the more often it can be reused. In section 7.2, the implicit available of the <:< class was used to add a convenience method directly on the Set class.

The next chapter covers the Scala collections library, and we make heavy use of the concepts defined in this chapter. In particular, the collections library attempts to return the most specific collection type possible after any method call. This has some interesting consequences, as you'll see.

Using the right collection

8

The Scala collections library is the single most impressive library in the Scala ecosystem. It's used in every project and provides myriad utility functions. The Scala collections provide many ways of storing and manipulating data, which can be overwhelming. Because most of the methods defined on Scala collections are available on every collection, it's important to know what the collection types imply in terms of performance and usage patterns.

Scala's collections also split into three dichotomies:

- Immutable and mutable collections
- Eager and delayed evaluation
- Sequential and parallel evaluation

Each of these six categories can be useful. Sometimes parallel execution can drastically improve throughput, and sometimes delaying the evaluation of a method can improve performance. The Scala collections library provides the means for developers to choose the attributes their collections should have. We'll discuss these in sections 8.2 through 8.4

The biggest difficulty with all the new power from the collections library is working generically across collections. We discuss a technique to handle this in section 8.5.

Let's look at the key concepts in the Scala collection library and when to use each.

8.1   Use the right collection

With all the new choices in the Scala collections library, choosing the right collection is important. Each collection has different runtime characteristics and is suited for different styles of algorithms. For example, Scala's `List` collection is a single linked-list and is suited for recursive algorithms that operate by splitting the head off the rest of the collection. In contrast, Scala's `Vector` class is implemented as a set of nested arrays that's efficient at splitting and joining. The key to utilizing the Scala collections library is knowing what the types convey.

In Scala, there are two places to worry about collection types: creating generic methods that work against multiple collections and choosing a collection for a datatype.

Creating generic methods that work across collection types is all about selecting the lowest possible collection type that keeps the generic method performant, but isn't so high up the collections hierarchy that it can't be used for lots of different collections. In fact, the type-system tricks we discuss in section 7.3 can allow you to use type-specialized optimizations generically. We'll show this technique in section 8.5.

Choosing a collection for a datatype is done by instantiating the right collection type for the use case of the data. For example, the `scala.collection.immutable` `.List` class is ideal for recursive algorithms that split collections by head and tail. The `scala.collection.immutable.Vector` collection is suited toward most general purpose algorithms, due to its efficient indexing and its ability to share much of its internal structure when using methods like `+:` and `++`. We'll show this technique in section 8.3.

The core abstractions in the collections library illustrate different styles of collections.

8.1.1   The collection hierarchy

The Scala collection hierarchy is rich in depth. Each level in the hierarchy represents a new set of abstract functions that can be implemented to define a new collection or add performance goals onto the parent class. The collections hierarchy starts with the `Traversable` abstraction and works it way toward `Map`, `Set`, and `IndexedSequence` abstractions. Let's look at the abstract hierarchy of the collections library.

Let's look at the collections hierarchy in figure 8.1.

The collections hierarchy starts with the trait `TraversableOnce`. This trait represents a collection that can be traversed at least once. This trait abstracts between

A rich set of collections

The Scala collections library is rich in choices. It provides a core set of abstractions for collections. This set is branched into several dichotomies:

- Sequential versus parallel
- Eager evaluation versus lazy evaluation
- Immutable versus mutable collections

The core set of abstractions has variants that allow one or more of these differentiators to be true.

Traversable and Iterator. An Iterator is a stream of incoming items where advancing to the next item consumes the current item. A Traversable represents a collection that defines a mechanism to traverse the entire collection but can be traversed repeatedly. The Iterable trait is similar to Traversable but allows the repeated creation of an Iterator. The hierarchy branches out into sequences, maps (also known as *dictionaries*), and sets.

THE GEN* TRAITS   In reality, the collection hierarchy has a duplicate generic variant. Every trait in the hierarchy has a Gen* trait that it inherits from, such as GenTraversableOnce, GenIterator, and GenSeq. The generic variants of collections offer no guarantees on serial or parallel execution, while the traits discussed here enforce sequential execution. The principles behind each collection are the same, but traversal ordering isn't guaranteed for parallel collections. We discuss parallel collections in detail in section 8.4.2.

Let's look at when to use each of the collection types.

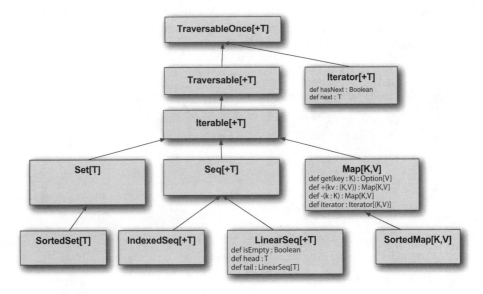

Figure 8.1   Generic collections hierarchy

8.1.2   *Traversable*

The `Traversable` trait is defined in terms of the `foreach` method. This method is an internal iterator—that is, the `foreach` method takes a function that operates on a single element of the collection and applies it to every element of the collection. Traversable collections don't provide any way to stop traversing inside the `foreach`. To make certain operations efficient, the library uses preinitialized exceptions to break out of the iteration early and prevent wasted cycles. This technique is somewhat efficient on the JVM, but some simple algorithms will suffer greatly. The index operation, for example, has complexity $O(n)$ for `Traversable`.

Internal versus external iterators

Iterators can either be internal or external. An internal iterator is one where the collection or owner of the iterator is responsible for walking it through the collection. An external iterator is one where the client code can decide when and how to iterate.

Scala supports both types of iterators with the `Traversable` and `Iterable` types. The `Traversable` trait provides the `foreach` method for iteration, where a client will pass a function for the collection to use when iterating. The `Iterable` trait provides an iterator method, where a client can obtain an iterator and use it to walk through the collection.

Scala also defines `Iterable` as a subclass of `Traversable`. The downside is that any collections that only support internal iterators must extend `Traversable` and nothing else.

When using `Traversable`s, it's best to utilize operations that traverse the entire collection, such as `filter`, `map`, and `flatMap`. `Traversable`s aren't often seen in day-to-day development, but when they are, it's common to convert them into another sort of collection for processing. For example, we'll define a `Traversable` that opens a file and reads its lines for every traversal.

```scala
class FileLineTraversable(file: File) extends Traversable[String] {
  override def foreach[U](f: String => U) : Unit = {
    val input = new BufferedReader(new FileReader(file))
    try {
      var line = input.readLine
      while(line != null) {
        f(line)
        line = input.readLine
      }
    } finally {
      input.close()
    }
  }
  override def toString =
    "{Lines of " + file.getAbsolutePath + "}"
}
```

The `FileLineTraversable` class takes a file in its constructor and extends the `Traversable` trait for `Strings`. The `foreach` method is overridden to open the file and read lines from the file. The lines are passed into the function `f`. The method uses a `try-finally` block to ensure the file is closed after iteration. This implementation means that every time the collection is traversed, the file is opened and all of its contents are enumerated. Finally, the `toString` method is overridden so that when it's called within the REPL, the entire file's contents aren't enumerated. Let's use this class.

```scala
scala> val x = new FileLineTraversable(new java.io.File("test.txt"))
x: FileLineTraversable = {Lines of
/home/.../chapter8/collections-examples/test.txt}

scala> for { line <- x
     |    word <- line.split("\\s+")
     | } yield word
res0: Traversable[java.lang.String] =
  List(Line, 1, Line, 2, Line, 3,
      Line, 4, Line, 5, ")
```

The first line constructs a `FileLineTraversable` against the `test.txt` file. This sample file contains lines that look like the following `Line 1`. The second line iterates over all the lines in the file and splits this line into words before constructing a new list with the words. The result is another `Traversable` of `String` that has all the individual words of the file.

The return type is `Traversable` even though the runtime type of the resulting list of words is a `scala.List`. The starting type in the `for` expression was a `Traversable`, so the resulting type of the expression will also be a `Traversable` without any outside intervention.

One concern with using the `FileLineTraversable` class is that the *entire* file would have to be traversed for any operation on the collection. Although we can't create efficient random element access, the traversable can be terminated early if necessary. Let's modify the definition of `FileLineTraversable` to include logging statements.

```scala
override def foreach[U](f: String => U): Unit = {
    println("Opening file")                          ⟵── Additional logging
     val input = new BufferedReader(new FileReader(file))
    try {
      var line = input.readLine
      while(line != null) {
        f(line)
        line = input.readLine
      }
      println("Done iterating file"
    } finally {
      println("Closing file")
       input.close()
    }
  }
```

The `foreach` method has been modified with logging statements in three places: The first is when the file is opened, the second is when the file has reached its termination state, and the third is when the file is closed. Let's see what happens with a previous example usage:

```
scala> val x = new FileLineTraversable(new java.io.File("test.txt"))
x: FileLineTraversable = {Lines of
  /home/.../scala-in-depth/chapter8/collections-examples/test.txt}

scala> for { line <- x
     |     word <- line.split("\\s+")
     | } yield word
Opening file
Done iterating file
Closing file
res0: Traversable[java.lang.String] =
  List(Line, 1, Line, 2, Line, 3, Line, 4, Line, 5, ")
```

The `FileLineTraversable` is constructed the same as before. But now when trying to extract all the individual words, the logging statements are printed. The file is opened, the iteration is completed, and the file is closed. Now what happens if only the top two lines of the file need to be read?

```
scala> for { line <- x.take(2)                          ◁——  Limit two lines
     |     word <- line.split("\\s+")
     | } yield word
Opening file
Closing file
res1: Traversable[java.lang.String] = List(Line, 1, Line, 2)
```

This time the `take` method is called against the FileLineTraversable. The `take` method is used to limit a collection to the first n elements, or in this case the first two elements. Now when extracting the lines of the file, the `Opening file` and `Closing file` logging statements print, but not the `Done iterating file` statement. This is because the `Traversable` class has an efficient means of terminating `foreach` early when necessary. We do this by throwing a `scala.util.control.ControlThrowable`. This preallocated exception can be efficiently thrown and caught on the JVM.

Carefully catching exceptions

In Scala, some control flows, such as nonlocal closure returns and break statements, are encoded using subclasses of the `scala .util.control.ControlThrowable`. Due to JVM optimizations, this leads to an efficient implementation but requires Scala users to practice restraint in capturing `Exception`s. For example, instead of catching all throwables, when using Scala you should make sure to rethrow `ControlThrowable` exceptions.

```
try { ... } catch {
  case ce : ControlThrowable => throw ce
  case t : Throwable => ...
}
```

It's usually considered bad practice to catch `Throwable` instead of `Exception`. In Scala, if you must catch `Throwable` make sure to rethrow `ControlThrowable`.

The downside to this approach is that the take method will read three lines of the file before the exception is thrown to prevent continued iteration.

Traversable is one of the most abstract and powerful traits in the collections hierarchy. The foreach method is the easiest method to implement for any collection type, but it's suboptimal for many algorithms. It doesn't support random access efficiently and it requires one extra iteration when attempting to terminate traversal early. The next collection type, Iterable, solves the latter point by using an external iterator.

8.1.3 *Iterable*

The Iterable trait is defined in terms of the iterator method. This returns an external iterator that you can use to walk through the items in the collection. This class improves slightly on Traversable performance by allowing methods that need to parse a portion of the collection stop sooner than Traversable would allow.

External iterators are objects you can use to iterate the internals of another object. The Iterable trait's iterator method returns an external iterator of type Iterator. The Iterator supports two methods, hasNext and next. The hasNext method returns true if there are more elements in the collection and returns false otherwise. The next method returns the next element in the collection or throws an exception if there are none left.

One of the downsides to having an external iterator is that collections such as the FileLineTraversable are hard to implement. The traversal of the collection is external to the collection itself, so the FileLineTraversable needs to know when all iterators are completed or no longer used before it can clean up memory/resources. In the worst case, the file may remain open for the entire life of an application. Because of this issue, subclasses of Iterable tend to be standard collections.

The major benefit of the Iterable interface is the ability to coiterate two collections efficiently. For example, let's imagine that there are two lists. The first is a list of names and the second is a list of addresses. We can use the Iterable interface to iterate through both lists at the same time efficiently.

```scala
scala> val names = Iterable("Josh", "Jim")
names: Iterable[java.lang.String] = List(Josh, Jim)

scala> val address = Iterable("123 Anyroad, Anytown St 11111",
                              "125 Anyroad, Anytown St 11111")
address: Iterable[java.lang.String] =
  List(123 Anyroad, Anytown St 11111, 125 Anyroad, Anytown St 11111)

scala> val n = names.iterator
n: Iterator[java.lang.String] = non-empty iterator

scala> val a = address.iterator
a: Iterator[java.lang.String] = non-empty iterator

scala> while(n.hasNext && a.hasNext) {
     |     println(n.next + " lives at " + a.next)
     | }
```

```
Josh lives at 123 Anyroad, Anytown St 11111
Jim lives at 125 Anyroad, Anytown St 11111
```

The first line constructs an `Iterable` of name strings. The second line constructs an `Iterable` of address strings. The value n is created as an external iterator on the name strings. The value a is created as an external iterator on the address strings. The while loop iterates over both the a and n iterators simultaneously.

Zipping collection

Scala defines a `zip` method that will convert two collections into a single collection of pairs. The coiteration program is equivalent to this line of Scala:

```
names.iterator zip address.iterator map { case (n, a) => n+" lives at
           "+a } foreach println
```

The `zip` method is used against names and addresses. The `map` method deconstructs the pairs and constructs the statement <name> lives at <address>". Finally, the statements are sent to the console using the `println` method.

When joining information between two collections, requiring the `Iterable` trait can greatly improve the efficiency of the operation. But we still have an issue with using external iterators on mutable collections. The collection could change without the external iterator being aware of the change:

```
scala> val x = collection.mutable.ArrayBuffer(1,2,3)
x: scala.collection.mutable.ArrayBuffer[Int] = ArrayBuffer(1, 2, 3)

scala> val i = x.iterator
i: Iterator[Int] = non-empty iterator
```

The first line constructs a new `ArrayBuffer` collection (a mutable collection that extends from `Iterable`) with the elements 1, 2, and 3. Next, the value i is constructed as an iterator over the array. Now let's remove all the elements from the mutable structure and see what happens to the i instance:

```
scala> x.remove(0,3)

scala> i.hasNext
res3: Boolean = true
scala> i.next
java.lang.IndexOutOfBoundsException: 0
...
```

The first line is a call to `remove`. This will remove all elements in the collection. The second line calls `hasNext` on the iterator. Because the iterator is external, it isn't aware that the underlying collection has changed and returns true, implying there's a next element. The next line calls the `next` method, which throws a `java.lang.Index-OutOfBoundsException`.

We should use the `Iterable` trait when explicit external iteration is required for a collection, but random access isn't required.

8.1.4 Seq

The Seq trait is defined in terms of the length and apply method. It represents collections that have a sequential ordering. We can use the apply method to index into the collection by its ordering. The length method returns the size of the collection. The Seq trait offers no guarantees on performance of the indexing or length methods. We should use the Seq trait only to differentiate Sets and Maps from sequential collections—that is, if the order in which things are placed into a collections is important and duplicates should be allowed, then the Seq trait should be required.

A good example of when to use a Sequence is when working with sampled data, such as audio. Audio data is recorded at a sampling rate and the order in which it occurs is important in processing that data. Using the Seq trait allows the computation of sliding windows. Let's instantiate some data and compute the sum of elements in sliding windows over the data.

```scala
scala> val x = Seq(2,1,30,-2,20,1,2,0)
x: Seq[Int] = List(2, 1, 30, -2, 20, 1, 2, 0)

scala> x.tails map (_.take(2)) filter (_.length > 1) map (_.sum) toList
res24: List[Int] = List(3, 31, 28, 18, 21, 3, 2)
```

The first line constructs an example input audio sequence. The second line computes the sum of sliding windows. The sliding windows are created using the tails method. The tails method returns an iterator over the tail of an existing collection. This means, each successive collection in the tails iterator has one less element. These collections can be converted into sliding windows using the take method, which ensures only N elements exist (in this case two). Next, we use the filter method to remove windows that are less than the desired size. Finally, the sum method is called on these windows and the resulting collection is converted to a list.

> **The sliding method**
> Scala defines a sliding method on collections that can be used rather than the tails method. The preceding example could be rewritten as follows:
>
> ```scala
> scala> Seq(2,1,30,-2,20,1,2,0).sliding(2).map(_.sum).toList
> res0: List[Int] = List(3, 31, 28, 18, 21, 3, 2)
> ```

Sequence tends to be used frequently in abstract methods when the algorithms are usually targeted at one of its two subclasses: LinearSeq and IndexedSeq. We prefer these where applicable. Let's look at LinearSeq first.

8.1.5 LinearSeq

The LinearSeq trait is used to denote that a collection can be split into a head and tail component. The trait is defined in terms of three "assumed to be efficient" abstract methods: isEmpty, head, and tail. The isEmpty method returns true if the collection is empty. The head method returns the first element of the collection if the collection isn't empty. The `tail` method returns the entire collection minus the head. This type of collection is ideal for tail recursive algorithms that split collections by their head.

The canonical example of a `LinearSeq` is a `Stack`. A `Stack` is a collection that operates like a stack of toys. It's easy to get the last toy placed on the stack, but it could be frustrating to continually remove toys to reach the bottom of the stack. A `LinearSeq` is similar in that it can be decomposed into the head (or top) element and the rest of the collection.

Let's look at how we can use a `LinearSeq` as a stack in a tree traversal algorithm. First, let's define a binary tree datatype.

```
sealed trait BinaryTree[+A]
case object NilTree extends BinaryTree[Nothing]
case class Branch[+A](value: A,
                      lhs: BinaryTree[A],
                      rhs: BinaryTree[A]) extends BinaryTree[A]
case class Leaf[+A](value: A) extends BinaryTree[A]
```

The trait `BinaryTree` is defined as covariant on its type parameter `A`. It has no methods and is sealed to prevent subclasses outside of the current compilation unit. The object `NilTree` represents a completely empty tree. It's defined with the type parameter specified to `Nothing`, which allows it to be used in any `BinaryTree`. The `Branch` class is defined such that it has a value and a left-hand tree and right-hand tree. Finally, the `Leaf` type is defined as a `BinaryTree` that contains only a value. Let's define an algorithm to traverse this `BinaryTree`.

```
def traverse[A, U](t: BinaryTree[A])(f: A => U): Unit = {
    @annotation.tailrec
    def traverseHelper(current: BinaryTree[A],
                       next: LinearSeq[BinaryTree[A]]): Unit =
      current match {
        case Branch(value, lhs, rhs) =>
          f(value)
          traverseHelper(lhs, rhs +: next)
        case Leaf(value) if !next.isEmpty =>
          f(value)
          traverseHelper(next.head, next.tail)
        case Leaf(value) => f(value)
        case NilTree if !next.isEmpty =>
          traverseHelper(next.head, next.tail)
        case NilTree => ()
      }
    traverseHelper(t, LinearSeq())
  }
```

The `traverse` method is defined to take a `BinaryTree` of content elements `A` and a function that operates on the contents and returns values of type `U`. The `traverse` method uses a nested helper method to implement the core of its functionality. The `traverseHelper` method is tail recursive and is used to iterate over all the elements in the tree. The `traverseHelper` method takes the current tree it's iterating over and a `nextLinearSeq`, which contains the elements of the binary tree that it should look at later.

The `traverseHelper` method does a match against the current tree. If the current tree is a branch, it'll send the value at the branch to the function `f` and then recursively call itself. When it does this recursive call, it passes the left-hand tree as the next node to look at and appends the right-hand tree to the *front* of the `LinearSeq` using the `+:` method. Appending the right-hand tree to the `LinearSeq` is a fast operation, usually *O(1)*, due to the requirements of the `LinearSeq` trait.

If the `traverseHelper` method encounters a `Leaf`, the value is sent to the function `f`. But if the `next` stack isn't empty, the stack is decomposed using the `head` and `tail` method. These methods are defined as efficient for the `LinearSeq`, usually *O(1)*. The `head` is passed into the `traverseHelper` method as the current tree and the `tail` is passed as the next stack.

Finally, if the `traverseHelper` method encounters a `NilTree` it operates similarly to when it encounters a `Leaf`. Because a `NilTree` doesn't contain data, only the recursive `traverseHelper` call is needed.

Now, let's construct a `BinaryTree` and see what traversal looks like:

```
scala> Branch(1, Leaf(2), Branch(3, Leaf(4), NilTree))
res0: Branch[Int] = Branch(1,Leaf(2),Branch(3,Leaf(4),NilTree))

scala> BinaryTree.traverse(res0)(println)
1
2
3
4
```

First, a `BinaryTree` is created with two branches and two leaves. Next the `BinaryTree.traverse` method is called against the tree with the method `println` for traversal. The resulting output is each value printed in the expected order: 1, 2, 3, 4.

This technique of manually creating a `Stack` on the `Heap` and deferring work onto it is a common practice when converting a general recursive algorithm into a tail recursive algorithm or an iterative algorithm. When using a functional style with tail recursion, the `LinearSeq` trait is the right collection to use. Let's look at a similar collection, the `IndexedSeq`.

8.1.6 *IndexedSeq*

The `IndexedSeq` trait is similar to the `Seq` trait except that it implies that random access of collection elements is efficient—that is, accessing elements of a collection should be constant or near constant. This collection type is ideal for most general-purpose algorithms that don't involve head-tail decomposition. Let's look at some of the random access methods and their utility.

```
scala> val x = IndexedSeq(1, 2, 3)
x: IndexedSeq[Int] = Vector(1, 2, 3)

scala> x.updated(1, 5)
```

```
res0: IndexedSeq[Int] = Vector(1, 5, 3)
```

An IndexedSeq can be created using the factory method defined on the IndexedSeq object. By default, this will create an immutable Vector, described in section 8.2.1. IndexedSeq collections have an updated method that takes an index and a new value and returns a new collection with the value at the index updated. In the preceding example, the value at index 1 is replaced with the integer 5.

Indexing into an IndexedSeq is done with the apply method. In Scala, a call to an apply method can be abbreviated so that indexing looks like the following:

```
scala> x(2)
res1: Int = 3
```

The expression x(2) is shorthand for x.apply(2). The result of the expression is the value at index 2 of the collection x. In Scala, indexing into any type of collection, including arrays, is done with an apply method rather than specialized syntax.

Sometimes it's more important to check whether or not a collection contains a particular item than it is to retain ordering. The Set collection does this.

8.1.7   Set

The Set trait denotes a collection where each element is unique, at least according to the == method. A Set is the ideal collection to use when testing for the existence of an element in a collection or to ensure there are no duplicates within a collection.

Scala supports three types of immutable and mutable sets: TreeSet, HashSet, and BitSet.

The TreeSet is implemented as a red black tree of elements. A red black tree is a data structure that attempts to remain balanced, preserving *O(log2n)* random access to elements. We find elements in the tree by checking the current node. If the current node is greater than the desired value, we check the left subbranch. If the current node is less than the desired value, then we check the right subbranch. If the elements are equal, then the appropriate node was found. To create a TreeSet, an implicit Ordering type class is required so that the less than and greater than comparisons can be performed.

The HashSet collection is also implemented as a tree of elements. The biggest difference is that the HashSet uses the hash of a value to determine which node in the tree to place an element. This means that elements that have the same hash value are located at the same tree node. If the hashing algorithm has a low chance of collision, HashSets generally outperform TreeSets for lookup speed.

The BitSet collection is implemented as a sequence of Long values. The BitSet collection can store only integer values. A BitSet stores an integer value by setting the bit corresponding to that value to true in the underlying Long value. BitSets are often used to efficiently track and store in memory a large set of flags.

One of the features of Sets in Scala is that they extend from the type (A) => Boolean—that is, a Set can be used as a filtering function. Let's look at mechanisms to limit the values in one collection by another.

```
scala> (1 to 100) filter (2 to 4).toSet
res6: scala.collection.immutable.IndexedSeq[Int] = Vector(2, 3, 4)
```

The range of numbers from 1 to 100 is filtered by the `Set` of numbers from 2 to 4. Note that any collection can be converted into a set (with some cost) using the `toSet` method. Because a `Set` is also a filtering function, it can be passed directly to the `filter` function on the range. The result is that only the numbers 2 through 4 are found in the result of the `filter` call.

Although Scala's `Set` collection provides efficient existence checking on collections, the `Map` collection performs a similar operation on key value pairs.

8.1.8 Map

The `Map` trait denotes a collection of key value pairs where only one value for a given key exists. `Map` provides an efficient lookup for values based on their keys:

```
scala> val errorcodes = Map(1 -> "O NOES", 2 -> "KTHXBAI", 3 -> "ZOMG")
errorcodes: scala.collection.immutable.Map[Int,java.lang.String] =
  Map(1 -> O NOES, 2 -> KTHXBAI, 3 -> ZOMG)

scala> errorcodes(1)
res0: java.lang.String = O NOES
```

The first statement constructs a map of error codes to error messages. The `->` method is from an implicit defined in `scala.Predef`, which converts an expression of the form `A -> B` to a tuple `(A,B)`. The second statement accesses the value at key 1 in the `errorcodes` map.

Scala's `Map` has implementation types for `HashMaps` and `TreeMaps`. These implementations are similar to the `HashSet` and `TreeSet` implementations. The basic rule of thumb is that if the key values have an efficient hashing algorithm with low chance of collisions, then `HashMap` is preferred.

Scala's `Map` provides two interesting use cases that aren't directly apparent from the documentation. The first is that, similarly to `Set`, a `Map` can be used as a partial function from the key type to the value type. Let's take a look.

```
scala> List(1,3) map errorcodes
res1: List[java.lang.String] = List(O NOES, ZOMG)
```

A list of values 1 and 3 is transformed using the `errorcodes` map. For each element in the list, a value is searched for in the `errorcodes` map. The result is a list of error messages corresponding to the previous list of error values.

Scala's `Map` also provides the ability to specify a default value to return in the event a key doesn't yet exist:

```
scala> val addresses =
     |   Map("josh" -> "123 someplace dr").withDefaultValue(
     |     "245 TheCompany St")
addresses: collection.immutable.Map[String,String] =
  Map(josh -> 123 someplace dr)

scala> addresses("josh")
```

```
res0: java.lang.String = 123 someplace dr

scala> addresses("john")
res1: java.lang.String = 245 TheCompany St
```

The addresses map is constructed as the configuration of what mailing address to use for a username. The Map is given a default value corresponding to a local company address where most users are assumed to be located. When looking up the address for user josh, a specific address is found. When looking up the address for the user john, the default is returned.

In idiomatic Scala, we usually use the generic Map type directly. This may be due to the underlying implementation being efficient, or from the convenience of three-letter collection names. Regardless of the original reason, the generic Map type is perfect for general purpose development.

Now that the basic collection types have been outlined, we'll look at a few specific immutable implementations.

8.2   Immutable collections

Immutable collections are the default in Scala and have many benefits over mutable collections in general purpose programming. In particular, immutable collections can be shared across threads without the need for locking.

Scala's immutable collections aim to provide both efficient and safe implementations. Many of these collections use advanced techniques to 'share' memory across differing versions of the collection. Let's look at the three most commonly used immutable collections: Vector, List, and Stream.

8.2.1   Vector

Vectors are the general-purpose utility collection of Scala. Vectors have a $log_{32}(N)$ random element access, which is effectively a small constant on the JVM using 32-bit integer indexes. They're also completely immutable and have reasonable sharing characteristics. In the absence of hard performance constraints, you should make Vectors the default collection. Let's look at its internal structure to see what makes it an ideal collection.

Vectors are composed as a trie on the index position of elements. A *trie* is a tree where every child in a given path down the tree shares some kind of common key as shown in figure 8.2:

This is an example trie storing index values from 0 to 7. The root node of the trie is empty. Each node of the tree contains two values and a left and right branch. Each branch is labeled 0 or 1. The path to any index in the trie can be determined from the binary representation of the number. For example, the number 0 (000) is the 0th index element in the 0 branch from

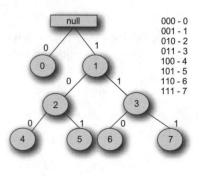

Figure 8.2   **Example index trie with a branching factor of two**

root, while the number 5 (101 in binary) is down the 1 branch from root, the 0 branch of the next node and the 1 branch of the final node. This gives us a well known path down the trie for any index given the binary number.

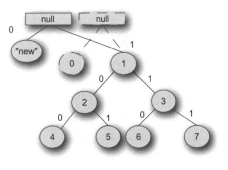

The binary trie can also be efficient. The cost of indexing any random element in the binary index trie is $log_2(n)$, but this can be reduced by using a higher branching factor. If the branching factor was increased to 32, the access time for any element would be

Figure 8.3   Update to trie with sharing

$log_{32}(n)$, which for 32-bit indices is about 7 and for 64-bit indices is about 13. For smaller collections, due to the ordering of the trie, the access time is less. The random access time of elements scales with the size of the trie.

The other property of the trie is the level of sharing that can happen. If nodes are considered immutable, then changing values at a given index can reuse portions of the trie. Let's take a look at this in figure 8.3.

Here's an updated trie where the value at index 0 is replaced with the value new. To create the new trie, two new nodes were created and the rest were reused as is. Immutable collections can benefit a great deal from sharing structure on every change. This can help reduce the overhead of changing the collections. In the worst case, the cost of changing a single element in the trie is $log_2(n)$ for a branching factor of 2. This can be reduced by increasing the branching factor.

Scala's Vector collection is similar to an indexed trie with a branch factor of 32. The key difference is that a Vector represents the branches of a trie as an array. This turns the entire structure into an array of arrays. Figure 8.4 shows what Scala's Vector with branching factor of 2 would look like.

The binary branched Vector has three primary arrays: display0, display1, and display2. These arrays represent the depth of the original trie. Each display element is a successively deeper nested array: display0 is an array of elements, display1 is an array of an array of elements, and display2 is an array of an array of an array of elements. Finding an element in the collection involves determining the depth of the tree and indexing into the appropriate display array the same way that the binary trie was indexed. To find the number 4, the display depth is 2, so the display2 array is chosen. The number 4 is 100 in binary, so the outer array is indexed by 1, the middle array indexed by 0 and the number 4 is located at index 0 of the resulting array.

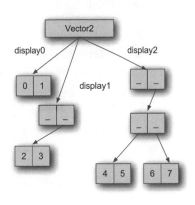

Figure 8.4   Vector's array structure with branching factor of 2

Because Scala's Vector is branched 32 ways, it provides several benefits. As well as scaling lookup times and modification times with the size of the collection, it also provides decent cache coherency because elements that are near each other in the collection are likely to be in the same array in memory. Essential, like C++'s vector, Scala's Vector should be the preferred collection for general-purpose computational needs. Its efficiency combined with the thread-safety gained from immutability make it the most powerful sequence in the library.

Rule 19	**When in doubt, use Vector**

Vector is the most flexible, efficient collection in the Scala collections library. Being immutable, it's safe to share across threads. Its indexing performance is excellent, as are append and prepend. Vector can also become a parallel collection efficiently. When unsure of the runtime characteristics of an algorithm, it's best to use a Vector.

In some situations, Vector isn't the most suited collection. When frequently performing head/tail decomposition, it's better to use an immutable descendant of Scala's LinearSeq trait: scala.collection.immutable.List

8.2.2 List

Scala's immutable List collection is a singly linked list. This can have decent performance if you're always appending or removing from the front of the list, but it can suffer with more advanced usage patterns. Most users coming from Java or Haskell tend to use List as a go-to default from habit. Although List has excellent performance in its intended use case, it's less general than the Vector class and should be reserved for algorithms where it's more efficient.

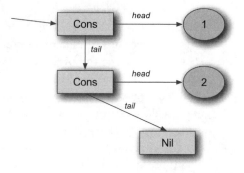

Figure 8.5   **Internal structure of a list**

Let's look at List's general structure in figure 8.5.

List is comprised of two classes: An empty list called Nil and a cons cell, sometimes referred to as a linked node. The cons cell holds a reference to a value and a reference to the rest of the list. Creating a list is as simple as creating cons cells for all the elements in the list. In Scala, the cons cell is called :: and the empty list is called Nil. A list can be constructed by appending elements to the empty list Nil.

```
scala> val x = 1 :: 2 :: 3 :: Nil
x: List[Int] = List(1, 2, 3)
```

This line appends 3 to the empty list and then appends 2 to that list and finally appends 1 to that list. The final effect is a linked list of 1, then 2, then 3. This uses a feature of Scala's operator notation. If an operator ends with the : character, it's considered right associative. The preceding line is equivalent to the following method calls:

```
scala> val x = Nil.::(3).::(2).::(1)
x: List[Int] = List(1, 2, 3)
```

In this version, it's easier to see how the list is constructed. Scala's treatment of the :
character in operator notation is a general concept designed to handle cases like this
where left associativity is not as expressive as right associativity.

The List collection extends from LinearSeq, as it supports *O(1)* head/tail decomposition and prepends.

Lists can support large amounts of sharing as long as you use prepends and
head/tail decomposition. But if an item in the middle of the list needs to be modified,
the front half of the list needs to be generated. This is what makes List less suited to
general-purpose development than Vector.

List is also an eagerly evaluated collection. The head and tail components of a list
are known when the list is constructed. Scala provides a different type of linked list
where the values aren't computed until needed. This collection is called a Stream.

8.2.3 *Stream*

Stream is a lazy persistent collection. A stream can lazily evaluate its members and persist them over time. A stream could represent an infinite sequence without overflow-
ing memory constraints. Streams remember values that were computed during their
lifetime, allowing efficient access to previous elements. This has the benefit of allowing backtracking but the downside of causing potential memory issues.

Scala's Stream class is similar to Scala's List class. A Stream is composed of cons
cells and empty streams. The biggest difference between Stream and List is that
Stream will lazily evaluate itself. Rather than storing elements, a stream stores *function-
objects* that can be used to compute the head element and the rest of the Stream
(tail). This allows Stream to store infinite sequences: a common tactic to join information with another collection. For example, this can be used to join indexes with elements in a sequence.

```
scala> List("a", "b", "c") zip (Stream from 1)
res5: List[(java.lang.String, Int)] = List((a,1), (b,2), (c,3))
```

The list of strings is zipped with an infinite stream of incrementing numbers starting
from 1. The from method on Stream creates an infinitely incrementing stream starting at the passed in number. The zip method does pairwise join at each index element of two sequences. The result is that the elements of the original list are joined
with their original indices. Even though the stream is infinite, the code compiles successfully because the stream is generated only for the indices required by the list.

Constructing a stream can be done similarly to list, except the cons (::) cell is constructed with the #:: method and an empty stream is referred to as Stream.empty.
Let's define a stream and see its execution behavior.

```
scala> val s = 1 #:: {
     |     println("HI")
     |     2
```

```
|  } #:: {
|    println("BAI")
|    3
|  } #:: Stream.empty
s: scala.collection.immutable.Stream[Int] = Stream(1, ?)
```

The stream s is created with three members. The first member is the number 1. The second is an anonymous function that prints HI and returns the value 2. The third is another anonymous function that prints BAI and returns the number 3. These three members are all prepended to an empty stream. The result is a stream of integers where the head is known to be the value 1. Notice that the strings HI and BAI aren't printed. Let's start accessing elements on the stream.

```
scala> s(0)
res39: Int = 1

scala> s(1)
HI
res40: Int = 2

scala> s(2)
BAI
res41: Int = 3
```

When accessing the first element in the stream, the head is returned without touching the rest of the stream. Nothing is printed to the console. But when the second index is accessed, the stream needs to compute the value. When computing the value, the string HI is printed to the console. Only the second value was computed. Next, when indexing into the third value, it must be computed and the BAI string is printed. Now, the stream has computed all of its elements.

```
scala> s
res43: scala.collection.immutable.Stream[Int] = Stream(1, 2, 3)
```

Now when printing the value of the stream to the console, it displays all three elements, because they're persisted. The stream won't recompute the values for indices it has already evaluated.

> **LISTS IN HASKELL VERSUS SCALA**   One area of confusion when coming to Scala from Haskell is the List class. The Haskell language has lazy evaluation by default while Scala has eager evaluation by default. When looking for something from a lazily evaluated list, like Haskell's list, use Scala's Stream, not its List.

One excellent use of Streams is computing the next value of the stream using previous values. This is evident when calculating the Fibonacci sequence, which is a sequence where the next number is calculated using the sum of the previous two numbers.

```
scala> val fibs = {
     |    def f(a:Int,b:Int):Stream[Int] = a #:: f(b,a+b)
     |    f(0,1)
     | }
fibs: Stream[Int] = Stream(0, ?)
```

The fibs stream is defined using a helper function. The helper function f is defined to take two integers and construct the next portion of the Fibonacci sequence from them. The #:: method is used to prepend the first input number to the stream and recursively call the helper function f. The recursive call puts the second number in place of the first and adds the two numbers together to send in as the second number. Effectively, the function f is keeping track of the next two elements in the sequence and outputs one every time it's called, delaying the rest of the calculation. The entire fibs sequence is created by seeding the helper function f with the numbers 0 and 1. Let's take a look at the fib sequence:

```scala
scala> fibs drop 3 take 5 toList
res0: List[Int] = List(2, 3, 5, 8, 13)

scala> fibs
res1: Stream[Int] = Stream(0, 1, 1, 2, 3, 5, 8, 13, ?)
```

This method call drops the first three values of the sequence and takes five values from it and converts them to a list. The resulting portion of the Fibonacci sequence is displayed to the screen. Next, the fibs sequence is printed to the console. Notice that now the fibs sequence prints out the first eight elements. This is because those eight elements of Stream were evaluated. This is the persistence aspect of the Stream working.

Streams don't work well when the eventual size of the stream won't fit into memory. In these instances, it's better to use a TraversableView to avoid performing work until necessary while allowing memory to be reclaimed. See section 8.1.1 for an example. If you need arbitrary high indices into a Fibonacci sequence, the collection could be defined as follows:

```scala
scala> val fibs2 = new Traversable[Int] {
     |   def foreach[U](f: Int => U): Unit = {
     |     def next(a: Int, b: Int): Unit = {
     |       f(a)
     |       next(b, a+b)
     |     }
     |     next(0,1)
     |   }
     | } view
fibs2: TraversableView[Int,Traversable[Int]] = TraversableView(...)
```

The fibs2 collection is defined as a Traversable of integers. The foreach method is defined in terms of a helper method next. The next method is almost the same as the helper method for the fibs stream except that instead of constructing a Stream, it loops infinitely, passing Fibonacci sequence values to the traversal function f. This Traversable is immediately turned into a TraversableView with the view method to prevent the foreach method from being called immediately. A view is a collection that lazily evaluates operations. Views are discussed in detail in section 8.4.1. Now, let's use this version of a lazily evaluated collection.

```
scala> fibs2 drop 3 take 5 toList
res52: List[Int] = List(2, 3, 5, 8, 13)

scala> fibs2
res53: TraversableView[Int,Traversable[Int]] = TraversableView(...)
```

The same drop 3 take 5 toList methods are operated on the fibs2 collection. Similarly to Stream, the Fibonacci sequence is calculated on the fly and values are inserted into the resulting list. But when reinspecting the fibs2 sequence after operating on it, none of the calculated indices are remembered on the TraversableView. This means indexing into the TraversableView repeatedly could be expensive. It's best to save the TraversableView for scenarios where a Stream would not fit in memory.

Stream provides an elegant way to lazily evaluate elements of a collection. This can amortize the cost of calculating an expensive sequence or allow infinite streams to be used. They're simple and easy to use when needed.

Sometimes, mutating collections is necessary for performance reasons. Although mutability should and can be avoided in general development, it's necessary in situations and can be beneficial. Let's look at how to achieve mutability in Scala's collection library.

8.3   *Mutable collections*

Mutable collections are collections that can conceptually change during their lifetime. The perfect example is an array. The individual elements of the array could be modified at any point during the array's lifetime.

In Scala, mutability isn't the default in the collections API. Using or creating mutable collections requires importing one or more interfaces from the scala.collections .mutable package and knowing which methods will mutate the existing collection vs. creating a new collection. For example, the map, flatMap, and filter methods defined on mutable collections will create new collections rather than mutate a collection in place.

The mutable collections library provides a few collections and abstractions that need to be investigated over and above the core abstractions:

- ArrayBuffer
- Mixin mutation event publishing
- Mixin serialization

Let's start looking at ArrayBuffer.

8.3.1   *ArrayBuffer*

The ArrayBuffer collection is a mutable Array that may or may not be the same size as that of the collection. This allows elements to be added without requiring the entire array to be copied. Internally, an ArrayBuffer *is* an Array of elements, as well as the stored current size. When an element is added to an ArrayBuffer, this size is checked. If the underlying array isn't full, then the element is directly added to the array. If the underlying array is full, then a larger array is constructed and all the elements are copied to the new array. The key is that the new array is constructed larger than required for the current addition.

Although the entire array is copied into the new array on some append operations, the *amortized* cost for append is a constant. Amortized cost is the cost calculated over a long time—that is, during the lifetime of an ArrayBuffer, the cost of appending averages out to be linear across all the operations, even though any given append operation could be *O(1)* or *O(n)*. This property makes ArrayBuffer a likely candidate for most mutable sequence construction.

The ArrayBuffer collection is similar to Java's java.util.ArrayList. The main difference between the two is that Java's ArrayList attempts to amortize the cost of removing and appending to the front *and* back of the list whereas Scala's ArrayBuffer is only optimized for adding and removing to the end of the sequence.

The ArrayBuffer collection is ideal for most situations where mutable sequences are required. In Scala, it's the mutable equivalent of the Vector class. Let's look at one of the abstractions in the mutable collections library, mixin mutation event publishing.

8.3.2 *Mixin mutation event publishing*

Scala's mutable collection library provides three traits, ObservableMap, Observable-Buffer, and ObservableSet, that can be used to listen to mutation events on collections. Mixing one of these traits into the appropriate collection will cause all mutations to get fired as events to observers. These events are sent to observers, and the observers have a chance to prevent the mutation. Here's an example:

```
scala>    object x extends ArrayBuffer[Int] with ObservableBuffer[Int] {
     |        subscribe(new Sub {
     |          override def notify(pub: Pub,
     |                              evt: Message[Int] with Undoable) = {
     |            Console.println("Event: " + evt + " from " + pub)
     |          }
     |        })
     |    }
defined module x
```

The object x is created as an ArrayBuffer that mixes in the ObservableBuffer. In the constructor, a subscriber is registered that prints events as they happen:

```
scala> x += 1
Event: Include(End,1) from ArrayBuffer(1)
res2: x.type = ArrayBuffer(1)

scala> x -= 1
Event: Remove(Index(0),1) from ArrayBuffer()
res3: x.type = ArrayBuffer()
```

Adding the element 1 to the collection causes the Include event to be fired. This event indicates that a new element is included in the underlying collection. Next the element 1 is removed from the collection. The result is a Remove event, indicating the index and value that was removed.

The full details of the event API for collection mutation is contained in the `scala.collection.script` package. The API is designed for advanced use cases such as data binding. Data binding is a practice where one object's state is controlled from another object's state. This is common in UI programming, where a list displayed onscreen could be tied directly to a Scala `ArrayBufferwithObservableBuffer`. That way, any changes to the underlying `ArrayBuffer` would update the display of the UI element.

Scala's mutable collection library also allows mixins to be used to synchronize operations on collections.

8.3.3   *Mixin synchronization*

Scala defines the traits `SynchronizedBuffer`, `SynchronizedMap`, `SynchronizedSet`, `SynchronizedStack`, and `SynchronizedPriorityQueue` for modifying the behavior of mutable collections. A `Synchronized*` trait can be used on its corresponding collection to enforce atomicity of operations on that collection.

These traits effectively wrap methods on collections with a `this.synchronized{}` call. Although this is a neat trick to aid in thread safety, these traits are little used in practice. It's better to use mutable collections in single threaded scenarios and promote immutable collections for cross thread data sharing.

Let's look at an alternative solution to parallelizing and optimizing collection usage: Views and Parallel collections.

8.4   *Changing evaluation with views and parallel collections*

The base collection in the collection hierarchy defaults to strict and sequential evaluation. Strict evaluation is when operations are performed immediately when they're defined. This is in contrast to lazy evaluation where operations can be deferred. Sequential evaluation is when operations are performed sequentially without parallelism against a collection. As shown in figure 8.6, this is in contrast to parallel evaluation where evaluation could happen on multiple threads across portions of the collection.

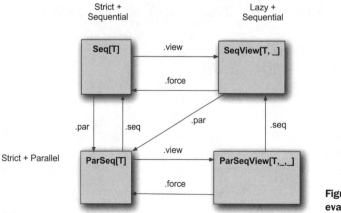

Figure 8.6   Changing evaluation semantics

The collections library provides two standard mechanisms to migrate from the default evaluation semantics into either parallel or lazy evaluation. These take the form of the view and par methods. The view method can take any collection and efficiently create a new collection that will have lazy evaluation. The force method is the inverse of the view method. It's used to create a new collection that has strict evaluation of its operations. Views will be covered in detail in section 8.4.1.

In a similar fashion, the par method is used to create a collection that uses parallel execution. The inverse of the par method is the seq method, which converts the current collection into one that supports sequential evaluation.

One important thing to note in the diagram is what happens when calling the par method on a View. As of Scala 2.9.0.1, this method call converts a sequential lazy collection into a parallel strict collection rather than a parallel lazy collection. This is due to how the encoding of types work. Let's investigate this mechanism some more.

8.4.1 Views

The collections in the collections library default to strict evaluation—that is, when using the map method on a collection, a new collection is immediately created before continuing with any other function call. Collections views are lazily evaluated. Method calls on a view will only be performed when they absolutely have to. Let's look at a simple example using List.

```
scala> List(1,2,3,4) map {  i => println(i); i+1 }
1
2
3
4
res1: List[Int] = List(2, 3, 4, 5)
```

This line constructs a list and iterates over each of its elements. During this iteration, the value is printed and the value is modified by one. The result is that each element gets printed to the string and the resulting list is created. Let's do the same thing, except this time we'll change from using a List to a ListView.

```
scala> List(1,2,3,4).view map {  i => println(i); i+1 }
res2: scala.collection.SeqView[Int,Seq[_]] = SeqViewM(...)
```

This expression is the same as the previous one, except the view method is called on List. The view method returns a view or window looking at the current collection that delays all functions as long as possible. The map function call against the view is not performed. Let's modify the result so that the values are printed.

```
scala> res2.toList
1
2
3
4
res3: List[Int] = List(2, 3, 4, 5)
```

The `toList` method is called against the `view` from the previous example. Because the `view` must construct a new collection, the map function that was deferred before is executed and the value of each item of the original list is printed. Finally, the value of the new list, with each element incremented by one, is returned.

Views pair well with `Traversable` collections. Let's reexamine the `FileLine-Traversable` class from before. This class opens a file and iterates over the lines for every traversal. This can be combined with a view to create a collection that will load and *parse* a file when it's iterated.

Rule 20

Use TraversableView for ephemeral streams of data

`Traversable` views provide the best flexibility between simplicity in implementation, runtime cost, and utility for ephemeral streams of data. If the data is only streamed once, a `TraversableView` can get the job done.

Let's imagine that a system has a simple property configuration file format. Every line of a `config` file is a key-value pair separated by the = character. Any = character is considered a valid identifier. Also, any line that doesn't have an = character is assumed to be a comment. Let's define the parsing mechanism.

```
def parsedConfigFile(file: java.io.File) = {
    val P = new scala.util.matching.Regex("([^=]+)=(.+)")
    for {
      P(key,value) <- (new FileLineTraversable(file)).view
    } yield key -> value
  }
```

The `parsedConfigFile` takes in the `config` file to parse. The value `P` is instantiated as a regular expression. The expression matches lines that have a single = sign with content on both sides. Finally, a `for` expression is used to parse the file. A `FileLine-Traversable` is constructed and the `view` method is called on this traversable, delaying any real execution. The regular expression `P` is used to extract key-value pairs and return them. Let's try it out in the REPL.

```
scala> val config = parsedConfigFile(new java.io.File("config.txt"))
config: TraversableView[(String, String),Traversable[_]] =
  TraversableViewFM(...)
```

The `parsedConfigFile` method is called with a sample `config` file. The `config` contains two attribute value pairs that are numbered. Notice that the file isn't opened and traversed. The return type is a `TraversableView` of (String,String) values. Now, when the configuration file should be read, the force method can be used to force evaluation of the view.

```
scala> config force
Opening file
Done iterating file
Closing file
res13: Traversable[(String, String)] =
  List((attribute1,value1), (attribute2,value2))
```

The force method is called on the config TraversableView. This causes strict evaluation of the deferred operations. The file is opened and iterated, pulling out all the parsable lines; these values are returned into the result.

Using views with Traversables is a handy way to construct portions of a program and delay their execution until necessary. For example, in an old Enterprise JavaBeans application, I constructed a parsable TraversableView that would execute an RMI call into the ApplicationServer for the current list of "active" data and perform operations on this list. Although there were several operations to whittle down and transform the data after it was returned from the ApplicationServer, these could be abstracted behind the TraversableView, similarly to how the config file example exposed a TraversableView of key value pairs rather than a TraversableView of the raw file.

Let's look at another way to change the execution behavior of collections: parallelization.

8.4.2 *Parallel collections*

Parallel collections are collections that attempt to run their operations in parallel.

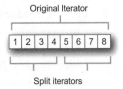

Original Iterator

Split iterators

Figure 8.7 Splitting parallel collection iterators

Parallel collections are implemented in terms of Splitable iterators. A Splitable iterator is an iterator that can be efficiently split into multiple iterators where each iterator owns a portion of the original iterator.

Figure 8.7 shows a Splitable iterator that originally points to a collection of the numbers 1 through 8. In the example, the Splitable iterator is split into two iterators. The first covers the numbers 1 through 4 and the second covers the numbers 5 through 8. These split iterators can be fed to different threads for processing.

The Parallel collection operations are implemented as tasks on Splitable iterators. Each task could be run using a parallel executor, by default a ForkJoinPool, initialized with a number of worker threads equal to the number of processors available on the current machine. Tasks themselves can be split, and each task defines a threshold it can use to determine whether it should be split further.

Let's look at figure 8.8 to see what might happen in parallel when calculating the sum of elements in a parallel collection.

The sum method on the collection of one to eight is split into seven tasks. Each task computes the sum of the numbers below it. If a task contains more numbers than the threshold, assumed to be two in this example, the collection is split and more sum tasks are thrown on the queue.

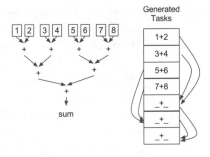

Figure 8.8 Parallel task breakdown of sum method

These tasks are farmed out to a `ForkJoinPool` and executed in parallel. A `ForkJoin-Pool` is like a thread pool, but with better performance for tasks that fork (split) first and join (combine) later.

When using parallel collections, there are two things to worry about:

- The efficiency of converting from a sequential to a parallel collection
- The parallelizability of a task

The collections library does its best to reduce the cost of the first. The library defines a `ParArray` collection that can take `Arrays`, and `Array`-based collections, and convert them into their parallel variant. The library also defines a `ParVector` collection that can efficiently, in *O(1)* time, convert from a `Vector` to a `ParVector`. In addition to these, the library has a mechanism to parallelize `Set`, `Map`, and the `Range` collections. The collections that aren't converted efficiently are those that subclass from `LinearSeq`. Let's take a look.

```scala
scala> List(1,2,3).par
res18: collection.parallel.immutable.ParSeq[Int] = ParVector(1, 2, 3)
```

In this example, a `List` of three numbers is converted to a parallel collection using the `par` method. The result is a `ParVector`. The runtime complexity of this operation is *O(N)* because the library has to construct a `Vector` from the `List`. If this overhead, combined with the overhead of parallelizing, is less than the runtime of an algorithm, it can still make sense to parallelize `LinearSeq`. But in most cases, it's best to avoid `LinearSeq` and its descendants when using parallel collections.

The second thing to worry about with parallel collections is the parallelizability of a task. This is the amount of parallelism that can be expected from a given task. For example, the `map` method on collections can have a huge amount of parallelism. The `map` operation takes each element of a collection and transforms it into something else, returning a new collection. This is ideal for parallel collections.

```scala
scala> ParVector(1,2,3,4) map (_.toString)
res22: collection.parallel.immutable.ParVector[java.lang.String] =
  ParVector(1, 2, 3, 4)
```

The preceding constructs a parallel vector of integers and converts all the elements to their string representation.

One method that doesn't have any parallelism is the `foldLeft` method. The `fold-Left` method on collections takes an initial value and a binary operation and performs the operation over the elements in a left-associative fashion. For example, given a collection of the values 1, 2, 3, and 4 and an initial value of 0, the binary operation + would be applied as follows: $(((0 + 1) + 2) + 3) + 4)$. The association requires that the operations be performed in sequence. If this were used on a parallel collection to compute the sum of elements in the collection, it would not execute in parallel. Let's take a look:

```scala
scala> (1 to 1000).par.foldLeft(0)(_+_)
res25: Int = 500500
```

A parallel range is constructed with the values 1 through 1,000. The `foldLeft` method is called with an initial value of `0` and an operation of `+`. The result is the correct sum, but there's no indication of whether this was parallelized. Let's use a cheap trick to figure out if the `foldLeft` is parallelized.

```scala
scala> (1 to 1000).par.foldLeft(Set[String]()) {
     |   (set,value) =>
     |     set + Thread.currentThread.toString()
     | }
res30: scala.collection.immutable.Set[String] =
  Set(Thread[Thread-26,5,main])
```

This time the `foldLeft` method is called with an empty `Set` of strings. The binary operation appends the current executing thread to the set. But if the same trick is used with the `map` operation, more than one thread will be displayed on a multicore machine:

```scala
scala> (1 to 1000).par map { ignore =>
     |   Thread.currentThread.toString
     | } toSet
res34: collection.parallel.immutable.ParSet[java.lang.String] = ParSet(
    Thread[ForkJoinPool-1-worker-0,5,main],
    Thread[ForkJoinPool-1-worker-1,5,main])
```

The parallel range from 1 to 1,000 is created and the `map` operation is called. The `map operation` converts each element to the current thread it's running in, and the resulting list of threads is converted to a `Set`, effectively removing duplicates. The resulting list on my dual-core machine has two threads. Notice that unlike the previous example, the threads are from the default `ForkJoinPool`.

So, using parallel collections for parallelism requires using the parallelizable operations. The API documentation does a good job marking which operations are parallelizable, so it's best to take a thorough read through the scaladoc in the `scala.collection.parallel` package.

With all these different collection types, it can be difficult to write generic methods that need to work against many collection types. We'll discuss some mechanisms to do this.

8.5 *Writing methods to use with all collection types*

The new collections library goes to great lengths to ensure that generic methods, like `map`, `filter`, and `flatMap` will return the most specific type possible. If you start with a `List`, you should expect to retain a `List` for the duration of computations unless you perform some sort of transformation. You can do this property through a few type system tricks. Let's look at implementing a generic sort algorithm against collections.

A naive approach would be the following:

```scala
object NaiveQuickSort {
  def sort[T](a: Iterable[T])(implicit n: Ordering[T]): Iterable[T] =
    if (a.size < 2) a
    else {
      import n._
```

```
      val pivot = a.head
      sort(a.filter(_ < pivot)) ++
      a.filter(_ == pivot) ++
      sort(a.filter(_ > pivot))
  }
}
```

The NaiveQuickSort object is defined with a single method sort. The sort method implements a quick sort. It takes in an Iterable of elements of type T. The implicit parameter list accepts the type class Ordering for the type T. This is what's used to determine if one of the elements of the Iterable is larger, smaller, or equal to another. Finally, the function returns an Iterable. The implementation pulls a pivot element and splits the collection into three sets: elements less than the pivot, elements greater than the pivot, and elements equal to the pivot. These sets are then sorted and combined to create the final sorted list.

This algorithm works for most collections but has one obvious flaw:

```
scala> NaiveQuickSort.sort(List(2,1,3))
res12: Iterable[Int] = List(1, 2, 3)
```

The NaiveQuickSort.sort method is called with an unsorted List. The result is a sorted collection, but the type is Iterable, not List. The method does work, but the loss of the List type is undesirable. Let's see if the sort can be modified to retain the original type of the collection, if possible.

```
object QuickSortBetterTypes {
  def sort[T, Coll](a: Coll)(implicit ev0: Coll <:< SeqLike[T, Coll],
                             cbf: CanBuildFrom[Coll, T, Coll],
                             n: Ordering[T]): Coll = {
    if (a.length < 2)
      a
    else {
      import n._
      val pivot = a.head
      val (lower : Coll, tmp : Coll) = a.partition(_ < pivot)
      val (upper : Coll, same : Coll) = tmp.partition(_ > pivot)
      val b = cbf()
      b.sizeHint(a.length)
      b ++= sort[T,Coll](lower)
      b ++= same
      b ++= sort[T,Coll](upper)
      b.result
    }
  }
}
```

The QuickSortBetterTypes object is created with a single method, sort. The guts of the algorithm are the same as before, except a generic builder is used to construct the sorted list. The biggest change is in the signature of the sort method, so let's deconstruct it.

T is the type parameter representing elements of the collection. T is required to have an Ordering in this method (the implicit n : Ordering[T] parameter in the second parameter list). The ordering members are imported on the first line of the method. This allows the < and > operations to be "pimped" onto the type T for convenience. The second type parameters is `Coll`. This is the concrete `Collection` type. Notice that *no type bounds are defined.* It's a common habit for folks new to Scala to define generic collection parameters as follows: `Col[T] <: Seq[T]`. Don't do this, as this type doesn't quite mean what you want. Instead of allowing any subtype of a sequence, it allows only subtypes of a sequence that *also* have type parameters (which is most collections). You can run into issues if your collection has no type parameters or more than one type parameter. For example:

```
object Foo extends Seq[Int] {...}
trait DatabaseResultSetWalker[T, DbType] extends Seq[T] {...}
```

Both of these will fail type checking when trying to pass them into a method taking `Col[T] <: Seq[T]`. For the `object Foo`, this is because it has no type parameters, but the constraint `Col[T] <: Seq[T]` *requires* a single type parameter. The `Database-ResultSetWalker` trait can't match `Col[T] <: Seq[T]` because it has two type parameters, where the requirement is for only one. Although there are workarounds, that requirement can be surprising to users of the function. The workaround is to defer the type-checking algorithm using the implicit system (see section 7.2.3).

To get the compiler to infer the type parameter on the lower bound, we have to defer the type inferencer long enough for it to figure out all the types. To do that, we don't enforce the type constraint until we do the implicit lookup using the `<:<` class. The first implicit parameter `ev0 : Coll <:< SeqLike[T, Coll]` is used to ensure that the type `Coll` is a valid collection type with elements of T. This signature uses the Seq-Like class. Although most consider the `SeqLike` classes to be an implementation detail, they're important when implementing any sort of generic method against collections. `SeqLike` captures the original fully typed collection in its second type parameter. This allows the type system to carry the most specific type through a generic method so that it can be used in the return value.

> **DEFERRING TYPE INFERENCE OF PARENT-CLASS TYPE PARAMETERS** The need to defer the type inference for a type parameter `Foo <: Seq[T]` is necessary for supporting the Scala 2.8.x series. As of the Scala 2.9.x, the type inference algorithm was improved such that the implicit `<:<` parameter is no longer necessary.

The next type parameter in the `sort` method is the `cbf : CanBuildFrom[Coll, T, Coll]`. The `CanBuildFrom` trait, when looked up implicitly, determines how to build new collections of a given type. The first type parameter represents the original collection type. The second type parameter represents the type of elements desired in the *built* collection—that is, the type of elements in the collection the method is going to return. The final type parameter of `CanBuildFrom` is the full type of the new collection. This is the same type as the input collection in the case of `sort`, because the sort algorithm should return the same type of collection that came in.

The CanBuildFrom class is used to construct the builder b. This builder is given a sizeHint for the final collection and is used to construct the final sorted collection rather than calling the ++ method directly. Let's look at the final result.

```
scala> QuickSortBetterTypes.sort(
     |    Vector(56,1,1,8,9,10,4,5,6,7,8))
res0: scala.collection.immutable.Vector[Int] =
  Vector(1, 1, 4, 5, 6, 7, 8, 8, 9, 10, 56)

scala> QuickSortBetterTypes.sort(
     |    collection.mutable.ArrayBuffer(56,1,1,8,9,10,4,5,6,7,8))
res1: scala.collection.mutable.ArrayBuffer[Int] =
  ArrayBuffer(1, 1, 4, 5, 6, 7, 8, 8, 9, 10, 56)
```

The first line calls the new sort method against an unordered Vector of Ints. The resulting type is also a Vector of Ints. Next, the sort method is called against an ArrayBuffer of Ints. The result is again an ArrayBuffer of Ints. The new collection method now preserves the most specific type possible.

LinearSeqLike and recursive type definitions

The method signature doesn't work as is against the LinearSeqLike trait, because the LinearSeqLike trait defines its type parameters as LinearSeqLike[T, Col <: LinearSeqLike[T,Col]]. The second type parameter is recursive. The type Col appears in its own type constraint. In Scala 2.9, the type inferencer can still correctly deduce subclasses of LinearSeqLike. Here's an example method that will do head-tail decomposition on subclasses of LinearSeqLike.

```
def foo[T, Coll <: LinearSeqLike[T, Coll]](t : Coll with
LinearSeqLike[T,Coll]) : Option[(T, Coll)]
```

The method foo has two type parameters. The parameter T is the type of elements in the collection. The type parameter Coll is the full type of the collection and is recursive, like in the definition of the LinearSeqLike trait. This alone won't allow Scala to infer the correct types. The parameter list accepts a single parameter t with type Coll with LinearSeqLike[T,Coll]. Although the Coll type parameter has the type bound that <: LinearSeqLike[T,Coll], the with keyword must also be used to explicitly join the Coll type with LinearSeqLike[T,Coll]. Once this is completed, type inference will work correctly for Coll.

This implementation of sort is generic but may be suboptimal for different types of collections. It would be ideal if the algorithm could be adapted such that it was optimized for each collection in the hierarchy. This is easy to do as a maintainer of the collections library, because the implementations can be placed directly on the classes. But when developing new algorithms outside the collections library, type classes can come to the rescue.

8.5.1 Optimizing algorithms for each collections type

You can use the type class paradigm to encode an algorithm against collections and *refine* that algorithm when speed improvements are possible. Let's start by converting the generic sort algorithm from before into a type class paradigm. First we'll define the type class for the sort algorithm.

```
trait Sortable[A] {
    def sort(a : A) : A
  }
```

The `Sortable` type class is defined against the type parameter `A`. The type parameter `A` is meant to be the full type of a collection. For example, sorting a list of integers would require a `Sortable[List[Int]]` object. The `sort` method takes a value of type `A` and returns a sorted version of type `A`. The generic sort method can now be modified to look as follows:

```
object Sorter {
  def sort[Col](col : Col)(implicit s : Sortable[Col]) = s.sort(col)
}
```

The `Sorter` object defines a single method `sort`. The generic `sort` method now takes in the `Sortable` type class and uses it to sort the input collection. Now the implicit resolution of default `Sortable` types needs to be defined.

```
trait GenericSortTrait {
  implicit def quicksort[T,Coll](
        implicit ev0: Coll <:< IterableLike[T, Coll],
        cbf: CanBuildFrom[Coll, T, Coll],
        n: Ordering[T]) =
    new Sortable[Coll] {
      def sort(a: Coll) : Coll =
        if (a.size < 2)
          a
        else {
          import n._
          val pivot = a.head
          val (lower: Coll, tmp: Coll) = a partition (_ < pivot)
          val (upper: Coll, same: Coll) = tmp partition (_ > pivot)
          val b = cbf()
          b.sizeHint(a.size)
          b ++= sort(lower)
          b ++= same
          b ++= sort(upper)
          b.result
        }
    }
}
```

The `GenericSortTrait` is defined to contain the implicit look up for the generic `QuickSort` algorithm. It has the single implicit method `quicksort`. The `quicksort` method defines the same type parameters and implicit parameters as the original sort method. Instead of sorting, it defines a new instance of the `Sortable` type trait.

The `Sortable.sort` method is defined the same as before. Now the `GenericSort-Trait` has to be placed onto the `Sortable` companion object so that it can be looked up in the default implicit resolution.

```
object Sortable extends GenericSortTrait
```

The `Sortable` companion object is defined to extend the `GenericSortTrait`. This places the implicit `quicksort` method in the implicit lookup path when looking for the `Sortable[T]` type trait. Let's try it out.

```
scala> Sorter.sort(Vector(56,1,1,8,9,10,4,5,6,7,8))
res0: scala.collection.immutable.Vector[Int] =
  Vector(1, 1, 4, 5, 6, 7, 8, 8, 9, 10, 56)
```

The `Sorter.sort` method is called. The appropriate `Sortable` type trait is found for `Vector` and the collection is sorted using the `quicksort` algorithm. But if we try to call the sort method against something that doesn't extend from `IterableLike`, it won't work. Let's try the sort method on `Array`.

```
scala> Sorter.sort(Array(2,1,3))
<console>:18: error: could not find implicit value for
  parameter s: Sorter.Sortable[Array[Int]]
      Sorter.sort(Array(2,1,3))
```

The `Sorter.sort` method is called with an unsorted array. The compiler complain that it can't find a `Sortable` instance for `Array[Int]`. This is because `Array` does *not* extend from `Iterable`. Scala provides an implicit conversion that will wrap an `Array` and provide it with standard collection methods. Let's provide an implementation of sort for `Array`. For simplicity, we'll use a selection sort.

```
trait ArraySortTrait {
  implicit def arraySort[T](implicit mf: ClassManifest[T],
                            n: Ordering[T]): Sortable[Array[T]] =
    new Sortable[Array[T]] {
      def sort(a : Array[T]) : Array[T] = {
        import n._
        val b = a.clone
        var i = 0
        while (i < a.length) {
          var j = i
          while (j > 0 && b(j-1) > b(j)) {
            val tmp = b(j)
            b(j) = b(j-1)
            b(j-1) = tmp
            j -= 1
          }
          i += 1
        }
        b
      }
    }
}
```

The trait `ArraySortTrait` is defined with a single method `arraySort`. This method constructs a `Sortable` type trait using a `ClassManifest` and an `Ordering`. Using raw `Arrays` in Scala requires a `ClassManifest` so that the bytecode will use the appropriate method against the primitive arrays. The `Sortable` type trait is parameterized against `Arrays`. The algorithm loops through each index in the array and looks for the smallest element in the remainder of the array to swap into that position. The selection sort algorithm isn't the most optimal, but it's a common algorithm and easier to understand than what's used classically in Java. This `Sortable` implementation needs to be added to the appropriate companion object for implicit resolution.

```
object Sortable extends ArraySortTrait with QuickSortTrait
```

The `Sortable` companion object is expanded to extend from both the `ArraySort-Trait`, containing the `Sortable` type class for `Array`, and the `QuickSort` trait, containing the `Sortable` type class for iterable collections. Let's use this implementation now.

```
scala> Sorter.sort(Array(2,1,3))
res0: Array[Int] = Array(1, 2, 3)
```

Now, when calling the `sort` method with `Arrays`, the call succeeds. You can use this technique to support any number of collections and to specialize behavior for collections using techniques shown in section 7.3.

Scala provides all the right tools to generically deal with collections. The complexity of doing so can be high, so it's a judgment call when and how much abstraction is required for a particular method against collections.

8.6   Summary

The Scala collections library is one of the most compelling reasons to use Scala. From the power and versatility of the collection to the ability to preserve specific types on generic methods, Scala collections provide a clean and elegant solution to most problems. Using the collections API is a matter of understanding what the various type signatures mean and knowing how to flow between collection semantics and evaluation styles. Although the API is geared for immutability, there's more than enough support for mutable collections and interfaces.

This chapter provides a great introduction to the key concepts behind the collections API, but knowing the methods defined on the collections and how to string them together is also important. Because the collections library is always improving, the best source for learning these methods is the scaladoc documentation for the current release.

The next chapter covers Scala actors, which are another important concept in the Scala ecosystem.

9

Actors

Actors are an abstraction on a synchronous processes. They communicate to the external world by sending and receiving messages. An actor will process received messages sequentially in the order they're received, but will handle only one message at a time. This is critical, because it means that actors can maintain state without explicit locks. Actors can also be asynchronous or synchronous. Most actors won't block a thread when waiting for messages, although this can be done if desired. The default behavior for actors is to share threads among each other when handling messages. This means a small set of threads could support a large number of actors, given the right behavior.

In fact, actors are great state machines. They accept a limited number of input messages and update their internal state. All communication is done through messages and each actor stands alone.

But actors won't solve all issues your system faces. You have to know how to use them.

9.1 Know when to use actors

Actors aren't parallelization factories; they process their messages in single-threaded fashion. They work best when work is conceptually split and each actor can handle a portion of the work. If the application needs to farm many similar tasks out for processing, this requires a large pool of actors to see any concurrency benefits.

Actors and I/O should be interleaved carefully. Asynchronous I/O and actors are a natural pairing, as the execution models for these are similar. Using an actor to perform blocking I/O is asking for trouble. That actor can starve other actors during this processing. This can be mitigated, as we'll discuss in section 9.4.

Although many problems can be successfully modeled in actors, some will benefit more. The architecture of a system designed to use actors will also change fundamentally. Rather than relying on classic Model-View-Controller and client-based parallelism, an actors system parallelizes pieces of the architecture and performs all communication asynchronously.

Let's look at a canonical example of a good system design using actors. This example uses several tools found in the old Message Passing Interface (MPI) specification used in supercomputing. MPI is worth a look, as it holds a lot of concepts that have naturally translated into actor-based systems.

9.1.1 Using actors to search

Let's design a classic search program. This program has a set of documents that live in some kind of search index. Queries are accepted from users and the index is searched. Documents are scored and the highest scored documents are returned to the users. To optimize the query time, a scatter-gather approach is used.

The scatter-gather approach involves two phases of the query: *scatter* and *gather* (see figure 9.1).

The first phase, scatter, is when the query is farmed out to a set of subnodes. Classically, these subnodes are divided topically and store documents about their topic. These nodes are responsible for finding relevant documents for the query and returning the results, as shown in figure 9.2.

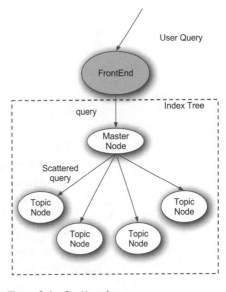

Figure 9.1   Scatter phase

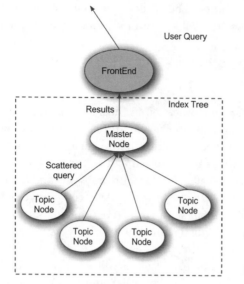

Figure 9.2   Gather phase

The second phase, gather, is when all the topic nodes respond to the main node with their results. These are pruned and returned for the entire query.

Let's start by creating a `SearchQuery` message that can be sent among the actors.

```
case class SearchQuery(query : String, maxResults : Int)
```

The `SearchQuery` class has two parameters. The first is the actual query, and the second is the maximum number of results that should be returned. We'll implement one of the topic nodes to handle this message.

```
trait SearchNode extends Actor {
  type ScoredDocument = (Double, String)
  val index : HashMap[String, Seq[ScoredDocument]] = ...
  override def act = Actor.loop {
    react {
      case SearchQuery(query, maxResults) =>
        reply index.get(query).getOrElse(Seq()).take(maxResults)
    }
  }
}
```

The `Search` node defines the type `Scored Document` to be a tuple of a double score and a string document. The index is defined as a `HashMap` of a query string to scored documents. The index is implemented such that it pulls in a different set of values for each `SearchNode` created. The full implementation of the index is included in the source code for the book.

The `act` method on `SearchNode` contains its core behavior. When it receives a `SearchQuery` message, it looks for results in its index. It replies to the sender of the `SearchQuery` all of these results in a truncated manner so that only `maxResults` are returned.

REACT VERSUS RECEIVE The `SearchNode` actor uses the `react` method for accepting messages. The actors library also supports a `receive` method. These methods differ in that `react` will defer the execution of the actor until there is a message available. The `receive` method will block the current thread until a message is available. Unless absolutely necessary, `receive` should be avoided to improve the parallelism in the system.

Now let's implement the `HeadNode` actor that's responsible for scattering queries and gathering results.

```
trait HeadNode extends Actor {
  val nodes : Seq[SearchNode] = ...
  override def act = Actor.loop {
    react {
      case s @ SearchQuery(_, maxResults) =>
        val futureResults = nodes map (n => n !! s)
        def combineResults(current : Seq[(Double, String)],
                           next : Seq[(Double, String)]) =
            (current ++ next).view sortBy (_._1) take maxResults force
        reply futureResults.foldLeft(Seq[ScoredDocument]()) {
          (current, next) =>
            combineResults(current,
                         next().asInstanceOf[Seq[ScoredDocument]])
        }
    }
  }
}
```

The `HeadNode` actor is a bit more complicated. It defines a member containing all the `SearchNodes` that it can scatter to. It then defines its core behavior in the `act` method. The `HeadNode` waits for `SearchQuery` messages. When it receives one, it sends it to all the `SearchNode` children awaiting a future result. The `!!` method on actors will send a message and expect a reply at some future time. This reply is called a `Future`. The `HeadNode` can block until the reply is received by calling the `apply` method on the `Future`. This is exactly what it does in the `foldLeft` over these futures. The `HeadNode` is aggregating the `next` future result with the `current` query results result to produce the final result list. This final result list is sent to the original query sender using the `reply` method.

USING VIEW TO COMBINE RESULTS In the example the `view` and `force` methods are used around a set of collection methods. Although they offer no benefit for the `sortBy` method, in practice the `take` method is usually used, and the `view` and `force` methods can help improve efficiency by avoiding the creation of intermediate collections.

The system now has a scatter-gather search tree for optimal searching. But there's still a lot to be desired. The casting of the result type in the `HeadNode` actor is less than ideal in a statically typed language like Scala. Also, the `HeadNode` blocks for an entire `SearchQuery`. This means that the amount of parallelism in the system could be expanded so that slow-running queries don't starve faster queries. Finally, the search tree has no failure handling. If a bad index or query string occurs, the whole system will crash.

Actors can improve these downsides. Let's start with fixing the type-safety issues.

9.2   *Use typed, transparent references*

One of the biggest dangers in the Scala standard actors library is to give actors references to each other. This can lead to accidentally calling a method defined on another actor instead of sending a message to that actor. Although that may seem innocuous to some, this behavior can break an actors system, especially if you use locking. Actors are optimized by minimizing locking to a few minor locations, such as when scheduling and working with a message buffer. Introducing more locking can easily lead to deadlocks and frustration.

Another disadvantage to passing direct references to actors is transparency, where the location of an actor is tied in to another actor. This locks them in place where they are. The actors can no longer migrate to other locations, either in memory or on the network, severely limiting the system's ability to handle failure. We'll discuss this in detail in section 9.3.

Another downside to sending actors directly in the Scala standard library is that actors are untyped. This means that all the handy type system utilities you could leverage are thrown out the window when using raw actors. Specifically, the compiler's ability to find exhausting pattern matches using sealed traits.

> **USING SEALED TRAITS FOR MESSAGE APIS**   It's a best practice in Scala to define message APIs for actors within a sealed trait hierarchy. This has the benefit of defining every message that an actor can handle and keeping them in a central location for easy lookup. With a bit of machinery, the compiler can be coerced to warn when an actor doesn't handle its complete messaging API.

The Scala standard library provides two mechanisms for enforcing type safety and decoupling references from directly using an actor: the InputChannel and Output-Channel traits.

The OutputChannel trait is used to send messages to actors. This is the interface that should be passed to other actors, and it looks like this:

```
trait OutputChannel[-Msg] {
  def !(msg: Msg @unique): Unit
  def send(msg: Msg @unique, replyTo: OutputChannel[Any]): Unit
  def forward(msg: Msg @unique): Unit
  def receiver: Actor
}
```

The OutputChannel trait is templatized by the type of messages that can be sent to it. It supports sending messages via three methods: !, send, and forward. The ! method sends a message to an actor and doesn't expect a reply. The send method sends a message to an actor and attaches an output channel that the actor can respond to. The forward method is used to send a message to another actor such that the original reply channel is preserved.

The receiver method on OutputChannel returns the raw actor used by the Output-Channel. You should avoid this method.

Notice the methods that OutputChannel doesn't have: !! and !?. In the Scala standard library, !! and !? are used to send messages and expect a reply in the current scope. This is done through the creation of an anonymous actor that can receive the response. This anonymous actor is used as the replyTo argument for a send call. The !? method blocks the current thread until a response is received. The !! method creates a Future object, which stores the result when it occurs. Any attempt to retrieve the result blocks the current thread until the result is available. Futures do provide a map method. This attaches a function that can be run on the value in the future when it's available without blocking the current thread.

In general, using !! and !? is discouraged. The potential for deadlocking a thread is great. But when used lightly or with caution, these methods can be helpful. It's important to understand the size and scope of the project and the type of problem being solved. If the problem is too complex to ensure !! and !? behave appropriately, avoid them altogether.

Let's modify the scatter-gather example to communicate using OutputChannels.

9.2.1 Scatter-Gather with OutputChannel

The scatter-gather example requires two changes to promote lightweight typesafe references: removing the direct Actor references in HeadNode and changing the query responses to go through a collection channel. The first change is simple.

```
/** The head node for the scatter/gather algorithm. */
trait HeadNode extends Actor {
  val nodes : Seq[OutputChannel[SearchNodeMessage]]
  override def act : Unit = {
    ...
  }
}
```

The nodes member of the HeadNode actor is changed to be a Seq[OutputChannel [SearchNodeMessage]]. This change ensures that the HeadNode will only send SearchNodeMessage messages to SearchNodes. The SearchNodeMessage type is a new sealed trait that will contain all messages that can be sent to SearchNodes.

The second change is a bit more involved. Rather than directly responding to the sender of the SearchQuery, let's allow an output channel to be passed along with the SearchQuery that can receive results.

```
sealed trait SearchNodeMessage
case class SearchQuery(query : String,
                       maxDocs : Int,
                       gatherer : OutputChannel[QueryResponse])
  extends SearchNodeMessage
```

The SearchQuery message now has three parameters: the query, the maximum number of results, and the output channel that will receive the query results. The SearchQuery message now extends from the SearchNodeMessage. The new SearchNodeMessage trait is sealed, ensuring that all messages that can be sent to the SearchNode are defined in the same file. Let's update the SearchNodes to handle the updated SearchQuery message.

```
trait SearchNode extends Actor {
  lazy val index : HashMap[String, Seq[(Double, String)]] = ...

  override def act = Actor.loop {
    react {
      case SearchQuery(q, maxDocs, requester) =>
        val result = for {
          results <- index.get(q).toList
          resultList <- results
        } yield resultList
        requester ! QueryResponse(result.take(maxDocs))
    }
  }
}
```

The SearchNode trait is the same as before except for the last line in the react call. Instead of calling reply with the QueryResponse, the SearchNode sends the response to the requestor parameter of the query.

This new behavior means that the head node can't just send the same SearchQuery message to the SearchNodes. Let's rework the communication of the system, as shown in figure 9.3.

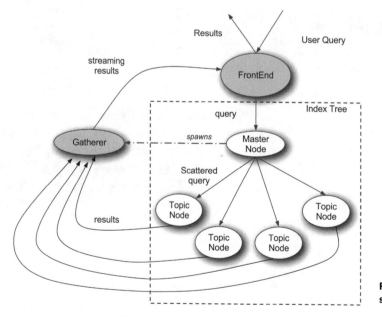

Figure 9.3   Modified scatter-gather search

The new design has a `Gatherer` actor. This actor is responsible for receiving all results from `SearchNodes` and aggregating them before sending back to the front end. The `Gatherer` could be implemented in many ways. One advanced implementation could use prediction to stream results to the front end as they're returned, attempting to ensure high priority results get sent immediately. For now, let's implement the `GathererNode` such that it aggregates all results first and sends them to the front end.

```
trait GathererNode extends Actor {
  val maxDocs: Int
  val maxResponses: Int
  val client: OutputChannel[QueryResponse]
  ..
}
```

The `GathererNode` is defined as an `Actor`. It has three members. The `maxDocs` member is the maximum number of documents to return from a query. The `maxResponses` member is the maximum number of nodes that can respond before sending results for a query. The `client` member is the `OutputChannel` where results should be sent. The `GathererNode` should be tolerant of errors or timeouts in the search tree. To do this, it should wait a maximum of one second for each response before returning the query results. Let's implement the `act` method for the `GathererNode`.

```
def act = {
  def combineResults(current: Seq[(Double, String)],
                 next: Seq[(Double, String)]) =
    (current ++ next).view.sortBy(_._1).take(maxDocs).force

  def bundleResult(curCount: Int,
                 current: Seq[(Double, String)]): Unit =
    if (curCount < maxResponses) {
      receiveWithin(1000L) {
        case QueryResponse(results) =>
          bundleResult(curCount+1, combineResults(current, results))
        case TIMEOUT =>
          bundleResult(maxResponses, current)
      }
    } else {
      client ! QueryResponse(current)
    }
  bundleResult(0, Seq())
}
```

The act method defines the core behavior of this actor. The `combineResults` helper method is used to take two sets of query results and aggregate them such that the highest scored results remain. This method also limits the number of results returned to be the same as the `maxDocs` member variable.

The `bundleResult` method is the core behavior of this actor. The curCount parameter is the number of responses seen so far. The current parameter is the aggregate of all collected query results from all nodes. The `bundleResult` method first checks to see if the number of responses is less than the maximum expected results. If so, it calls receiveWithin to wait for another response. The receiveWithin method will wait for a given time for messages before sending the special scala.actors.TIMEOUT message. If another query result is received, the method combines the result with the previous set of results and recursively calls itself with bumped values. If receiving the message times out, the bundleResult method calls itself with the number of responses set to the maximum value. If the number of responses is at or above the maximum, the current query results are sent to the client.

Finally, the act method is implemented by calling the bundleResult method with an initial count of zero and an empty Seq of results.

The GathererNode stops trying to receive messages after the query results have been sent. This effectively ends the life of the actor and allows the node to become garbage-collected. The Scala standard actors library implements its own garbage collection routine that will have to remove references to the GathererNode before the JVM garbage collection can recover memory.

The last piece of implementation required is to adapt the HeadNode to use the GathererNode instead of collecting all the results in futures.

```
trait HeadNode extends Actor {

  val nodes : Seq[OutputChannel[SearchNodeMessage]]

  override def act : Unit = {
    this.react {
      case SearchQuery(q, max, responder) =>
        val gatherer = new GathererNode {
          val maxDocs = max
          val maxResponses = nodes.size
          val client = responder
        }
        gatherer.start                              <—— Must start the actor
        for (node <- nodes) {
          node ! SearchQuery(q, max, gatherer)
        }
        act
    }
  }
  override def toString = "HeadNode with {\n" +
    "\t" + nodes.size + " search nodes\n" +
    nodes.mkString("\t", "\n\t", "\n}")
}
```

The HeadNode has been changed so that when it receives a SearchQuery, it constructs a new GathererNode. The gatherer is instantiated using the parameters from the SearchQuery. The gatherer must also be started so that it can receive messages. The last piece is to send a new SearchQuery message to all the SearchNodes with the OutputChannel set to the gatherer.

Splitting the scatter and gather computations into different actors can help with throughput in the whole system. The HeadNode actor only has to deal with incoming messages and do any potential preprocessing of queries before scattering them. The GathererNode can focus on receiving responses from the search tree. A Gatherer node could even be implemented such that it stopped `SearchNodes` from performing lookups if enough quality results were received. Most importantly, if there's any kind of error gathering the results of one particular query, it won't adversely affect any other query in the system.

This is a key design issue with actors. Failures should be isolated as much as possible. This can be done through the creation of failure zones.

9.3 Limit failures to zones

Architecting and rationalizing distributed architecture can be difficult. Joe Armstrong, the creator of Erlang, popularized the notion of actors and how to handle failure. The recommended strategy for working with actors is to let them fail and let another actor, called a *supervisor* handle that failure. The supervisor is responsible for bringing the system it manages back into a working state.

Looking at supervisors and actors from a topological point of view, supervisors create zones of failure for the actors they manage. The actors in a system can be partitioned by the supervisors such that if one section of the system goes down, the supervisor has a chance to prevent the failure from reaching the rest of the system. Each supervisor actor can itself have a supervisor actor, creating nested zones of failure.

The error handling of supervisors is similar to exception handling. A supervisor should handle any failure that it knows how to, and bubble up those it doesn't to outer processes. If no supervisor can handle the error, then this would bring down the entire system, so bubbling up errors should be done carefully!

Supervisors can be simpler to write than exception handling code. With exception handling, it's difficult to know if a `try-catch` block contained any state-changing code and whether it can be retired. With supervisors, if an actor is misbehaving, it can restart the portion of the system that's dependent on that actor. Each actor can be passed an initial good state and continue processing messages.

Notice the relationship between the supervisor of an actor and the creator of the actor. If the supervisor needs to recreate an actor upon destruction, the supervisor is also the ideal candidate to start the actor when the system initializes. This allows all the initialization logic to live in the same location. Supervisors may also need to act as proxy to the subsystem they manage. In the event of failure, the supervisor may need to buffer messages to a subsystem until after it has recovered and can begin processing again.

Supervisors are created differently in the various Scala actor libraries. In the core library, supervisors are created through the `link` method. The Akka actors library provides many default supervisor implementations and mechanisms of wiring actors and supervisors together. One thing that's common across actor libraries is that supervisors are supported and failure zones are encouraged.

9.3.1 Scatter-Gather failure zones

Let's adapt the scatter-gather example to include failure zones. The first failure zone should cover the `HeadNode` and `SearchNode` actors. Upon failure, the supervisor can reload a failing search node and wire it back into the head node. The second failure

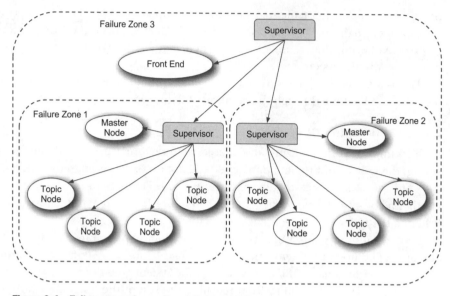

Figure 9.4   Failure zones for scatter-gather example

zone should cover the `FrontEnd` actor and the supervisors of the first failure zone. In the event of failure in this outer zone, the supervisor can restart any failed inner zones and inform the front end of the new actors. A topological view of this failure handling is shown in figure 9.4.

Rule 21 | **Design for failure with topological zones**

When designing with actors, it's important to prepare what zones are allowed to fail separately. The system should be designed such that any one zone does not take down the entire application.

Failure Zones 1 and 2 in the diagram show the `HeadNode` and `SearchNode` failure zones for two parallel search hierarchies. The supervisor for these zones is responsible for restarting the entire tree, or a particular `SearchNode`, on failure. Zones 1 and 2 are each encompassed in Zone 3. This zone manages the search on the front end. In the event of failure, it restarts the underlying search trees or the front end as needed.

We'll start by defining the supervisor for the search nodes:

Listing 9.1   Supervisor for search nodes

```
trait SearchNodeSupervisor extends Actor {
  val numThreadsForSearchTree = 5

  private def createSearchTree(size : Int) = {          ◁——  Subtree constructor
    val searchNodes = for(i <- 1 to size) yield {
    val tmp = new SearchNode {
      override val id = i
    }                                                          Supervise
    SearchNodeSupervisor.this link tmp           ◁——│        subnodes
      tmp.start
```

```
        tmp
    }
    val headNode = new HeadNode {
      val nodes = searchNodes
      override val scheduler = s
    }
    this link headNode
    headNode.start
    headNode
  }
  def act() : Unit = {
    trapExit = true
    def run(head : Actor) : Nothing = react {
      case Exit(deadActor, reason) =>
        run(createSearchTree(10))
      case x =>
        head ! x
        run(head)
    }
    run(createSearchTree(10))
  }
}
```

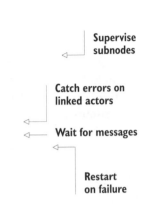

Supervise subnodes

Catch errors on linked actors

Wait for messages

Restart on failure

The SearchNodeSupervisor contains two methods: createSearchTree and act. The create-SearchTree is responsible for instantiating nodes of the search tree and returning the top node. This method iterates over the desired size of the tree and creates the SearchNode class from the previous examples. Remember that each SearchNode uses its assigned ID to load a set of indexed documents and make them available for queries. Each search node created is linked to the supervisor. In the Scala standard library actors, linking is what creates a supervisor hierarchy. Linking two actors means that if one fails, both are killed. It also allows one of them to trap errors from the other. This is done from the call to trapExit = true in the act method.

The second method is the standard library actor's act method. This defines the core behavior of the

Common linking pitfalls

The link method has two restrictions that simplify its use.

- It must be called from inside a live actor—that is, from the act method or one of the continuations passed to react.

- It should be called on the supervisor with the other actor as the method argument.

Because link alters the behavior of failure handling, it needs to lock both actors it operates against. Because of this synchronization, it's possible to deadlock when waiting for locks. Ordering the locking behavior can prevent this behavior. The link method also requires, through runtime asserts, that it's called against the current live actor. The actor must be actively running in its scheduled thread. This means linking should be done *internal* to the supervisor actor. This is why all the topological code is pushed down into the supervisor and why it acts as a natural proxy to the actors it manages.

supervisor actor. The first line here is the `trapExit = true`, which allows this actor to catch errors from others. The next line is a helper function called `run`, which accepts one parameter, the current head actor, and calls `react`, which will block waiting for messages. The first message it handles is the special `Exit` message. An `Exit` message is passed if one of the linked actors fails. Notice the values that come with an `Exit` message: `deadActor` and `reason`. The `deadActor` link allows the supervisor to attempt to pull any partial state from the `deadActor` if needed, or remove it from any control structures as needed. Note that the `deadActor` is already gone and won't be scheduled anymore at the time of receiving this message.

For the `SearchNodeSupervisor`, when handling errors, the entire search tree is reconstructed and passed back into the `run` method. This may not be ideal in a real-life situation because reconstructing the entire tree could be expensive or the tree might be sprawled over several machines. In that case, the `SearchNodeSupervisor` could restart the failed node and notify the search tree of the replacement.

If the `SearchNodeSupervisor` encounters any other message, it's forwarded to the current `HeadNode`. This means that the supervisor can block incoming messages when restarting the system. When the main node crashes, the supervisor receives the `Exit` message and stops processing messages while it fixes the system. After restoring things, it will again pull messages from its queue and delegate them down to the search tree.

9.3.2   General failure handling practices

The supervisor for the scatter-gather search system demonstrates ways to handle the issues of failure in an actors system. When designing an actors-based system and outlining failure zones, table 9.1 helps make decisions appropriate for that module.

These three decisions are crucial in defining robust concurrent actor systems. The first point is the most important. Creating a fail-safe zone implies ensuring that if that

Table 9.1   Actor design decisions

Decision	Scatter-Gather example	Other options
Providing transparent way to restart failed components	Forward messages through the supervisor. If supervisor fails, restart outer failure zone.	Update name service with references to actors. Directly communicate new location to connected components.
Granularity of failure zones	The entire search tree fails and restarts.	Single `Search` node inner failure zone with `Search Tree` outer failure zone.
Recovery of failed actor state	Actor data is statically pulled from disk. Doesn't change during its lifetime.	Periodic snapshotting to persistent store. Pulling live state from dead actor and sanitizing. Persisting state after every handled message

zone crashes and restarts, it won't affect external zones. The Scala actors library makes it easy to lose transparency for actors. This can be done by passing the reference to a specific actor rather than a proxy or namespace reference.

The second decision can affect the messaging API for actors. If a subsystem needs to tolerate failure of one of its actors, the other actors need to be updated to communicate with the replacement actor. Again, transparent actor references can be a boon here. For the Scala standard library, using the supervisors as proxies to sub-components is the simplest way to provide transparency. This means that for fine-grained failure zones, many supervisors must be created, possibly one per actor.

The third decision is one not discussed in the example—that of state recovery. Most real-life actors maintain some form of state during their lifetimes. This state may or may not need to be reconstructed for the system to continue functioning. Although not directly supported in the Scala standard library, one way to ensure state sticks around is to periodically snapshot the actor by dumping its state to a persistent store. This could then be recovered later.

A second method of keeping state would be to pull the last known state from a dead actor and sanitize it for the reconstructed actor. This method is risky, as the state of a previous actor isn't in a consistent state and the sanitization process may not be able to recover. The sanitization process could also be hard to reason through and write. This mechanism isn't recommended.

Another mechanism for handling state is to persist the state after every message an actor receives. Although not directly supported by the Scala standard library, this could easily be added through a subclass of actor.

> **AKKA TRANSACTORS** The Akka actors library provides many ways to synchronize the state of live actors, one of which is transactors. Transactors are actors whose message handling functions are executed within a transactional context.

One item not on this list is threading strategies. Because actors share threads, an actor that fails to handle its incoming messages could ruin the performance of other actors that share the same threading resources. The solution to this is to split actors into scheduling zones, similar to splitting them into failure zones.

9.4 *Limit overload using scheduler zones*

One type of failure that a supervisor can't handle well is thread starvation of actors. If one actor is receiving a lot of messages and spending a lot of CPU time processing them, it can starve other actors. The actor schedulers also don't have any notion of priority. Maybe a high-priority actor in the system must respond as quickly as possible, and could get bogged down by lower priority actors stealing all the resources.

Schedulers are the solution to this problem. A scheduler is the component responsible for sharing actors among threads. The scheduler selects the next actor to run and assigns it to a particular thread. In the Scala actors library, a scheduler implements the `IScheduler` interface.

Table 9.2 Schedulers

Scheduler	Purpose
ForkJoinScheduler	Parallelization optimized for tasks that are split up, parallelized, and recovered—that is, things that are forked for processing, then joined together.
ResizableThreadPoolScheduler	Starts up a persistent thread pool for actors. If load is increased, it'll automatically create new threads up to an environment-specified limit.
ExecutorScheduler	Uses a `java.util.concurrent.Executor` to schedule actors. This allows actors to use any of the standard Java thread pools and is the recommended way to assign fixed size thread pool.

A variety of scheduling mechanisms are available for the standard library actors, as shown in table 9.2.

The ForkJoinScheduler is the default scheduler for Scala actors. This is done through a nifty work-stealing algorithm where every thread has its own scheduler. Tasks created in a thread are added to its own scheduler. If a thread runs out of tasks, it steals work from another thread's scheduler. This provides great performance for a lot of situations. The scatter-gather example is a perfect fit for the fork join parallel executor. Queries are distributed to each SearchNode for executions, and results are aggregated to create the final query results. The work-stealing pulls and distributes the forked work for a query. If the system is bogged down, it could degrade to performing similarly to a single-threaded query engine. Although generally efficient, the ForkJoinScheduler isn't optimal in situations where task sizes are largely variable.

The ResizableThreadPoolScheduler constructs a pool of threads that share the processing of messages for a set of actors. Scheduling is done on a first-come, first-serve basis. If the workload starts to grow beyond what the current thread pool can handle, the scheduler will increase the available threads in the pool up until a maximum pool size. This can help a system handle a large increase in messaging throughput and back off resources during downtime.

The ExecutorScheduler is a scheduler that defers scheduling actors to a `java.util.Executor` service. There are many implementations of `java.util.Executor` in the Java standard library as well as common alternatives. One of these, from my own codebases, was an Executor that would schedule tasks on the Abstract Windows Toolkit (AWT)-rendering thread. Using this scheduler for an actor guarantees that it handles messages within a GUI context. This allowed the creation of GUIs where actors could be used to respond to backend events and update UI state.

Each of these schedulers may be appropriate to one or more components in a system. Some components scheduling may need to be completely isolated from other components. This is why scheduling zones are important.

9.4.1 Scheduling zones

Scheduling zones are groupings of actors that share the same scheduler. Just as failure zones isolate failure recovery, so do scheduling zones isolate starvation and contention of subsystems. Scheduling zones can also optimize the scheduler to the component.

Figure 9.5 shows what a scheduling zone design might be for the scatter-gather example.

Rule 22	**Limit starvation using scheduling zones**

Prevent low-latency services from getting clobbered by low-priority processes using scheduling zones to carve out dedicated resources.

The scatter-gather search service can be split into four scheduling zones: Search Tree 1, Search Tree 2, Front End, and Supervisor.

The first scheduling zone handles all actors in a search tree. The `ForkJoin-Scheduler` is optimized for the same behavior as the scatter-gather algorithm, so it makes an ideal choice of scheduler for this zone. The replicated `Search` tree uses its own `ForkJoinScheduler` to isolate failures and load between the two trees.

The front end scheduling zone uses a customized scheduler that ties its execution to an asynchronous HTTP server; the handling of messages is done on the same thread as input is taken, and the results are streamed back into the appropriate socket using one of the front-end threads. These actors could also use their own thread pool. This would be ideal if the HTTP server accepting incoming connections used a thread pool of the same size.

The last scheduling zone, not shown, is the scheduling of error recovery. Out of habit, I tend to place these on a separate scheduling routine so they don't interfere with any other subcomponent. This isn't strictly necessary. Error recovery, when it happens, is the highest priority task for a given subcomponent and shouldn't steal

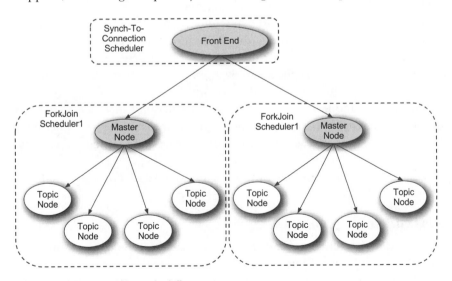

Figure 9.5   Scatter-gather scheduling zones

more important work from other threads. But if more than one subcomponent is sharing the same scheduling zone, then I prefer to keep recovery work separate from core work.

Let's add scheduling zones to the scatter-gather search tree example. The only changes required are in the constructor function defined on the supervisor, as shown in the following listing:

Listing 9.2 `SearchTree` factory

```
private def createSearchTree(size : Int) = {
    val numProcessors =
        java.lang.Runtime.getRuntime.availableProcessors
    val s = new ForkJoinScheduler(                              Create
        initCoreSize = numProcessors,                           scheduler
      maxSize = numThreadsForSearchTree,                        for zone
      daemon = false, fair = true)
    val searchNodes = for(i <- 1 to size) yield new SearchNode {
        override val id = i
        override val scheduler = s
    }
    searchNodes foreach this.link
    searchNodes.foreach(_.start)
    val headNode = new HeadNode {                               Assign
      val nodes = searchNodes                                  scheduler
        override val scheduler = s                              to actor
    }
    this link headNode
    headNode.start
    headNode
  }
```

The original code has two new additions. The first is the creation of the `ForkJoin-Scheduler`. This scheduler takes four arguments. The `initCoreSize` and `maxSize` arguments are the minimum and maximum number of threads it should store in its thread pool. The `daemon` argument specifies whether threads should be constructed as daemons. This scheduler can shut itself down if the actors within are no longer performing any work. The last argument is whether or not the scheduler should attempt to enforce fairness in the work-stealing algorithm.

The second additions are the overridden scheduler member of the `SearchNode` and `HeadNode` actors. This override causes the actor to use the new scheduler for all of its behavior. It can do this only at creation time, so the scheduling zones must be known a-priori.

The actors are now operating within their own fork-join pool, isolated from load in other actors.

9.5   *Dynamic actor topology*

One of the huge benefits of using actors is that the topology of your program can change drastically at runtime to handle load or data size. For example, let's redesign the scatter-gather search tree so that it can accept new documents on the fly and add them to the index. The tree should be able to grow in the event that a specific node gets to be too large. To accomplish this, we can treat an actor as a state machine.

Rule 23

Just use Akka

Akka is the most performant actors framework available on the JVM. It's designed with actor best practices baked into the API. Writing efficient, robust actors systems is simplest in the Akka framework.

The entire scatter-gather tree is composed of two node types: search (leaves) and head (branches). A search node holds an index, like the previous topic nodes. It's responsible for adding new documents to the index and for returning results to queries. A head node holds the number of children. It's responsible for delegating queries to all children and setting up a gatherer to aggregate the results.

USING AKKA The following examples will use the Akka actors library. Although the Scala standard library is elegant, the Akka library makes the robust usage of actors easy. Akka builds in the notion of transparent actor references, while providing a good set of useful supervisors and schedulers. Creating failure zones and scheduling zones is much easier in Akka, and the library is standalone. In general, there's little reason not to use Akka, especially when attempting to design a distributed topology, as shown in the following listing:

Listing 9.3 `AdaptiveSearchNode`

```
trait LeafNode { self: AdaptiveSearchNode =>
  ...
  def leafNode: PartialFunction[Any, Unit] = {
    case SearchQuery(query, maxDocs, handler) =>
      executeLocalQuery(query, maxDocs, handler)
    case SearchableDocument(content) =>
      addDocumentToLocalIndex(content)
  }
  ...
}
```

The `LeafNode` trait is defined with a single `PartialFunction[Any,Unit]` named `leafNode`. This function contains the message handling behavior for the adaptive search nodes when the node is a leaf. When the node receives a `SearchQuery` it executes that query against the local index. When the node receives a `Searchable-Document`, it adds that document to the local index:

Listing 9.4 `LeafNode.executeLocalQuery`

```
trait LeafNode { self: AdaptiveSearchNode =>

  var documents: Vector[String] = Vector()
  var index: HashMap[String, Seq[(Double, String)]] = HashMap()
  ...
  private def executeLocalQuery(query: String,
```

```
                                        maxDocs: Int,
                                        handler: ActorRef) = {
        val result = for {
          results <- index.get(query).toList
          resultList <- results
        } yield resultList
        handler ! QueryResponse(result take maxDocs)
      }
    }
```

The executeLocalQuery function extracts all the results for a given word. These are then limited by the desired maximum number of results in the query and sent to the handler. Note that the handler is of type ActorRef not Actor. In Akka, there's no way to gain a direct reference to an actor. This prevents accessing its state directly from a thread. The only way to talk with an actor is to send a message to it using an ActorRef, which is a transparent reference to an actor. Messages are still sent to actors using the ! operator. The executeLocalQuery function didn't change from the Scala actors version to the Akka actors version besides the use of ActorRef:

> **Listing 9.5   LeafNode.addDocumentToLocalIndex**

```
trait LeafNode { self: AdaptiveSearchNode =>

  private def addDocumentToLocalIndex(content: String) = {
    documents = documents :+ content
    if (documents.size > MAX_DOCUMENTS) split()
    else for( (key,value) <- content.split("\\s+").groupBy(identity)) {
      val list = index.get(key) getOrElse Seq()
      index += ((key, ((value.length.toDouble, content)) +: list))
    }
  }
  protected def split(): Unit
}
```

After updating the index, the document is added to the list of stored documents. Finally, if the number of documents in this node has gone above the maximum desired per node, the split method is called. The split method should split this leaf node into several leaf nodes and replace itself with a branch node. Let's defer defining the split method until after the parent node is defined. If the index doesn't need to be split, the index is updated.

To update the index, the document string is split into words. These words are grouped together such that the key refers to a single word in a document and the value refers to a sequence of all the same words in the document. This sequence is later used to calculate the score of a given word in the document. The current index for a word is extracted into the term list. The index for the given word is then updated to include the new document and the score for that word in the document.

Let's first define the branch node functionality before defining the split method:

Listing 9.6 `BranchNode`

```
trait ParentNode { self: AdaptiveSearchNode =>
 var children = IndexedSeq[ActorRef]()
 def parentNode: PartialFunction[Any, Unit] = {
   case SearchQuery(q, max, responder) =>
       val gatherer: ActorRef = Actor.actorOf(new GathererNode {
         val maxDocs = max
         val maxResponses = children.size
         val query = q
         val client = responder
       })
       gatherer.start
       for (node <- children) {
         node ! SearchQuery(q, max, gatherer)
       }
   case s @ SearchableDocument(_) => getNextChild ! s
 }
 ...
}
```

The `ParentNode` is also defined with a self type of `AdaptiveSearchNode`. The parent node also contains a list of children. Again, the reference to child actors is the `ActorRef` type. The method `parentNode` defines a partial function that handles incoming messages when an actor is a parent. When the parent receives a `SearchQuery` it constructs a new gatherer and farms the query down to its children.

Notice the difference from Scala actors. In Akka, an actor is constructed using the `Actor.actorOf` method. Although the actor is constructed as a gatherer node, the term *gatherer* is of type `ActorRef` *not* `GathererNode`.

When the `ParentNode` receives a `SearchableDocument` it calls `getNextChild` and sends the document to that child. The `getNextChild` method, not shown, selects a child from the `children` sequence in a round-robin fashion. This is the simplest attempt to ensure a balanced search tree. In practice, there would be a lot more effort to ensure the topology of the tree was as efficient as possible (see figure 9.6).

The key behavior of the new adaptive search tree is that it should dynamically change shape. Any given node should be able to change its state from being a leaf node to a parent node that has children. Let's call the new state changing actor an `AdaptiveSearchNode`.

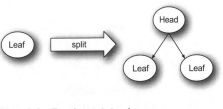

Figure 9.6 Topology state change

Listing 9.7 `AdaptiveSearchNode`

```
class AdaptiveSearchNode extends Actor with ParentNode with LeafNode {

  def receive = leafNode

  protected def split(): Unit = {
```

```
    children = (for(docs <- documents grouped 5) yield {
      val child = Actor.actorOf(new AdaptiveSearchNode)
      child.start()
      docs foreach (child ! SearchableDocument(_))
      child
    }).toIndexedSeq
    clearIndex()
    this become parentNode
  }
```

Similar to Scala actors, an Akka actor must extend the `Actor` trait. The largest difference between Akka and Scala actors is the `receive` method. In Akka, `receive` defines the message handle for all messages, not just the next message received. There's no need to explicitly loop. Also, `receive` is called via the Akka library when a message is ready, so `receive` is *not* a blocking call.

The `receive` method is defined to return the `leafNode` behavior by default. This means any `AdaptiveSearchNode` instantiated will start of as a leaf node. In Akka, to switch the behavior of an actor, there's a `become` method that accepts a different message handler.

The `split` method is defined to:

- Create new `AdaptiveSearchNode` actors for every five documents in the current index (see listing 9.8. This will begin acting as leaf nodes. These nodes are then sent the portion of documents they will be responsible for.
- The local index is cleared to allow it to be garbage–collected. In a production system, this wouldn't happen until the children acknowledged that they had received the documents and were ready to begin serving traffic.
- The behavior of the current actor is switched to the parent behavior in the expression `this become parentNode`.

Listing 9.8 Creating an adaptive scatter-gather tree

```
def makeTree = {
    val searchTree = Actor.actorOf(new AdaptiveSearchNode {
      self.dispatcher = searchnodedispatcher
    })
    searchTree.start()
    submitInitialDocuments(searchTree)
    searchTree
  }
```

Now, creating a scatter-gather search tree is much easier. Only the root `Adaptive-SearchNode` needs to be created and the documents sent into the root node. The tree will dynamically expand into the size required to handle the number of documents.

AKKA'S SCHEDULER AND SUPERVISORS Akka provides an even richer set of actor supervisors and schedulers than the Scala actors library. These aren't discussed in the book, but can be found in Akka's documentation at http://akka.io/docs/

This technique can be powerful when distributed and clustered. The Akka 2.0 framework is adding the ability to create actors inside a cluster and allow them to be dynamically moved around to machines as needed.

9.6 *Summary*

Actors provide a simpler parallelization model than traditional locking and threading. A well-behaved actors system can be fault-tolerant and resistant to total system slowdown. Actors provide an excellent abstraction for designing high-performance servers, where throughput and uptime are of the utmost importance. For these systems, designing failure zones and failure handling behaviors can help keep a system running even in the event of critical failures. Splitting actors into scheduling zones can ensure that input overload to any one portion of the system won't bring the rest of the system down. Finally, when designing with actors, you should use the Akka library for production systems.

The Akka library differs from the standard library in a few key areas:

- Clients of an actor can never obtain a direct reference to that actor. This drastically simplifies scaling an Akka system to multiple servers because there's no chance an actor requires the direct reference to another.
- Messages are handled in the order received. If the current message handling routine can't handle an input message, it's dropped (or handled by the unknown message handler). This prevents out-of-memory errors due to message buffers filling up.
- All core actors library code is designed to allow user code to handle failures without causing more. For example, Akka goes to great lengths to avoid causing out-of-memory exceptions within the core library. This allows user code, your code, to handle failures as needed.
- Akka provides most of the basic supervisor behaviors that can be used as building blocks for complex supervision strategies.
- Akka provides several means of persisting state "out of the box."

So, while the Scala actors library is an excellent resource for creating actors applications, the Akka library provides the features and performance needed to make a production application. Akka also supports common features out of the box.

Actors and actor-related system design is a rich subject. This chapter lightly covered a few of the key aspects to actor-related design. These should be enough to create a fault-tolerant high-performant actors system.

Next let's look into a topic of great interest: Java interoperability with Scala.

Integrating Scala with Java

In this chapter

- The benefits of using interfaces for Scala-Java interaction
- The dangers of automatic implicit conversions of Java types
- The complications of Java serialization in Scala
- How to effectively use annotations in Scala for Java libraries

One of the biggest advantages of the Scala language is its ability to seamlessly interact with existing Java libraries and applications. Although this interaction isn't completely seamless, Scala offers the tightest integration to Java of any JVM language.

The key to knowing how to integrate Scala and Java lies in the Java Virtual Machine specification and how each language encodes onto that specification. Scala does its best to translate simple language features directly onto JVM features. But complicated Scala features are implemented with some compiler tricks, and these tricks are usually the cause of issues when integrating with Java. For the most part, the Java language translates simply into JVM bytecode; however, it too has language features that use compiler tricks. These will also cause rough spots in Scala/Java interaction.

Another benefit of understanding how to interface Scala with Java is that it helps to integrate Scala with every other JVM language. Because Java is king on the JVM, all alternative JVM languages provide means of using existing Java code. This means that communications from Scala to another JVM language can be accomplished through Java in the worst case. Scala is working on language features to integrate directly with dynamic languages, but even with the 2.9.0 release, these features are considered experimental.

This chapter focuses on four big issues in Scala/Java interaction. The first issue is that Scala treats all types as objects, and Java supports primitives within the language. This leads to issues that can be solved by creating appropriate interfaces for communication between Java and Scala. Other mismatches can be alleviated with judicious use of implicit conversions.

The second issue is implicit conversions, which tend to be overutilized. While extremely useful, they can cause subtle bugs in Scala/Java interaction. We'll cover these in detail in section 10.2.

The third issue is Java serialization. Scala does a lot to support Java serialization seamlessly and succeeds for the most part. A few advanced Scala features can cause issues with Java serialization. We'll discuss these in section 10.3.

The fourth issue is with annotations. Scala adheres to a uniform access principle—that is, Scala makes no distinction between methods and fields; they share the same namespace. Java does distinguish between fields and methods. Some Java libraries require specific methods or fields to have annotations. Scala provides some advanced annotation features that enable this to succeed. We'll discuss these in section 10.4.

Let's look into the mismatch between Java primitives and Scala objects.

10.1 The language mismatch between Scala and Java

The Scala and Java languages offer tight integration. Scala classes can be instantiated and extended within Java. Java interfaces and classes can be extended within Java. Scala trait can be extended within Java using a bit of trickery. But this seemingly tight integration runs afoul of three rough patches: primitive boxing, visibility differences, and inexpressible language features.

Primitive boxing is the (semi-)automatic conversion of primitive values on the JVM into objects. This is done because generic parameters are implemented through type-erasure. *Type-erasure* refers to the practice where, although the generic parameters are known to the compiler at compile time, they get erased to `java.lang.Object` at run-time. This was one of the means with which Java retained backwards compatibility when it introduced generics. Scala and Java implement this differently, which we'll look into in section 10.1.1.

Visibility refers to using protected and private modifiers to change the access restrictions on classes and their members. Scala prefers to make everything visible at runtime (that is, in the bytecode) while Java prefers to enforce as much runtime visibility restrictions as the JVM allows. These competing goals can lead to runtime visibility problems. We'll discuss these in section 10.1.2.

Inexpressible language features are features within the Scala language that can't be expressed within the Java language. Things like curried methods, implicit parameters and higher-kinded types are examples. It's best to avoid or hide these features in any code that needs to interface with Scala and Java. We'll discuss these in more detail in section 10.1.3.

The first difference between Scala and Java is the special treatment of *primitives*, things created directly on the stack and passed by value, and *objects*, things created on the heap and passed by reference. In Java, primitives are isolated from objects. Specifically, code using generic type parameters in Java can't use primitives. To get around this, Java defines a set of classes that mimic the types of primitives. When an object is required, the primitive can be placed into an object. This technique is known as boxing the primitive. The object makes a box in which to carry the primitive. Scala makes no distinction between primitives and objects, and performs boxing behind the scenes on behalf of the developer.

10.1.1 *Differences in primitive boxing*

In the Scala language, *everything* is an object and the compiler does its best to hide the fact that primitives aren't objects. In the Java language, the programmer is forced to pay attention to the difference between a primitive and an object containing the same value. This means that `java.util.List<int>` isn't a valid type in Java, but `java.util.List<Integer>` is valid.

To relieve the overhead of boxing, Java introduced *auto-(un)boxing* in version 1.5. Autoboxing is an implicit conversion from a primitive type to its boxed type. This allows you to write a `for` loop as the following:

```
List<Integer> foo = ...
for (int item : foo) {                                      ⟵   item is unboxed
  ...
}
```

In the example, the line `int item : foo` is a `for` expression that's unboxing all integers in the list `foo`. Although not seen, this is the same code as the following:

```
List<Integer> foo = ...
for (Integer item_ : foo) {
  int item = item_.intValue();                              ⟵   Explicit unboxing
  ...
}
```

This example is similar except that the `int item` is explicitly unboxed from the `Integer` returned from the list. Although boxing happens automatically in Java, it can be an expensive operation at runtime.

In Scala, there's no distinction between primitives and objects. The language treats `scala.Int` as an object. The compiler tries to optimize the usage of `scala.Int` such that it remains in primitive form throughout the life of a program. For example, we'll define the following Scala object:

```
object Test {
  def add(x: Int, y: Int) = x + y
}
```

This object defines one method, add. The add method takes two scala.Int values and returns a scala.Int. The bytecode emitted by the compiler is as follows:

```
public int add(int, int);
  Code:
    0:  iload_1
    1:  iload_2
    2:  iadd
    3:  ireturn

}
```

The signature for the add method uses the primitive int type. The bytecode emitted uses iload, iadd, and ireturn. These three bytecodes operate on primitive integers. What happens if we use a generic type with scala.Int? The compiler will generate boxing code as needed:

```
object Test {
  def add2(items: List[Int]) = {
    var sum = 0
    val it = x.iterator
    while (it.hasNext) {
      sum += it.next
    }
    sum
  }
}
```

The object Test defines a new method add2. This method take a generic List class parameterized to have scala.Int elements. The code creates a sum variable, grabs an iterator to the list, and iterates over the values in the list. Each of these values is added to the sum variable and the sum is returned. Let's take a look at the bytecode in the following listing.

Listing 10.1   The add2 method

```
public int add2(scala.collection.immutable.List);
  Code:
    0: iconst_0
    1: istore_2
    2: aload_1
    3: invokeinterface #28,   1;
      //InterfaceMethod
  scala/collection/LinearSeqLike.iterator:()Lscala/collection/Iterator;
    8: astore_3
    9: aload_3
    10: invokeinterface #34,   1;
```

```
   //InterfaceMethod scala/collection/Iterator.hasNext:()Z
15: ifeq 33
18: iload_2
19: aload_3
20: invokeinterface #38,  1;
   //InterfaceMethod
scala/collection/Iterator.next:()Ljava/lang/Object;
25: invokestatic #44;
   //Method
scala/runtime/BoxesRunTime.unboxToInt:(Ljava/lang/Object;)I
28: iadd
29: istore_2
30: goto 9
33: iload_2
34: ireturn
}
```

The add2 method is compiled so that it takes the scala.collection.immutable.List type as a parameter and returns a primitive integer. The List class is generic and suffers from the same problem as Java generics. The implementation of Generic types in Java forces the use of Object at runtime; therefore, primitives can't be generic type parameters. Label 20 in the byte code shows that invoking next against the List's iterator returns the type Object. Label 25 shows Scala's version of autoboxing: the Boxes-RunTime class. Scala uses the scala.runtime.BoxesRunTime class to implement all boxing/unboxing operations as efficiently as possible.

Avoiding boxing in Scala

Starting in Scala 2.8.0 the @specialized keyword can be used on generic classes to avoid boxing entirely. This is done through method overloading and type-specific subclasses. For example, the Iterator class in specialization would be written as follows:

```
trait Iterator[@specialized(Int) T] {
 def hasNext: Boolean
 def next: T
}
```

This results in the following JVM interface:

```
public interface Iterator {
 public abstract boolean hasNext();
 public abstract java.lang.Object next();
 public abstract int next$mcI$sp();
}
```

The next method is defined to return an Object, as is standard in generic implementations in Java and Scala. But there's a specialized version of next called nextmcIsp that returns a primitive int. When the compiler knows that the Iterator has a type parameter of Int, it will generate calls to the nextmcIsp rather than next. This can be used to remove the cost of boxing, albeit by creating larger classes.

The important point here is that both Scala and Java use boxing with generic classes. Scala hides boxing entirely behind `scala.Int` while `Java` promotes boxing into the language itself. This mismatch can cause issues when working with Scala from Java or Java from Scala. These issues can be solved using one simple rule: Use primitives in methods used from both Scala and Java.

Rule 24 | **Prefer primitives in methods when integrating Java and Scala**

Scala attempts to preserve primitives throughout your code. It's best to use primitives, and arrays, for the simplest interface between Java and Scala.

This simple rule can avoid a few of the issues with Scala/Java interaction. We still have the issue of generic parameters. In Java, a list of integers has the type `java.util .List<java.lang.Integer>`. In Scala, a list of integers has the type `java.util.List [scala.Int]`. Although the runtime implementation of the two lists is the same, Scala's type system does not automatically convert from Java's boxed primitives to Scala's unified object types—the Scala compiler won't automatically convert a `java .util.List[java.lang.Integer]` into a `java.util.List[scala.Int]` even if such a conversion would be type-safe.

Two solutions to this issue exist. One is to perform a cast from `java.util.List [java.lang.Integer]` to `java.util.List[scala.Int]`. The other is to define an implicit conversion that will shim Java types into Scala types. Let's look at the casting:

```
scala> val x = new java.util.ArrayList[java.lang.Integer]
x: java.util.ArrayList[java.lang.Integer] = []

scala> x.add(java.lang.Integer.valueOf(1))
res0: Boolean = true

scala> x.add(java.lang.Integer.valueOf(2))
res1: Boolean = true

scala> val z = x.asInstanceOf[java.util.List[Int]]
z: java.util.List[Int] = [1, 2]

scala> z.get(0)
res3: Int = 1
```

The first line constructs a new `java.util.ArrayList` with a generic parameter equal to `java.lang.Integer`. The next two lines add data to the list. The third line defines a new list z, which is a cast from `java.util.ArrayList[java.lang.Integer]` to `java .util.List[scala.Int]`. The REPL prints the values in the list when describing the return types. Notice that the correct values are shown and there are no runtime exceptions. The next retrieves the first value from the cast list. Notice that the return type is `scala.Int` and there are no `ClassCastExceptions`. The `asInstanceOf` cast was legal because Scala and Java box their primitive integers to the same type: `java.lang.Integer`.

These casts may be considered dangerous. They subvert the type system in Scala and prevent it from discovering future errors. For example, if a method is changed from taking a `java.util.List[java.lang.Integer]` to a `java.util.List [MySpecialClass]`, the cast to `java.util.List[scala.Int]` will still compile and prevent other compile-time errors.

The second solution can avoid this pitfall by operating within the type system. The second solution is to create an implicit conversion from `java.util.List [java.lang.Integer]` to `java.util.List[scala.Int]`:

```
scala> implicit def convertToScala(
     |   x: java.util.List[java.lang.Integer]) =
     |     x.asInstanceOf[java.util.List[Int]]
convertToScala:
  (x: java.util.List[java.lang.Integer])java.util.List[Int]

scala> def foo(x: java.util.List[Int]) = x.get(0)
foo: (x: java.util.List[Int])Int

scala> foo(x)
res4: Int = 1
```

The implicit `convertToScala` is defined to take a `java.util.List[java.lang.Integer]`. It performs the same cast from the previous example. The difference here is that the dangerous cast is hidden behind the method such that it can only be used in a type-safe fashion; the method can only take lists of `java.lang.Integer` types, so if the generic type parameter of the list is changed, the implicit view won't be used at all and the compiler will issue the appropriate type error.

The scalaj-collections library provides primitive-safe implicit conversions between Scala and Java collection types. This offers the best mechanism to handle primitives in collections, but noncollection types may still require a hand-rolled implicit conversion.

The next big issue is the difference in visibility implementation.

10.1.2 *Differences in visibility*

Java enforces visibility both statically and dynamically. Visibility is enforced both by the Java compiler and by the JVM runtime. Java embeds visibility restrictions directly into the bytecode that the JVM uses to enforce at runtime.

Scala enforces visibility statically, and does its best to encode visibility constraints for the JVM. Scala's visibility design is far more powerful than Java's and can't be directly encoded into bytecode for runtime enforcement. Scala tends to make methods publicly visible and enforces all constraints at compile time, unless the visibility rule in Scala lines up directly with one from Java.

Let's look at a simple example. Java's `protected` modifier differs from Scala's. Specifically, in Scala, companion objects are allowed to access protected members of their companion classes. This means that Scala can't encode protected members using the JVM's protected bytecode because that would restrict companion classes from accessing protected members. Let's look at an example.

```
class Test {
 protected val x = 10
}
```

The Test class is defined with a single member x. The val x is protected and holds the value 10. Let's look at the generated bytecode for this class.

```
public class Test extends java.lang.Object implements scala.ScalaObject{
private final int x;

public int x();
  Code:
    0: aload_0
    1: getfield #11; //Field x:I
    4: ireturn
```

. . .

The Test class is defined with a private field x and a public accessor called x. This means that in Java an external user of the Test class could access the protected x method. Here's an example:

```
class Test2 {
  public static void main(String[] args) {
    Test obj = new Test();
    System.out.println(obj.x());                    ◁──── Sneaky access
  }
}
```

The Test2 class is defined in Java. The main method is defined to construct a new Scala Test instance. The next line calls the protected x method and prints its value to the console. Even though the value is protected within Scala, the call succeeds in Java. Let's run the Test2 class:

```
$ java -cp /usr/share/java/scala-library.jar:. Test2
10
```

The program outputs the value 10 with no runtime visibility exception. Java doesn't see Scala's visibility constraints. This means that Java clients of Scala classes need to be on their best behavior to prevent modifying or accessing values that they shouldn't.

Rule 25	**Don't call methods with $ in the name from Java**
	Scala's visibility rules are more advanced than Java and cannot be expressed. When calling into Scala from Java, avoid calling methods with $ in the name, as these are implementation details of Scala's encoding.

Visibility issues are a subset of a bigger issue with Java/Scala integration—that of inexpressible language features.

10.1.3 *Inexpressible language features*

Java and Scala both have features that are inexpressible in the other language.

Java has static values on classes. These are values that are constructed when a class is loaded and aren't associated with any particular instance of the class. In Scala, everything is an object and there are no static values. We might argue that Scala's objects are static values. Scala's objects are implemented in terms of static values on the JVM but aren't themselves static values. Consequently, Java libraries that require static values are hard to interact with from Scala.

Scala has many features unavailable in Java, such as traits, closures, named and default parameters, implicit parameters, and type declarations. When interacting with Scala, Java can't use implicit resolution to find missing parameters to methods. Java can't use Scala's default parameter definitions.

For each of these issues, there's usually a workaround somewhere, but it's best to avoid these issues entirely. You can do this with a simple mechanism: Construct interfaces in Java that define all the types that will be passed between Java and Scala.

SCALA/JAVA INTEGRATION TIP   Construct interfaces in Java that define all types that will be passed between Java and Scala. Place these interfaces into a project that can be shared between the Java portions of code and the Scala portions of code. By limiting the features used in the integration points, there won't be any feature mismatch issues.

Because Java is more limited in features and compiles more directly to bytecode, it makes for a great integration language. Using Java interfaces ensures you avoid the corner case issues of integration, besides those of boxing.

One example where using Java is required is on the Android platform which has an interface called `Parcelable`. You can use this interface to allow objects to be passed between processes. Because this could involve serializing the data, the `Parcelable` interface requires a static field that the Android platform can use to instantiate a `Parcelable`.

For example, say that an application needs to pass addresses between processes on the Android platform. In Java, the `Address` class would look as shown in the following listing:

Listing 10.2   Parcelable Address for Android

```java
public class Address implements Parcelable {
    public String street;
    public String city;
    public String state;
    public String zip;
    public void writeToParcel(Parcel out, int flags) {
        out.writeString(street);
        out.writeString(city);
        out.writeString(state);
        out.writeString(zip);
    }

    private Address(Parcel in) {
        street = in.readString();
        city = in.readString();
        state = in.readString();
        zip = in.readString();
    }
```

```
public int describeContents() {
    return 0;
}

public static final Parcelable.Creator<Address> CREATOR
        = new Parcelable.Creator<MyParcelable>() {
    public Address createFromParcel(Parcel in) {
        return new Address(in);
    }

    public Address[] newArray(int size) {
        return new Address[size];
    }
};
}
```

The Address class is composed of four members: street, city, state, and zip. It has a writeToParcel method that's Android's way of flattening or serializing the class to send to another process. The private constructor for Address is used to deserialize the values from the Parcel it was stored in. The describeContents method returns a bit-mask that tells the Android platform the types of data that are contained in the parcel, in case any need special treatment. Finally, there's a public static instance called CREATOR defined on the class of type Parcelable.Creator<Address>. The Android system uses this type to create and parse incoming Addresses from other processes. This mechanism is also inexpressible in Scala.

The solution in this case is to create a split between the pieces that require Java and the pieces that require Scala. In the case of Address, it's such a simple class, that writing it completely in Java could be a fine solution. But if Address were more complex, this splitting would be appropriate. Let's pretend that Address uses some advanced Scala type features in some of its member functions. To get Address to still be Parcelable in Android *and* to keep the advanced Scala features, it must be split. The Scala features can stay in an abstract class that the Java statics can extend. The Scala class would look as follows:

```
abstract class AbstractAddress(
    val street: String,
    val city: String,
    val state: String,
    val zip: String) extends Parceable {
  override def writeToParcel(out: Parcel, flags: Int) {
    out.writeString(street)
    out.writeString(city)
    out.writeString(state)
    out.writeString(zip)
  }
  override def describeContents = 0
}
```

The AbstractAddress class is defined with street, city, state, and zip as constructors and as val members. The abstract class can also define all the methods required by the Parcelable interface: writeToParcel and describeContents. But the static

CREATOR instance can't be made in Scala. This can be done in Java. Let's extend the AbstractAddress class in Java to allow for usage in Android:

```
public class Address extends AbstractAddress {
  private Address(Parcel in) {
    super(in.readString(),
          in.readString(),
          in.readString(),
          in.readString());
  }
  public static final Parcelable.Creator<Address> CREATOR
    = new Parcelable.Creator<MyParcelable>() {
        public Address createFromParcel(Parcel in) {
          return new Address(in);
        }
        public Address[] newArray(int size) {
          return new Address[size];
        }
    };
}
```

The Address class is defined with a private constructor that takes in a Parcel and delegates to the constructor defined in Scala. Then the static CREATOR instance is defined similarly to the Java-only version.

Due to Scala's tight integration with Java, interfacing with constructors and extending abstract classes can be seamless. This simple Address Parcelable example highlights what to do when running into APIs developed for Java without Scala in mind.

Another area of concern when integrating with Java is the overuse of implicit conversions to adapt Java libraries into Scala idioms.

10.2   *Be wary of implicit conversions*

One common mechanism of supporting the Scala/Java interaction is to create implicit conversions within Scala that promote Java types into a more Scala-friendly form. This can help ease the pain of using classes not designed for Scala but comes at a cost. Implicit conversions carry a few dangers that developers need to be aware of:

- Object identity and equality
- Chaining implicits.

The most common example of using implicit conversions to ease integration between Java and Scala are found in the Scala object scala.collection.JavaConverters. This object contains a set of implicit conversions to convert collections from Java to their Scala equivalents and vice versa. These implicit conversions are immensely handy but also suffer from all the issues associated with this design. Let's look into how object identity and equality can become a problem when using JavaConversions.

10.2.1 *Object identity and equality*

One of the dangers of using implicits to wrap Scala or Java objects for interoperability is that it can alter object identity. This breaks equality in any code that might require equality. Let's look at a simple example of converting a Java collection into a Scala one:

```scala
scala> import collection.JavaConversions._
import collection.JavaConversions._

scala> val x = new java.util.ArrayList[String]
x: java.util.ArrayList[String] = []

scala> x.add("Hi"); x.add("You")

scala> val y : Iterable[String] = x
y: Iterable[String] = Buffer(Hi, You)

scala> x == y
res1: Boolean = false
```

The first line imports the `JavaConversions` implicit conversions. The next line creates the Java collection `ArrayList`. The values `"Hi"` and `"You"` are added to the array list. The `val y` is constructed with the type of `scala.Iterable`. This invokes an implicit conversion to adapt the Java `ArrayList` into a Scala `Iterable`. Finally, when testing equality of the two collections, the value is `false`. When wrapping a Java collection, the wrapped collection isn't equal to the original.

Rule 26 | **Avoid implicit views**

Implicit views, when interfacing with Java, can cause silent object identity issues and other problems. It's best to be explicit.

The nuance of this issue can be subtle. For example, the implicit conversion from a Java collection to a Scala collection isn't as obvious as in the previous example. Imagine there's a Java class that looks as follows:

```java
import java.util.ArrayList;

class JavaClass {
  public static ArrayList<String> CreateArray() {
    ArrayList<String> x = new ArrayList<String>();
    x.add("HI");
    return x;
  }
}
```

The class `JavaClass` has one method called `CreateArray` that returns an `ArrayList` containing the value `"HI"`. Now imagine the following Scala class:

```scala
object ScalaClass {
  def areEqual(x : Iterable[String], y : AnyRef) = x == y
}
```

The object `ScalaClass` is defined with one method, `areEqual`. This method takes a `scala.Iterable` and an `AnyRef` and checks the equality. Now let's use these two classes together.

```
scala> import collection.JavaConversions._
import collection.JavaConversions._

scala> val x = JavaClass.CreateArray()
x: java.util.ArrayList[String] = [HI]

scala> ScalaClass.areEqual(x,x)
res3: Boolean = false
```

The first line imports the implicit conversions for Collection. The next line calls the Java class and constructs the new ArrayList. Finally, the same variable is placed into both sides of the areEqual method. Because the compiler is running the implicit conversions behind the scenes, the fact that x is being wrapped is less apparent in this code. The result of areEqual is false.

Although this example is contrived, it demonstrates how the issue can become hidden behind method calls. In real-world programming, this issue can be difficult to track down when it occurs, as the method call chains are often more complex.

10.2.2 Chaining implicits

The second issue facing implicits as a means to ease Java integration is that of chaining implicits. Scala and Java both support generic types. Collections in both languages have one generic parameter. The implicits that convert from Java to Scala and back again will alter the collection type, but usually not the underlying generic parameter. This means that if the generic parameter type also needs to be converted for smooth Java/Scala integration, then it's possible the implicit won't be triggered.

Let's look at a common example: boxed types and Java collections.

```
scala> val x = new java.util.ArrayList[java.lang.Integer]
x: java.util.ArrayList[java.lang.Integer] = []

scala> val y : Iterable[Int] = x
<console>:17: error: type mismatch;
 found    : java.util.ArrayList[java.lang.Integer]
 required: Iterable[Int]
       val y : Iterable[Int] = x
```

The first line constructs a new Java ArrayList collection with generic parameter set to java.lang.Integer. In Scala, because the compiler doesn't differentiate between primitives and objects, the type scala.Int can be safely used for generic parameters. But Java's boxed integer, java.lang.Integer, isn't the same type as scala.Int, but the two can be converted seamlessly. Scala provides an implicit conversion from java.lang.Integer to scala.Int:

```
scala> val x : Int = new java.lang.Integer(1)
x: Int = 1
```

This line constructs a java.lang.Integer with the value 1 and assigns it to the value x with the type scala.Int. The implicit in scala.Predef kicks in here and automatically converts from the java.lang.Integer type into scala.Int. This implicit doesn't kick in when looking for implicit conversions from Java to Scala.

Let's naively try to construct an implicit that can convert from a collection type and modify its nested element all in one go.

```
implicit def naiveWrap[A,B](
  col: java.util.Collection[A])(implicit conv: A => B) =
    new Iterable[B] { ... }
```

The naiveWrap method is defined with two type parameters: one for the original type in the Java collection, A, and another for the Scala version of that type, B. The naive-Wrap method takes another implicit conversion from the Java type A to the Scala type B. The hope is that an implicit view will bind the type parameter A to java.lang .Integer and B to scala.Int and the conversion from java.util.ArrayList [java.lang.Integet] to scala.Iterable[Int] will succeed.

Let's try this out in the REPL:

```
scala> val x = new java.util.ArrayList[java.lang.Integer]
x: java.util.ArrayList[java.lang.Integer] = []

scala> val y : Iterable[Int] = x
<console>:17: error: type mismatch;
 found    : java.util.ArrayList[java.lang.Integer]
 required: Iterable[Int]
       val y : Iterable[Int] = x
```

This is the same error as before. The Java list x isn't able to be converted to an Iterable[Int] directly. This is the same problem we saw before where the type inferencer doesn't like inferring the A and B types from the naiveWrap method.

The solution to this problem is one used from 7.2.3: We can defer the type inference of the parameters. Let's try to implement the wrap method again.

```
trait CollectionConverter[A] {
  val col: java.util.Collection[A]
  def asScala[B](implicit fun: A => B) =
    new Iterable[B] { ... }
}
object Test {
  implicit def wrap[A](i: ju.Collection[A]) =
    new CollectionConverter[A] {
      override val col = i
    }
}
```

The CollectionConverter type is implemented to capture the original A type from the naiveWrap method. The Converter trait holds the Java collection that needs to be converted. The asScala method is defined to capture the B type from the naiveWrap method. This method takes an implicit argument that captures the conversion from A to B. The asScala method is what constructs the Scala Iterable. The Test object is defined with a new implicit wrap method. This method captures the original A type and constructs a new CollectionConverter.

The new implicit conversions requires the asScala method to be called directly. Let's take a look:

```
scala> import Test.wrap
import Test.wrap

scala> val x = new java.util.ArrayList[java.lang.Integer]
x: java.util.ArrayList[java.lang.Integer] = []

scala> x.add(1); x.add(2);

scala> val y: Iterable[Int] = x.asScala
y : Iterable[Int] = CollectionConverter(1, 2)
```

First, the new implicit wrap method is imported. Next a Java `ArrayList[java` `.lang.Integer]` is constructed and values are added to it. Finally, the conversion is attempted using the `asScala` method, and this time it succeeds.

The downside to this approach is the requirement of the additional method call to ensure the types are inferred correctly. But as a general solution, this is more ideal. The explicit `asScala` method call denotes a transformation to a new object. This makes it easy to know when a collection is being converted between the Scala and Java libraries.

> **SCALAJ-COLLECTIONS**   The scalaj-collections library from Jorge Ortiz provides collection conversions to and from Scala and Java collections. The library uses the same technique of having an `asScala` and `asJava` method implicitly added to collections of the respected types. The scalaj library offers a more robust solution than what's available in the standard library.

Although using implicits to wrap Java libraries into Scala libraries can be dangerous, it's still a helpful technique and is used throughout the standard library. It's important to know when only simple implicit conversions won't be enough and how to solve these issues. Chaining implicit conversions can solve a lot of the remaining issues.

The important point here is that implicits aren't magic and can't automatically convert between Scala and Java types for all situations. Implicits can and should be used to *reduce* the overhead of these interaction points.

The next potential issue with Java integration is that of serialization.

10.3   *Be wary of Java serialization*

For most applications, Java serialization works well within Scala. Scala's closures are automatically made serializable and most of the classes are serialization friendly.

> **SCALA 2.7.X AND SERIALIZATION**   The Scala 2.7.x series had a lot of issues with Java serialization that have been fixed in 2.8.x and beyond. When using Scala with Java serialization, it's recommended you use one of the newer releases.

A corner case is where Scala's generation of anonymous classes can cause issues with serialization. Let's look at an example.

We'll define a set of objects to model characters within a game. This game will be composed of different people. Each person could be in one of two states: alive or dead. Let's define the person class.

```
object PlayerState {
  sealed trait PlayerStatus extends Serializable
```

```
  val ALIVE = new PlayerStatus { override def toString = "ALIVE" }
  val DEAD = new PlayerStatus { override def toString = "DEAD" }
}
case class Player(s : PlayerState.PlayerStatus)
```

The object `PlayerState` is used to encapsulate the status enumeration. The sealed trait `PlayerStatus` represents the status enumeration. Two status values are defined: `ALIVE` and `DEAD`. Finally, the `Player` class is constructed with a single member `s` that holds the player status.

Now, imagine a few of these players are created and stored in some semipermanent fashion using Java serialization. The game server is running smoothly and everyone's happy, even those who have dead players. To simulate this, let's serialize a single dead player to disk.

```
scala> val x = new Player(PlayerState.DEAD)
x: test.Player = Player(DEAD)

scala> val out = new ObjectOutputStream(
     | new FileOutputStream("player.out"))
out: java.io.ObjectOutputStream = java.io.ObjectOutputStream@5acac877

scala> out.writeObject(x); out.flush()
```

The value `x` is created with a player in the `DEAD` status. The value `out` is constructed as a Java `ObjectOutputStream` for the file `player.out`. The output stream is used to serialize the dead player to disk.

Around this time, there's a new feature request to allow players to sleep during the game. The `PlayerStatus` enumeration is updated to have a new state: sleeping.

```
object PlayerState {
  sealed trait PlayerStatus extends Serializable
  val ALIVE = new PlayerStatus { override def toString = "ALIVE" }
  val SLEEPING = new PlayerStatus { override def toString = "SLEEPING"}
  val DEAD = new PlayerStatus { override def toString = "DEAD" }
}
```

The `SLEEPING` value is added between the `ALIVE` and `DEAD` status. Other than the new value, nothing in the original code has changed. But when trying to load dead players from disk, there's an issue:

```
scala> val input =
     | new ObjectInputStream(new FileInputStream("player.out"))
input: java.io.ObjectInputStream = java.io.ObjectInputStream@7e98f9c2

scala> val x = input.readObject
java.io.InvalidClassException: PlayerState$$anon$2;
  local class incompatible: stream classdesc
    serialVersionUID = -1825168539657690740,
  local class serialVersionUID = 6026448029321119659
```

A new `ObjectInputStream` is constructed to deserialize the object using Java's serialization. The next line attempts to read the serialized player object and throws an `InvalidClassException`. What's happened is the class that used to represent the `DEAD` value has moved. The `ALIVE`, `SLEEPING`, and `DEAD` classes are constructed anonymously: they aren't given named classes.

Scala generates anonymous class names using a simple formula: location in source code + current count of anonymously generated classes for this location. This means that the original `ALIVE` class is generated with the name `PlayerState$$annon$1` and the original `DEAD` class is generated with the name `PlayerState$$annon$2`. But when adding the new `SLEEPING` status, the anonymous class names are changed. `ALIVE` stays the same, but `SLEEPING` is named `PlayerState$$annon$2` and `DEAD` is moved to `PlayerState$$annon$3`.

The mistake here was using anonymous classes rather than named classes. This issue could prevent refactoring in the code. Let's dig deeper into anonymous classes and their interaction with Java serialization.

10.3.1 *Serializing anonymous classes*

Scala will generate anonymous classes to express core language features. Here are the situations where anonymous classes are created:

- Anonymous type refinements
  ```
  new X { def refinement = ... }
  ```
- Anonymous mixin inheritance
  ```
  new X with Y with Z
  ```
- Closures and lambda functions.
  ```
  List(1,2,3).map(_.toString)
  ```

Each of these scenarios has the potential to create a serializable class that can become a refactoring burden. Let's see what happens when compiling these three lines. First, let's create a Scala file:

```
trait X extends java.io.Serializable
class Y

object Foo {
  def test1 = new X { def foo = "HI" }        ⟵  Type refinement
  def test2 = new Y with X                     ⟵  Mixin inheritance
  def test3 = List(1,2,3).map(_.toString)      ⟵  Closure
}
```

The X and Y traits are defined to illustrate the class generation. The `Foo` object contains all three scenarios. The `test1` method creates an anonymous class for the type refinement. The `test2` method creates an anonymous class from the mixin inheritance. The `test3` method creates an anonymous class for the closure `_.toString`. Let's look at the class files that are generated:

```
> ls
anon.scala              Foo$$anonfun$test3$1.class   X.class
Foo$$anon$1.class       Foo.class                    Y.class
Foo$$anon$2.class       Foo$.class
```

The `test1` method generated the `Foo$$anon$1.class` file. The `test2` method generated the `Foo$$anon$2.class` file and the `test3` method created the `Foo$$anonfun$test3$1.class` file. Notice that anonymous classes are numbered on a per file basis and anonymous functions are numbered based on their class/method scope. This means that anonymous classes make it easier to break long-term serializability of data, because any anonymous class defined in the file can change the numbering.

For anonymous classes, the simple solution is to ensure that any long-term persisted objects define named objects or classes. Doing this, the preceding example becomes:

```
class One extends X { def foo = "HI" }
class Two extends Y with X

object Foo {
  def test1 = new One
  def test2 = new Two
  def test3 = List(1,2,3).map(_.toString)
}
```

The classes `One` and `Two` are created to correspond to the anonymous classes from the earlier `test1` and `test2` methods. The `test1` and `test2` methods are changed to use the new named classes. The benefit to this approach is that the generated classfiles are file-order independent. Let's look at the generated classfile directory.

```
> ls
anon.scala    Foo$$anonfun$test3$1.class   Foo.class
Foo$.class    One.class                    Two.class
X.class       Y.class
```

The result is that the only remaining anonymous class is the closure defined in the `test3` method. The class `One` and `Two` are now explicitly named and can be moved around within the file or into other files. The only remaining issue is the long-term serializability of the anonymous function.

> **AVOID LONG-TERM SERIALIZATION OF CLOSURES** Scala's closure syntax is highly convenient and used frequently in development. But because of the volatile nature of randomly generated class names, it's best to avoid persisting closures for any long-running applications. When no other option is available, you should ensure that closure deserialization issues are properly handled.

When it comes to anonymous functions, it's best to avoid long-term serialization. This grants the most amount of flexibility in syntax and usage. Sometimes this isn't an option. For example, imagine the following scheduling service:

```
trait SchedulingService {
  def schedule( cron_schedule: String, work: () => Unit) : Unit
}
```

The trait `SchedulingService` defines the interface for a long-term scheduler. The single method `schedule` is used to schedule tasks to be performed at a later time. The `schedule` method takes two parameters, a configuration for when to run the task and an anonymous closure to run. The `SchedulingService` could leverage the fact that closures are serializable and store the task on the filesystem. This would let the `SchedulingService` allow persistent schedules in the face of restarts.

In the face of closure class name instability, this is a bad long-term strategy. The simple solution to fix the problem is to force users away from using closures, as best as possible. For example, the `SchedulingService` could use a `Job` trait instead of a closure.

```
trait Job extends java.io.Serializable {
  def doWork(): Unit
}
trait SchedulingService {
  def schedule(cron_schedule: String, work: Job): Unit
}
```

The `Job` trait is defined as `Serializable` and has one abstract method, `doWork`. The `doWork` method will contain the same implementation that used to be in the anonymous closure. The `SchedulingService` is updated to take `Job`s instead of `Function0` `[Unit]`. Although this doesn't prevent users from creating anonymous subclasses of `Job`, it does make it easier for them to explicitly name their `Job` classes and avoid volatile classnames.

   The upside to serialization issues in Scala is that Java serialization is often not used for long-term serialization. Java's serialization frequently gets related to remote method invocations and live machine-to-machine messaging or temporary data storage. Long-term persistence tends to take the form of SQL databases, NoSQL databases (using something like Protocol Buffers), XML, or JSON (JavaScript Serialized Object Notation). This means that in the general case, no special care needs to be taken around anonymous classes. But in those few situations that are troublesome, there are solutions you can use to avoid refactoring hell.

   . The next potential wart in Java integration is that of annotations.

10.4   *Annotate your annotations*

Many libraries use annotations for runtime code generation and inspection. Annotations are pieces of metadata that can be attached to expressions or types. Annotations can be used to accomplish many different goals, including the following:

- Ensuring or altering compiler warnings and errors (`@tailrec`, `@switch`, `@implicitNotFound`).
- Alter the bytecode output from compilation (`@serializable`, `@scala` `.annotations.BeanProperty`).
- Configure external services (the Java Persistence API uses annotations like `@Column` and `@ManyToOne`, to denote how to serialize classes into a relational database system [RDBMS]).
- Create and enforce additional type system constraints (the continuations plugin defines `@cpsParam` on types to create additional type-system checks for delimited continuations).

In the JVM ecosystem, many libraries rely on annotations to work properly. Scala prefers annotations instead of keywords for features like Java serialization. Understanding annotations in Scala and where they wind up within the bytecode of a class is important for interoperability with Java frameworks.

One of the largest issues facing Scala and Java interoperability is the mismatch of how Scala compiles class members and annotations compared to how Java compiles class members and annotations. In Java, there's a separate namespace for class fields and class methods. Both of these can be created, named, and annotated separately. In Scala, there's one namespace for all members of a type. The compiler takes responsibility for creating fields on a class as needed. Annotations on a member of a Scala class could compile to multiple methods and fields in the bytecode. Let's look at an example:

```
class Simple {
   @Id
   var value = 5
}
```

The `Simple` class defines a single member value. The value member is of type `Int` and is variable. It is also annotated with the `ID` annotation. In Scala 2.9.0, this class is compiled approximately into the following Java class:

```
class Simple {
  @Id private int value = 5;
  public int value() { return value; }
  public void value_$eq(int value) { this.value = value; }
}
```

The `Simple` class has three members: A `value` field, a `value` method, and a `value_$eq` method. The methods are defined `public` and the field is defined `private`. The annotation is only placed on the field representing the value. Even though the single member `var value` compiles into three separate locations in a classfile, the annotation is being placed on only one of them.

JavaBean style getters and setters

Some frameworks in Java rely on a Java naming convention for access properties on objects. This is a convention of the JavaBean specification, where property accessors and setters usually take the names `getFoo` and `setFoo`. Although the JavaBean specification doesn't require that methods have the string `get` and `set` in them, some Java libraries aren't implemented against the specification, but rather against the naming convention. To support these frameworks, Scala provides the `@Bean-Property` annotation. The simple class mentioned earlier can be modified to support these libraries, as follows:

```
class Simple {
 @reflect.BeanProperty
 var value = 5
}
```

This leads to the creation of the following methods: `value`, `value_$eg`, `getValue`, and `setValue`.

For libraries and frameworks that support the full JavaBean specification, the only annotation required is `@reflect.BeanInfo`. This can be applied to the class itself and the compiler will generate an appropriate `BeanInfo` class for all `vars` and `vals` on the class.

In the best case, this mismatch where one definition can compile to several locations in a classfile can confuse annotation libraries designed to work with Java. In the worst case, the libraries are completely unusable. The solution to this is to use annotations targets.

10.4.1 Annotation targets

Annotation targets are used to assign where in the resulting class files annotations should be placed. Scala provides the annotation targets shown in table 10.1:

Table 10.1   Annotation target types

Annotation	Bytecode location
`@annotation.target.field`	The field associated with a `var` or `val`.
`@annotation.target.getter`	The method used to obtain the value of a `var` or `val`. The method has the same name as the `val` or `var`.
`@annotation.target.setter`	The method used to set the value of a `var`. The method has the name of the `var` with `_$eq` appended for its name.
`@annotation.target.beanGetter`	The JavaBean style `get` method. This only works if the `@reflect.BeanProperty` annotation is specified on the Scala member.
`@annotation.target.beanSetter`	The JavaBean style `set` method. This only works if the `@reflect.BeanProperty` annotation is specified on the Scala member.

The different annotations each target a separate area of generated bytecode. These allow complete customization of where annotations are applied. To use one of these annotations, you must apply them against *another* annotation—that is, the target annotations annotate other annotations with the desired bytecode location. Here's an example:

```
import javax.persistence.Id

class Data {
  @(Id @annotation.target.getter)
  var dataId = 1
}
```

The class `Data` is defined with a single member `dataId`. The annotation `Id` is applied against the `dataId` member. The annotation `Id` also has the annotation `annotation.target.getter` applied to it. Scala allows annotations to be placed on expressions, types, members, and classes. The annotation target classes need to be placed against the annotation type that they wish to change. The expression `@(Id @annotation.target.getter)` is an annotation of the type `Id  @annotation.target.getter`, which is the annotated type `Id`. This can be simplified by creating a type alias for the annotated type.

```
object AnnotationHelpers {
  type Id = javax.persistence.Id @annotation.target.getter
}

import AnnotationHelpers._

class Data {
  @Id
  var dataId = 1
}
```

The `AnnotationHelpers` object defines a type alias `Id`. The type alias is the annotated type `javax.persistence.Id @annotation.target.getter`. The next line imports the type alias. The `Data` class is now modified to use the type alias for its annotation. This results in the same bytecode as the previous example.

When using a library or framework designed to annotate JavaBeans, it's helpful to create a wrapper for Scala. This wrapper should consist of an object, similar to `AnnotationHelpers`, that has the Java framework's annotations assigned to the appropriate generated code locations. This can ease usage within Scala. This technique is helpful for defining Scala classes that work with the Java Persistence API (JPA).

A second issue needs to be dealt with: some libraries require annotations in locations that Scala doesn't generate.

10.4.2 *Scala and static fields*

As discussed in section 10.1, Scala doesn't have a way to express static fields on classes. Although the JVM allows fields associated with class instances at runtime, the Scala language doesn't support this notion. You might argue that you can annotate Scala's objects because they are compiled to static values. But this doesn't work in practice.

Let's look at a quick example:

```
object Foo {}
```

This defines a simple object `Foo` in the raw namespace. Scala compiles to bytecode an equivalent to this Java class:

```
class Foo$ {
  public static Foo$ MODULE$ = null;

  private Foo$() {}

  static {
    MODULE$ = new Foo$
  }
}
```

The `Foo$` class is defined with a single static member: `MODULE$`. The static block is run when the class is loaded into the JVM. This instantiates the `Foo` object and assigns it to the `MODULE$` static field. Scala converts all objects to JVM classes with the same name as the object but with a `$` appended to the name. This prevents trait/class/object name clashes.

In this example, note that there's only one static field. You also have no way to provide an annotation on the static field. If a Java library requires static fields or annotations on static fields to work, this library is unusable against Scala classes.

But the Java library isn't completely unusable. The solution here is the same as before: Use Java for the portion of code that needs to interact with Java.

This is the unfortunate reality of interacting with Java libraries. A few were designed in such a way as to not be usable from Scala.

10.5   Summary

Using Java from Scala is usually a painless process. This chapter covered the areas of concern and offered solutions to each.

First, is the mismatch between Java's primitive with boxing and Scala's unified Any-Val types. You can simplify this mismatch by preferring primitive types on the Java side. Because Scala always prefers using the primitive value at runtime, this reduces the total amount of boxing/unboxing overhead within a program.

The second area of concern is when there exists a solution to a problem in both Scala and Java. The canonical example is the differing collections libraries. The Scala collections API isn't friendly to use from Java, and the Java collections API lacks many of the functional features found in the Scala version. To ease integration between Java portions of code and Scala portions, providing implicit conversions on the Scala side can be beneficial. It's important to be careful here to ensure you don't make assumptions about equality. Using explicit conversion functions can help highlight where object identities are changing. They can also be used to perform more than one implicit coercion.

The next area of concern is Java serialization. This works well in Scala. The downside is when Java serialization is used for long-term persistence. Scala allows the easy creation of anonymous classes, classes that could be serialized. If an object is intended for long-term serialization, the class should be formalized and named. Otherwise the source code structure may become locked for the lifetime of the serialized object, or worse. The persistent storage may need to be flushed and migrated.

Finally, when faced with a Java library that won't work from Scala, it's best to avoid such a library. If this isn't possible, then constructing the portion of code required to interact with the library in Java and exposing a Scala-friendly interface is the only solution.

The next chapter covers functional programming, which is a way of writing programs that may be foreign to those of us coming from an object-oriented or imperative background. Let's look into a world where no effects are side effects and operations are deferred as long as possible.

11
Patterns in functional programming

Functional programming is the practice of composing programs using functions. It's an area of software design and architecture that has been neglected in mainstream books and classes since the emergence of object-oriented programming. Functional programming offers a lot to the object-oriented developer and can nicely complement standard object-oriented practices.

Functional programming is a relatively large topic to try to compress into a single chapter. Instead, this chapter introduces a few key abstractions used in functional programming and demonstrates their usage in two different situations. The goal is to show one of the many styles of functional programming, rather than turn you into an expert functional programmer.

First, a discussion on some fundamental concepts behind the patterns in functional programming.

11.1 *Category theory for computer science*

Category theory is the mathematical study of collections of concepts and arrows. For the purposes of computer science, a concept is a type, like String, Int, and so on. An arrow is a morphism between concepts—something that converts from one concept to another. Usually in computer science, a morphism is a function defined against two types. A category is a grouping of concepts and arrows. For example, the category of cats includes all the various types of cats in the world as well as the captions needed to convert from a serious cat into a lol cat. Category theory is the study of categories like these and relationships between them. The most used category in programming is the categories of types: the classes, traits, aliases and object self types defined in your program.

Category theory shows up in many corners of programming but may not always be recognized. This section will introduce a library to configure software and introduce the concepts from category theory that are used in the library.

A good way to think of category theory, applied to functional programming, is design patterns. Category theory defines a few low-level abstract concepts. These concepts can be directly expressed in a functional language like Scala and have library support. When designing software, if a particular entity fits one of these concepts, a whole slew of operations immediately becomes available as well as the means to reason through usage. Let's look at this concept in the context of designing a configuration library.

In section 2.4 we explored the usage of Scala's Option class as a replacement for nullable values. In particular, this section showed how we can use Options to create *walled gardens*—that is, functions can be written as if all types aren't null. These functions can be lifted into functions that will propagate empty values. Let's look at the lift3 function from chapter 2:

```scala
scala>   def lift3[A,B,C,D](f: Function3[A,B,C,D]) = {
     |       (oa: Option[A], ob: Option[B], oc: Option[C]) =>
     |         for(a <- oa; b <- ob; c <- oc) yield f(a,b,c)
     |   }
lift3: [A,B,C,D](f: (A, B, C) => D)(
  Option[A], Option[B], Option[C]) => Option[D]
```

The lift3 function takes a function defined against raw types and converts it to a function that works with Option types. This lets us wrap Java's DriverManager.getConnection method directly and make it option-safe.

The lift3 function uses Scala's for expression syntax. Scala's for expressions are syntactic sugar for the map, flatMap, foreach, and withFilter operations defined on a class. The for expression

```scala
for(a <- oa; b <- ob; c <- oc) yield f(a,b,c)
```

is desugared into the following expression:

```scala
oa.flatMap(a => ob.flatMap(b => oc.map(c => f(a,b,c))))
```

Each <- of the for expression is converted into a map or flatMap call. These methods are each associated with a concept in category theory. The map method is associated with functors, and the flatMap method is associated with monads. For expressions make an excellent way to define workflows, which we define in section 11.4.

A monad is something that can be flattened. Option is a monad because it has both a flatten and flatMap operation that abide by the monadic laws. We'll cover the details of monads in section 11.2.2. For now, let's first generalize the advanced Option techniques from section 2.4.1.

Imagine that we're designing a configuration library. The goal is to use this library, in combination with a variant of the lift3 method, to construct database connections based on the current configuration parameters. This library could read configuration parameters from different locations. If any of these locations are updated, the program should automatically alter its behavior the next time a database connection is requested. Let's define a new trait, Config, that will wrap this logic for us. Because the filesystem is volatile and configuration isn't guaranteed to exist, the Config library will also make use of the Option trait to represent configuration values that weren't found. Let's define a minimal Config trait.

```
trait Config[+A] {
  def map[B](f : A => B) : Config[B]
  def flatMap[B](f : A => Config[B]): : Config[B]
  def get : A
}
```

The Config trait consists of three methods. The first, map, takes a function that operates on the data stored in the Config object and returns a new Config object. This is used to transform the underlying configuration data. For example, when reading environment variables of strings, the map method could be used to convert an environment variable into an Integer.

The next method is flatMap. This method takes a function against the current Config object and returns a second Config object. You can use this to construct new Config objects based on values stored in an initial Config object. For example, imagine we have a Config[java.io.File] that holds the location of a secondary configuration file. We can use the flatMap operation to read this location and then extract more configuration values from that location.

The final method is called get. This method is unsafe, in that it will attempt to read the current configuration environment, wherever configuration is defined to be, and return the resulting configuration values. As with Option, you shouldn't use this method until the code calling it knows what to do in the event of failure. Also, because the get method will read the environment, it can be expensive if performed within a tight loop of the software.

Let's define a construction operation for Config. Creating a new Config object is the case of defining the get method, because map and flatMap can be implemented in terms of get. For now, let's assume that map and flatMap are implemented appropriately (see the source code for implementations).

```
object Config {
  def apply[A](data : => A) = new Config[A] {
    def get = data
  }
}
```

The Config object defines a single method called apply, which is the constructor for Config objects. The apply method takes one parameter, a *by-name parameter*. By-name parameters in Scala are similar to no-argument functions in that they'll evaluate their associated expressions every time they're referenced. This means that defining the get method to reference the data argument will cause the data parameter to be reevaluated each time it's referenced. Here's an example:

```
scala> var x = 1
x: Int = 1

scala> Config({ x += 1; x})
res2: java.lang.Object with config.Config[Int] = ...

scala> res2.get
res3: Int = 2

scala> res2.get
res4: Int = 3
```

First, the variable x is defined as equal to 1. Next, a Config object is constructed. The argument is the expression { x +=1; x}. This expression should be evaluated every time the Config's get method is called. The next line calls the get method, and the returned value is 2. The next line calls the get method again and the return value is now 3. Let's create a few convenience methods to read configuration locations.

```
def environment(name : String) : Config[Option[String]] =
    Config(if (System.getenv.containsKey(name))
      Some(System.getenv.get(name))
    else None)
```

The environment method will read configuration values from the process environment. The method takes a string of the environment variable to read. The Config object is constructed using an if expression. If the environment variable is available, the value is returned inside an Option. If the variable isn't available, a None is returned. The full type returned is a Config[Option[String]]. Let's try this out on the command line:

```
> export test_prop="test_prop"
> scala -cp .
...
scala> val test = environment("test_prop")
test: Config[String] = Config$$anon$1@659c2931

scala> test.get
res0: String = test_prop
```

First, the environment variable test_prop is exported. Next, the Scala REPL is started and a Config object pointing to the test_prop property value is created. When calling get on this test property, the correct value is displayed.

Now let's look into constructing database connections based on environment variables. Here's the original code from section 2.4:

```
scala>   def lift3[A,B,C,D](f : Function3[A,B,C,D]) = {
     |        (oa : Option[A], ob : Option[B], oc : Option[C]) =>
     |          for(a <- oa; b <- ob; c <- oc) yield f(a,b,c)
     |    }
lift3: [A,B,C,D](f: (A, B, C) => D)(
  Option[A], Option[B], Option[C]) => Option[D]

scala> lift3(DriverManager.getConnection)
```

The `lift3` method takes a three-argument function and converts it into a three-argument function that works against `Option` arguments. This is used on the `Driver-Manager.getConnection` method to construct a new method that operates on `Options`.

Using `DriverManager` with the new `Config` library requires lifting the `get-Connection` function to take `Config[Option[String]]` rather than just `Option[String]`. Let's take the simple approach of defining a new `lift` function to convert three-argument methods into methods that operate on `Config` objects.

```
def lift3Config[A,B,C,D](f : Function3[A,B,C,D]) = {
  (ca : Config[A], cb : Config[B], cc : Config[C]) =>
    for(a <- ca; b <- cb; c <- cc) yield f(a,b,c)
}
```

The `lift3Config` method takes a three-argument function as its own argument. It returns a new function that takes `Config` traits of the original parameters. The implementation uses `for` expressions to call the underlying `flatMap` and `map` operations on the `Config` object. The final result is a `Config` object wrapping the underlying data. Let's use this to define a `DatabaseConnection` that uses environment variables.

```
scala> val databaseConnection =
     |   lift3Config(DriverManager.getConnection)(
     |   Config.environment("jdbc_url"),
     |   Config.environment("jdbc_user"),
     |   Config.environment("jdbc_password"))
databaseConnection: Config[java.sql.Connection]
```

The `lift3Config` method is called against the `lift3` method called on `DriveManager.getConnection`. This creates a three-argument function that works on `Config[Option[String]]` types. Finally, this new function is passed three arguments, one for each environment variable. The resulting `Config` object will construct a new database connection if the environment variables `jdbc_url`, `jdbc_user`, and `jdbc_password` are all available.

This implementation of `lift3Config` should look familiar. It's almost identical to the `lift3` method because both the `Config` trait and the `Option` trait are instances of the same abstract concept from category theory. Let's try to reverse engineer the raw concepts behind the `lift` method to see if we can rescue it for both `Option` and `Config`.

11.2   *Functors and monads, and how they relate to categories*

Functors are transformations from one category to another that can also transform and preserve morphisms. A *morphism* is the changing of one value in a category to another in the same category. In the example of the category of cats, a morphism would be akin to a box that takes a dim cat and converts it into a neon glowing cat. In the category of types, the most commonly used in computer science, a morphism is a function that converts from one type to another. The functor would be something that converts cats into dogs. The functor would be able to convert dim cats into dim dogs and glowing cats into glowing dogs. The functor could *also* convert the box so that it can convert dim dogs into glowing dogs.

Figure 11.1 illustrates functors.

The circle on the bottom represents the category of all possible types. Inside are the standard `String`, `Double`, `Int`, and any other type that can be defined in Scala. The functor `F` is a type constructor in Scala. For any type `T` that's in the category on the bottom, you can place that type in the type constructor `F[_]` and get a new type `F[T]` shown on the top category. For example, for any type `T`, a `Config[T]` can be made. The `Config` class is a functor.

> **LAWS OF FUNCTORS AND OTHER PROPERTIES**   Functors, and the other concepts described in this chapter, have mathematical laws that govern their behavior. These laws provide a default set of unit tests as well as standard transformations that can be performed on code. This book doesn't cover the laws in detail, but we give sufficient grounding in `Category` theory for you to investigate these laws as needed.

For the transformation to be a functor transformation, it means that all morphisms must be preserved in the transformation. If we have a function that manipulates types

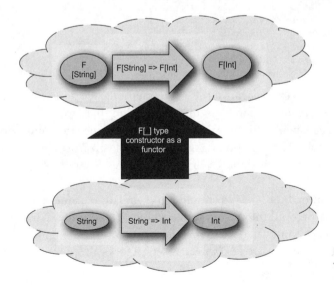

Figure 11.1   Functor transforming types and functions

in the first category, we should have a transformed function that operates on the transformed types. For example, if I have a function that takes a `String` and converts it to an `Int`, I should be able to also take a `Config[String]` instance and convert it to a `Config[Int]` instance. This is what the `map` method on `Option` and `Config` grant. Let's convert this into an interface:

Listing 11.1　Functor typeclass

```
trait Functor[T[_]] {
    def apply[A](x: A): T[A]
    def map[A,B](x : T[A])(f: A=>B) : T[B]
}
```

The `apply` method grants the first property of functors. For any type `A`, a `Functor` can construct a type `T[A]` in the new category. The `map` method grants the second property of functors. Given a transformed type `T[A]` and a morphism in the original category `A=>B`, a value `T[B]` can be created. We have a new function that takes `T[A]` and returns `T[B]`.

Let's implement the `Functor` interface for `Config`.

```
object ConfigAsFunctor extends Functor[Config] {
  def apply[A](x : A): Config[A] = Config(x)
  def map[A,B](x : Config[A])(f: A=>B) = x.map(f)
}
```

The `Functor` implementation for `Config` is defined such that the `apply` method calls the `Config` companion object's `apply` method. The `map` method can delegate to the underlying map method on the `Config` class.

Finally, let's create a bit of syntactic sugar so that the `map` method on the `Functor` typeclass appears to be on the raw type.

```
implicit def functorOps[F[_] : Functor, A](ma: F[A]) = new {
  val functor = implicitly[Functor[F]]
  final def map[B](f: A => B): F[B] = functor.map(ma)(f)
}
```

The implicit method `functorOps` creates a new anonymous class that has a local `map` method that accepts only a function `A => B`. This simplifies the remaining code samples using `Functor`.

Now, we'll create the `lift` method so that it's generic against the `Functor` abstraction.

```
def lift[F[_] : Functor] = new {
  val functor = implicitly[Functor[F]]
  def apply3[A,B,C,D](f: (A,B,C) => D): (
    F[A],F[B],F[C]) => F[F[F[[D]]] = {
      (fa, fb, fc) =>
        fa map { a =>
          fb map { b =>
            fc map { c =>
              f(a,b,c)
```

```
            }
          }
        }
      }
    }
```

The new `lift` method uses a `Functor` to promote elements of the function. The `apply3` method accepts a three-argument function and calls `map` against each of these methods to chain the method calls. The resulting function is one that accepts all the original arguments inside the `FunctorF[_]` and returns a nested result type `F[F[F[D]]]`.

The issue with this method is that the resulting type is `F[F[F[D]]]`, not `F[D]`. This means for the config library, creating a database connection will result in a `Config[Config[Config[Connection]]]` instead of a `Config[Connection]`. To resolve this, let's create a new type trait the extends `Functor` and adds a `flatten` method. This method will be responsible for collapsing the pattern `F[F[D]]` to `F[D]`, which should allow the above function to work as desired. This new trait is called a `Monad`.

11.2.1 Monads

Monads are a means of combining a functor application, if that functor is an `endofunctor`. An `endofunctor` is a functor that converts concepts and morphisms in its category back into the same category. Using the cat example, an `endofunctor` would be a way of converting cats and genetic cat manipulations into different types of cats and cat genetic manipulations. Transforming a cat more than once by the same functor could be reduced into single functor application. Similarly, altering cat genetic manipulations more than once can be reduced into a single alteration.

In computer science, monads are often used to represent computations. A monad can be used to abstract out the execution behavior of a program. Some monads can be used to handle concurrency, exceptions, or even side effects. Using monads in workflows or pipelines is discussed in section 11.4.

Let's look at the programming definition of a monad in the following listing:

Listing 11.2 Monad typeclass

```
trait Monad[T[_]] {
  def flatten[A](m : T[T[A]]): T[A]
  def flatMap[A,B](x : T[A])(f : A => T[B]
    )(implicit func: Functor[T]): T[B] =
      flatten(func.map(x, f))
}
```

The `Monad` trait defines the `flatten` and `flatMap` methods. The `flatten` method is used to take a double wrapped type and turn it into a wrapped type. If a `Functor T[_]` is applied twice, the monad knows how to combine this to one application. For example, the `List` monad can convert a list of lists into a single list with all the underlying elements of the nested lists. The `Monad` trait also provides a convenience function `flatMap`, which chains the `flatten` and `map` calls for convenience.

Monad and functor differences

In reality, a monad is the `flatten` operation for a functor. If you were to encode the category theory directly into the type system, the `flatMap` method would require an implicit `Functor`. For category theory applied to computer science, in this instance at least, everything is in the category of types. The type constructor `F[_]` applied to a type `T` results in the type `F[T]`, which is in the same category of types. A monad is a means of taking two such applications and reducing them to a single—that is, `F[F[T]]` becomes `F[T]`.

If you think of monads as functions, then it's equivalent to taking the function `def addOne(x: Int) = x +1` and the expression `addOne(addOne(5))` and converting it to the function `def addTwo(x: Int) = x +2` and the resulting expression `addTwo(5)`. Now imagine such a translation done against types.

Monads are means of combining functor applications on types, hence `F[F[T]]` being shortened to `F[T]` through use of a monad.

Monads are, among other things, a means of preventing bloat in types and accessors. We can take a nested list of lists and treat it as a single list, which has a more convenient syntax.

Again, let's create a convenience implicit to reduce the syntactic noise of using the `Monad` type trait.

```
implicit def monadOps[M[_] : Functor : Monad, A](ma: M[A]) = new {
  val monad = implicitly[Monad[M]]
  def flatten[B](implicit $ev0: M[A] <:< M[M[B]]): M[B] =
    monad.flatten(ma)
  def flatMap[B](f: A => M[B]): M[B] =
    monad.flatMap(ma)(f)
}
```

The implicit method `monadOps` creates a single anonymous class. The `flatten` method uses the implicit type constraint trick from section 7.2.3 to ensure that the value inside the monad `M[_]` is another `M[_]` value. The `flatMap` method delegates to the `Monad` trait's `flatMap` method.

Now, let's modify the `lift` function to make use of the `Monad` trait.

```
def lift[F[_] : Monad : Functor] = new {
  val m = implicitly[Monad[F]]
  val func = implicitly[Functor[F]]
  def apply3[A,B,C,D](f: (A,B,C) => D): (F[A], F[B], F[C]) => F[D] = {
      (fa, fb, fc) =>
        m.flatMap(fa) { a =>
          m.flatMap(fb) { b =>
            func.map(fc) { c =>
              f(a,b,c)
            }
          }
        }
    }
}
```

The new `lift` method uses a `Monad` type class instead of a `Functor`. This `lift` method looks similar to the original `lift` method for `Option`, except that it can generically `lift` functions to operate against monads. Let's try it out.

```scala
scala> lift[Option] apply3 java.sql.DriverManager.getConnection
res4: (Option[String], Option[String],
      Option[String]) => Option[java.sql.Connection] =
    <function3>
```

The `lift` method is called using `Option` as the type parameter. The `apply3` method is called directly against `java.sql.DriverManager.getConnection(...)`. The result is a new function that accepts three `Option[String]` values and returns an `Option[Connection]`.

Monads and functors form the basic building blocks of lots of fundamental concepts in programming. We'll explore these more in depth in section 11.4. An abstraction lives between monads and functors. This abstraction can be used as an alternative mechanism of writing the `lift` function. Instead of relying on a `flatMap` operation, a function can curried and values fed into it in an applicative style.

11.3   *Currying and applicative style*

Currying is the conversion of a function of multiple parameters into a chain of functions that accept a single parameter. A curried function accepts one of its arguments and returns a function that accepts the next argument. This chain continues until the last function returns a result. In Scala, any function of multiple parameters can be curried.

Applicative style refers to using curried functions to drive parameters in applicative functors through them. Applicative functors are functors that also support a method to convert mapped morphisms into morphisms against mapped types. In English, this means that if we have a list of functions, an applicative functor can create a single function that accepts a list of argument values and returns a new list of results.

11.3.1   *Currying*

Currying is taking a function of several arguments and turning it into a function that takes a single argument and returns a function that takes the next argument that returns a function that takes the next argument and so on, until finally one of the functions returns a value. In Scala, all functions have a `curried` method that can be used to convert them from multiargument functions into curried functions. Let's try it out:

```scala
scala> val x = (x:Int, y:Double, z: String) => z+y+x
x: (Int, Double, String) => java.lang.String = <function3>

scala> x.curried
res0: (Int) => (Double) => (String) => java.lang.String = <function1>
```

The first line constructs a function that takes three arguments: an integer, a double, and a string. The second calls `curried` against it, which returns a function of the type

`Int => Double => String => String`. This function takes an `Int` and returns another function `Double => String => String`. This function takes a `Double` and returns a function that takes a `String` and returns a `String`. A single function of multiple arguments is converted into a chain of functions, each returning another function until all arguments have been satisfied and a return value is made. Currying is pretty easy to do by hand; let's try it out.

```scala
scala> val y = (a: Int) => (b: Double) => (c: String) => x(a,b,c)
y: (Int) => (Double) => (String) => java.lang.String = <function1>
```

This line constructs an anonymous function y that takes an `Int`, called a, and returns the function defined by the rest of the expression. This same trick defines a nested anonymous function, until eventually the function x defined earlier is called. Note that this function has the same signature as `x.curried`. The trick is that each call to a function captures a portion of the argument list of the original function and returns a new function for the remaining values.

This trick can be used when attempting to promote a function of multiple simple parameters to work with values inside a `Functor`. Let's redefine the `lift` method to use only a `Functor`.

```scala
def lift[F[_]: Functor] = new {
   def apply3[A,B,C,D](f: (A,B,C) => D): (F[A], F[B], F[C]) => F[D] = {
      (fa, fb, fc) =>
         val tmp: F[B => C => D] = fa.map(f.curried)
         ...?...
   }
}
```

The new implementation for the `apply3` method in `lift` uses the map operation on `Functor` against the curried function. The result is a function `B => C => D` wrapped inside the `F[_]` functor.

Let's break this down to see what's happening in the types. First a curried function is created.

```scala
scala> f.curried
res0: A => (B => C => D) = <function1>
```

The parentheses in the resulting expression have been adjusted to show the true type. The result is a single function that takes an `A` and produces a value. Because the `fa` parameter is a value of `F[A]`, we can combine the curried function with the `fa` value using the `map` method.

```scala
scala> fa.map[B => C => D](f.curried)
res0: F[B => (C => D)] = Config(<function1>)
```

The `map` method on `fa` is called against the curried function. The result is a `F[_]` containing the rest of the function. Remember the `Functor` defines its map method as `def map[A,B](m: F[A])(f: A=> B): F[B]`. In this case the second type parameter is a function B=>C=>D.

Now there's a problem. The code can't continue to use the map method defined on Functor because the remaining function is wrapped inside the functor F[_]. To solve this, let's define a new abstraction, Applicative, as shown in the following listing:

Listing 11.3 Applicative typeclass

```
trait Applicative[F[_]] {
  def lift2[A,B](f: F[A=>B])(ma: F[A]): F[B]
}
```

The Applicative trait is defined for the type F[_]. It consists of one method, lift2, that takes a function inside an F[_] and a value inside an F[_] and returns the result inside an F[_]. Notice that this is different from a monad, which can flatten F[F[_]]. The lift method can now be completed using applicative functors.

```
def lift[F[_]: Functor: Applicative] = new {
    val func = implicitly[Functor[F]]
    val app = implicitly[Applicative[F]]
    def apply3[A,B,C,D](f: (A,B,C) => D): (F[A], F[B], F[C]) => F[D] = {
      (fa, fb, fc) =>
        val tmp: F[B => C => D] = func.map(fa)(f.curried)
        val tmp2: F[C => D] = app.lift2(tmp)(fb)
        app.lift2(tmp2)(fc)
    }
  }
```

The lift function now requires both a Functor and an Applicative context bound. As before, the function is curried and applied against the first argument using the functor's map method. But the applicative functor's lift2 method can be used to apply the second argument of the function. Finally, the lift2 method is used again to apply the third argument of the original function. The final result is the value of type D wrapped inside the functor F[_].

Now, let's try the method against the previous example of using the Driver-Manager.getConnection method.

```
scala> lift[Config] apply3 java.sql.DriverManager.getConnection
res0: (Config[String], Config[String],
      Config[String]) => Config[java.sql.Connection] =
    <function3>
```

The result is the same as it was for using functor and monad. The two reasons to choose this style instead is that there are more things that can implement the lift2 method for applicative functors than can implement the flatten method for monads and that applicative functors can compute in parallel while monadic workflows are sequential.

11.3.2 *Applicative style*

An alternative syntax to lifting functions into applicative functors is known as *applicative style*. This can be used in Scala to simplify the construction of complex function dependencies, keeping the values inside an applicative functor. For example, using the `Config` library defined earlier, you can construct an entire program from functions and applicative applications. Let's take a look.

Rule 27　**Use applicative style to join parallel processes**

Applicative functors provide a way to take two computations and join them together using a function. The `Traversable` example highlights how two collections can be parallelized into pairs. Applicative functors and parallel processing go together like bread and butter.

Assuming there's a software system that's composed of two subsystems: the `DataStore` and the `WorkerPool`. The class hierarchy for this system looks as follows:

```
trait DataStore { ... }
trait WorkerPool { ... }
class Application(ds: DataStore, pool: WorkerPool) { ... }
```

The `DataStore` class and `WorkerPool` class are defined with all the methods required for their subcomponent. The `Application` class is defined as taking a `DataStore` instance and a `WorkerPool` instance. Now, when constructing the application, the following can be done with applicative style:

```
def dataStore: Config[DataStore]
def workerPool: Config[WorkerPool]
def system: Config[Application] =
  (Applicative build dataStore).and(
    workerPool) apply (new Application(_,_))
```

The `dataStore` and `workerPool` methods are defined as abstraction constructors of `DataStore` inside a `Config` object. The entire system is composed by creating an `Applicative` instance on the `dataStore`, combining the `workerPool` and applying that to an anonymous function (`new Application(_,_)`). The result is an `Application` embedded in a `Config` object. The `Applicative` call creates a builder that will use the `Config[_]` instances to construct something that can accept a function of raw types and return a resulting `Config` object.

> **HASKELL VERSUS SCALA**　Applicative style came to Scala from the Haskell language, where functions are curried by default. The syntax presented here is a Scala idiom and doesn't mimic the Haskell directly. In Haskell, applicative style uses the `<*>` operator, called *apply*, against a curried function on Applicative functors—that is, Haskell has a `<*>` method that performs the same function as the `lift2` method in the `Applicative` trait.

This applicative style, combined with the `Config` class, can be used to do a form of dependency injection in Scala. Software can be composed of simple classes that take their dependencies in the constructor and a separate configuration can be used to wire all the pieces together using functions. This is an ideal blend of object orientation and functional programming in Scala. For example, if the `DataStore` trait had an implementation that used a single JDBC connection like the following:

```
class ConnectionDataStore(conn: java.sql.Connection) extends DataStore
```

Then the entire application can be configured as shown in the following listing:

Listing 11.4   Configuring an application using the `Config` class and applicative builder

```
def jdbcUrl: Config[String] = environment("jdbc.url")
def jdbcUser: Config[String] = environment("jdbc.user")
def jdbcPw: Config[String] = environment("jdbc.pw")
def connection: Config[Connection] =
  (Applicative build jdbcUrl).and(jdbcUser).and(jdbcPw).apply(
    DriverManager.getConnection)

def dataStore: Config[DataStore] =
  connection map (c => new ConnectionDataStore(f))
def workerPool: Config[WorkerPool] = ...

def system: Config[Application] =
  Applicative build dataStore and workerPool apply (
    new Application(_,_))
```

The `environment` function is defined in 11.7. This function pulls the value of an environment variable if it exists and is used to pull values for the JDBC connection's URL, user, and password. The applicative builder is then used to construct a `Config[Connection]` using these config values and the `DriverManager.getConnection` method directly. This connection is then used to construct the `dataStore` configuration using the map method on `Config` to take the configured JDBC connection and use it to instantiate the `ConnectionDataStore`. Finally, the applicative builder is used to construct the application from the `dataStore` and `workerPool` configuration.

Although this is pure Scala code, the concept should look familiar to users of Java inversion-of-control containers. This bit of code represents the configuration of software separate from the definition of its components. There's no need to resort to XML or configuration files in Scala.

Let's look at how the `Applicative` object build method works.

```
object Applicative {
  def build[F[_]: Functor: Applicative, A](m: F[A]) =
    new ApplicativeBuilder[F,A](m)
}
```

The `build` method on `Applicative` takes two types, `F[_]` and `A`. The `F[_]` type is required to have an applicative and functor instance available implicitly. The `build` method accepts a parameter of type `F[A]` and returns a new `ApplicativeBuilder` class. Let's look at the `ApplicativeBuilder` class in the following listing:

Listing 11.5   `ApplicativeBuilder` class

```
class ApplicativeBuilder[F[_],A](ma: F[A])(
    implicit functor: Functor[F], ap: Applicative[F]) {
  import Implicits._

  def apply[B](f: A => B): F[B] = ma.map(f)

  def and[B](mb: F[B]) = new ApplicativeBuilder2(mb)
```

```
class ApplicativeBuilder2[B](mb: F[B]) {

    def apply[C](f: (A, B) => C): F[C] =
        ap.lift2((ma.map(f.curried)))(mb)

    def and[C](mc: F[C]) = new AppplicativeBuilder3[C](mc)

    class AppplicativeBuilder3[C](mc: F[C]) {

        def apply[D](f: (A,B,C) => D): F[D] =
            ap.lift2(ap.lift2((ma.map(f.curried)))(mb))(mc)


        ...
    }
  }
}
```

The ApplicativeBuilder class takes in its constructor the same arguments as the
Applicative.build method. The class consists of two methods, apply and and, as well
as a nested class ApplicativeBuilder2. The apply method takes a function against
raw types A and B and applies the captured member ma against it, creating an F[B].
The and method takes another applicative functor instance of type F[B] and constructs an ApplicativeBuilder2. The ApplicativeBuilder2 class also has two methods: apply and and. The apply method is a bit more odd. Like the lift example
earlier, this method curries the raw function f and uses the map and lift2 methods to
feed arguments to the lifted function inside the functor. The and method constructs
an ApplicativeBuilder3 that looks a lot like ApplicativeBuilder2 but with one
more parameter. This chain of nested builder classes goes all the way to Scala's limit
on anonymous function arguments of 23.

Applicative style is a general concept that can be applied in many situations. For
example, let's use it to compute all the possible pairings of elements from two
collections.

```
scala> (Applicative build Traversable(1,2) and
    Traversable(3,4) apply (_ -> _))
res1: Traversable[(Int, Int)] =
    List((1,3), (1,4), (2,3), (2,4))
```

The Applicative builder is used to combine two Traversable lists. The apply
method is given a function that takes two arguments and creates a pairing of the two.
The resulting list is each element of the first list paired with each element of the second list.

Functors and monads help express programs through functions and function
transformations. This applicative style, blended with solid object-oriented techniques,
leads to powerful results. As seen from the config library, applicative style can be used
to blend pure functions and those that wall off dangers into things like Option or
Config. Applicative style is usually used at the interface between raw types like String
and wrapped types like Option[String].

Another common use case in functional programming is creating reusable
workflows.

11.4 *Monads as workflows*

A monadic workflow is a pipeline of computation that remains embedded inside the monad. The monad can control the execution and behavior of the computation that's nested inside it. Monadic workflows are used to control things like side effects, control flow, and concurrency. A great example is using monadic workflows for automated resource management.

Rule 28

Use monadic workflows for sequential computations

Monadic workflows can be used to encapsulate a complicated sequential process. Monadic workflows are often used with collections to search through a domain model for relevant data. In the managed resource example, monadic workflows are used to ensure that when a sequential process is complete, resources are cleaned up. if you need parallelism, use applicative style, if you need sequencing, use monadic workflows.

Automated resource management is a technique where a resource, such as a file handle, closes automatically for the programmer when that resource is no longer needed. Though there are many techniques to perform this function, one of the simplest is to use the *loaner* pattern. The loaner pattern is where one block of code owns the resource and delegates its usage to a closure. Here's an example:

```
def readFile[T](f: File)(handler: FileInputStream => T): T = {
  val resource = new java.io.FileInputStream(f)
  try {
    handler(resource)
  } finally {
    resource.close()
  }
}
```

The `readFile` function accepts a `File` and a handler function. The file is used to open a `FileInputStream`. This stream is loaned to the handler function, ensuring that the stream is closed in the event of an exception. This method can then be used as follows:

```
readFile(new java.io.File("test.txt")) { input =>
  println(input.readByte)
}
```

The example shows how to use the `readFile` method to read the first byte of the `test.txt` file. Notice how the code doesn't open or close the resource; it's merely *loaned* the resource for usage. This technique is powerful, but it can be built up even further.

It's possible that a file may need to be read in stages, where each stage performs a portion of the action. It's also possible that the file may need to be read repeatedly. All of this can be handled by creating an automated resource management *monad*. Let's take a cut at defining the class, as shown in the following listing:

Listing 11.6 Automated resource management interface

```
trait ManagedResource[T] {
  def loan[U](f: T => U): U
}
```

The ManagedResource trait has a type parameter representing the resource it manages. It contains a single method, loan, which external users can utilize to modify the resource. This captures the loaner pattern. Now let's create one of these in the read-File method.

```
def readFile(file: File) = new ManagedResource[InputStream] {
    def loan[U](f: InputStream => U): U = {
      val stream = new FileInputStream(file)
      try {
        f(stream)
      } finally {
        stream.close()
      }
    }
  }
```

Now the readFile method constructs a ManagedResource with type parameter InputStream. The loan method on the ManagedResource first constructs the input stream, and then loans it to the function f. Finally, the stream is closed regardless of thrown errors.

The ManagedResource trait is both a functor *and* a monad. Like the Config class, ManagedResource can define the map and flatten operations. Let's look at the implementations.

Listing 11.7 ManagedResource functor and monad instances

```
object ManagedResource {
  implicit object MrFunctor extends Functor[ManagedResource] {
    override final def apply[A](a: A) = new ManagedResource[A] {
      override def loan[U](f: A => U) = f(a)
      override def toString = "ManagedResource("+a+")"
    }
    override final def map[A,B](ma: ManagedResource[A]
                             )(mapping: A => B) =
      new ManagedResource[B] {
        override def loan[U](f: B => U) = ma.loan(mapping andThen f)
        override def toString =
          "ManagedResource.map("+ma+")("+mapping+")"
      }
  }
  implicit object MrMonad extends Monad[ManagedResource] {
    type MR[A] = ManagedResource[A]
    override final def flatten[A](mma: MR[MR[A]]): MR[A] =
      new ManagedResource[A] {
        override def loan[U](f: A => U): U = mma.loan(ma => ma.loan(f))
        override def toString = "ManagedResource.flatten("+mma+")"
      }
  }
}
```

The ManagedResource companion object contains the Functor and Monad implementation so that Scala will find them by default on the implicit context. The Functor .apply method is implemented by loaning the captured value when the loan method is called. The Functor.map method is implemented by calling the loan value of the ma resource and first wrapping this value with the mapping function before calling the passed in function. Finally, the Monad.flatten operation is performed by calling loan on the outer resource and then calling loan on the inner resource that was returned from the outer resource.

Now that the ManagedResource trait has been made monadic, we can use it to define a workflow against a resource. A *workflow* is a euphemism for a collection of functions that perform a large task in an incremental way. Let's create a workflow that will read in a file, do some calculations, and write out the calculations.

The first task in reading the file is iterating over all the textual lines in the file. We can do this by taking the existing readFile method and converting the underlying InputStream into a collection of lines. First, let's construct a method to convert an input stream into a Traversable[String] of lines.

```
def makeLineTraversable(input: BufferedReader) =
  new Traversable[String] {
    def foreach[U](f: String => U): Unit = {
      var line = input.readLine()
      while (line != null) {
        f(line)
        line = input.readLine()
      }
    }
  } view
```

The makeLineTraversable method takes a BufferedReader as input and constructs a Traversable[String] instance. The foreach method is defined by calling readLine on the BufferedReader until it's out of input. For each line read, as long as it's not null, the line is fed to the anonymous function f. Finally, the view method is called on the Traversable to return a lazily evaluated collection of lines.

```
type LazyTraversable[T] = collection.TraversableView[T, Traversable[T]]
```

The LazyTraversable type alias is constructed to simplify referring to a Traversable view of type T where the original collection was also a Traversable. From now on, we'll use this alias to simplify the code samples. Now let's define the portion of workflow that will read the lines of a file.

```
def getLines(file: File): ManagedResource[LazyTraversable[String]] =
  for {
    input <- ManagedResource.readFile(file)
    val reader = new InputStreamReader(input)
    val buffered = new BufferedReader(reader)
  } yield makeLineTraversable(buffered)
```

The getLines method takes a file and returns a ManagedResource containing a collection of strings. The method is implemented by a single for expression, workflow. The workflow first reads the file and pulls the InputStream. This InputStream is converted into an InputStreamReader, which is then converted into a BufferedReader. Finally, the BufferedReader is passed to the makeLineTraversable method to construct a

LazyTraversable[String], which is yielded or returned. The result is a Managed-Resource that loans a collection of line strings, rather than a raw resource.

Scala's for expressions allow the creation of workflows. If a class is a monad or functor, then we can use a for expression to manipulate the types *inside* the functor without extracting them. This can be a handy tactic. For example, the getLines method could be called early in an application's lifecycle. The input file won't be read until the loan method is called on the resulting ManagedResource[LazyTraversable [String]]. This allows the composition of *behavior* to be part of the composition of the application.

Let's finish off the example. We should read the input file by line and calculate the lengths of each line. The resulting calculations will be written to a new file. Let's define a new workflow to make this happen.

```
def lineLengthCount(inFile: File, outFile: File) =
    for {
        lines <- getLines(inFile)
        val counts = lines.map(_.length).toSeq.zipWithIndex
        output <- ManagedResource.writeFile(outFile)
        val writer = new OutputStreamWriter(output)
        val buffered = new BufferedWriter(writer)
    } yield buffered.write(counts.mkString("\n"))
```

The lineLengthCount method takes in two File parameters. The for expression defines a workflow to first obtain a TraversableView of all the lines in a file using the getLines method. Next, the line length counts are calculated by calling the length method on each line and combining that with the line number. Next, the output is grabbed using the ManagedResource.writeFile method. This method is similar to the readFile method, except that it returns an OutputStream rather than an Input-Stream. The next two lines in the workflow adapt the OutputStream into a Buffered-Writer. Finally, the BufferedWriter is issued to write the counts calculations into the output file.

> **MONADIC I/O** The Haskell language has a monadic I/O library in which every side effecting input or output operation is wrapped inside a monad called I/O. Any kind of file or network manipulation is wrapped into workflows called do-notation, akin to Scala's do-notation.

This method doesn't perform any calculations. Instead it returns a Managed-Resource[Unit] that will read, calculate, and write the results when its loan method is called. Again, this workflow has just composed the *behavior* of calculating counts but didn't execute it. This gives the flexibility of defining portions of program behavior as first-class objects and passing them around or injecting them with a dependency injection framework.

A contingent of functional programmers believes that all side-effecting functions should be hidden inside a monad to give the programmer more control over when things like database access and filesystem access occur. This is similar to placing a workflow inside the `ManagedResource` monad and calling `loan` when that workflow should be executed. Though this mind-set can be helpful, it's also viral in that it contaminates an entire code base with monadic workflows. Scala comes from the ML family of languages, which don't mandate the use of a monad for side effects. Therefore, some code may make heavy use of monads and workflows while others won't.

Monadic workflows can be powerful and helpful when used in the right situations. Monads work well when defining a pipeline of tasks that need to be executed but without defining the execution behavior. A monad can control and enforce this behavior.

> **MONADIC LAWS AND WADLER'S WORK**   Monads follow a strict set of mathematical laws that we don't cover in this book. These laws—left identity, right identity and association—are covered in most monad-specific material. In addition, Philip Wadler, the man who enlightened the functional world on monads, has a series of papers that describe common monads and common patterns that are well worth the read.

Monads can also be used to annotate different operations in a pipeline. In the `Config` monad, there were several ways to construct a `Config` instance. In the case where a `Config` instance was constructed from a file, the `Config` monad could use change-detection to avoid reading the file multiple times. The monad could also construct a dependency graph for calculations and attempt to optimize them at runtime. Though not many libraries exist that optimize staged monadic behavior in Scala, this remains a valid reason to encode sequences of operations into monadic workflows.

11.5   Summary

Functional programming has a lot to offer the object-oriented developer. Functional programming offers powerful ways to interact with functions. This can be done through applicative style, such as configuring an application, or through monadic workflows. Both of these rely heavily on concepts from category theory.

One important thing to notice in this chapter is the prevalence of typeclass pattern with functional style. The typeclass pattern offers a flexible form of object orientation to the functional world. When combined with Scala's traits and inheritance mechanisms, it can be a powerful foundation for building software. The type classes we presented in this chapter aren't available in the standard library but are available in the Scalaz extension library (http://mng.bz/WgSG). The Scalaz library uses more advanced abstractions than those we presented here, but it's well worth a look.

Scala provides the tools needed to blend the object-oriented and functional programming worlds. Scala is at its best when these two evenly share a codebase. The biggest danger to misusing Scala is to ignore its object orientation or its functional programming. But combining the two is the sweet spot that the language was designed to fulfill.

index